LOCH LOMOND AND THE TROSSACHS
IN HISTORY AND LEGEND

Christmas, 2009
To Sandy —
Lets plan a trip!

love,
xx Martin
oo

Some other books by P.J.G. Ransom

The Archaeology of Canals
The Archaeology of Railways
The Archaeology of the Transport Revolution 1750–1850
Scottish Steam Today (Trains, ships and stationary engines)
The Victorian Railway and How It Evolved
Loch Earn: A Guide for Visitors
Narrow Gauge Steam: Its origins and world-wide development
Scotland's Inland Waterways
The Mont Cenis Fell Railway
Locomotion: Two Centuries of Train Travel (anthology)
Snow, Flood and Tempest: Railways and Natural Disasters

LOCH LOMOND AND THE TROSSACHS IN HISTORY AND LEGEND

P.J.G. RANSOM

JOHN DONALD PUBLISHERS
EDINBURGH

First published in 2004 by
John Donald Publishers,
an imprint of
Birlinn Limited
West Newington House
10 Newington Road
Edinburgh
EH9 1QS

www.birlinn.co.uk

ISBN 0 85976 586 5

British Library Cataloguing-in-Publication Data
A catalogue record for this book is available
from the British Library

Typesetting and prepress origination by Brinnoven, Livingston
Printed and bound by Cromwell Press, Trowbridge, Wiltshire

CONTENTS

ACKNOWLEDGEMENTS

I am most grateful for assistance rendered by: Keith Verden Anderson; Gavin Arneil, Hannah Stirling (Friends of Loch Lomond); Jack Bisset (Loch Lomond & The Trossachs National Park Authority); Peter Clapham (Stirling Council Archives); Graham Courtney; John Danielewski; Peter Dundas; Robert Forsythe; Geoff. Holliman (Loch Lomond Shores); Graham Hopner, Arthur Jones, Rhoda MacLeod (West Dunbartonshire Libraries); Cilla Jackson (St Andrews University Library); James Miller; David Munro (Royal Scottish Geographical Society); Trevor Rees; Andrew Saul; Susan Scobie, Heather Ward (Scottish & Southern Energy plc); David Stirling; Michael Wrottesley; and the staffs of: House of Lords Record Office; National Archives of Scotland; National Library of Scotland; Strathyre Learning Centre.

Dr John McGregor has generously exchanged information about railways at Crianlarich while his own detailed account of the early years of the West Highland – *The West Highland Railway: Plans, Politics and People* – has been going through the press.

I am also particularly grateful to Robert Greig for bringing the remarkable geography of Verdi's *Aroldo* to my attention, and to my wife Elisabeth and my agent Duncan McAra for their support as ever.

Views expressed, and interpretation of events described, are my own.

PREFACE

This is a book about certain aspects of the history of the region in which Scotland's first national park has been established. It is a border region, across which the Highland Line divided not merely two landscapes but also two cultures. Travel to, though, across and around the region has ever been one of its most important characteristics. So a large part of the book is devoted to the history and legends of people who travelled here – of their motives for doing so, of their means of travel, and particularly of the manner in which changes in means of travel have hindered as well as helped our ability to move around.

Yet there is more to it than that, as a glance at the list of contents shows. I must admit that those aspects of the region's history about which I have chosen to write are those which appeal most to me – but I hope they will appeal to you too. In places I have strayed outside the national park boundaries. This applies particularly to the story of travel and trade up and down the River Leven, without which any attempt to tell the story of that aspect of Loch Lomond would be incomplete. Even within the park, coverage of some areas is less complete than others. This applies particularly to its eastern part, of which Archie McKerracher has already written much in *Perthshire in History and Legend*. I have also endeavoured to avoid simply retelling well-known tales. This is not an encyclopedia, but a personal selection; if you find little about your own favourite place or personality, please do not write to tell me. On second thoughts, please do, and should there be a second edition I will endeavour to fit something in.

Nevertheless there are some aspects of the region's history covered in this book which have not been described so fully elsewhere, or indeed at all. Here for example for the first time is a comprehensive account of the use of Loch Lomond as a waterway – an element central to trade and travel in the region. The hesitant transformation of the military roads of the region into turnpike roads has not, so far as I am aware, been described elsewhere. Even the effect of Parliamentary action – or inaction – in the 1890s upon the railway map of the region in the 1960s has not previously had the spotlight turned upon it. But above all, I hope that what follows will prove not merely informative but also readable and entertaining.

P.J.G.R.

LOCH LOMOND AND THE TROSSACHS
IN HISTORY AND LEGEND

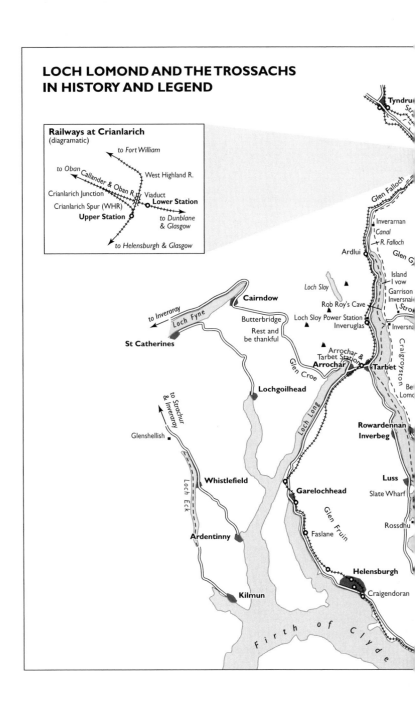

Railways at Crianlarich
(diagramatic)

to Fort William

to Oban

Callander & Oban R.

West Highland R.

Crianlarich Junction

Viaduct

Lower Station

Crianlarich Spur (WHR)

Upper Station

to Dunblane
& Glasgow

to Helensburgh & Glasgow

Tyndru

Glen Falloch

Inverarnan
Canal
R. Falloch

Ardlui

Glen G

Island
I vow

Loch Sloy

Garrison
Inversnai

Cairndow

Rob Roy's Cave

Stro

to Inveraray

Loch Fyne

Butterbridge

Loch Sloy Power Station

Inveruglas

Inversn

St Catherines

Rest and
be thankful

Craigroyston

Arrochar &
Tarbet Station

Glen Croe

Arrochar

Tarbet

Be
Lom

Lochgoilhead

Loch Long

Rowardennan

to Strachur
& Inveraray

Inverbeg

Glenshellish

Luss

Whistlefield

Slate Wharf

Loch Eck

Garelochhead

Glen Fruin

Rossdhu

Ardentinny

Faslane

Helensburgh

Kilmun

Craigendoran

Firth of Clyde

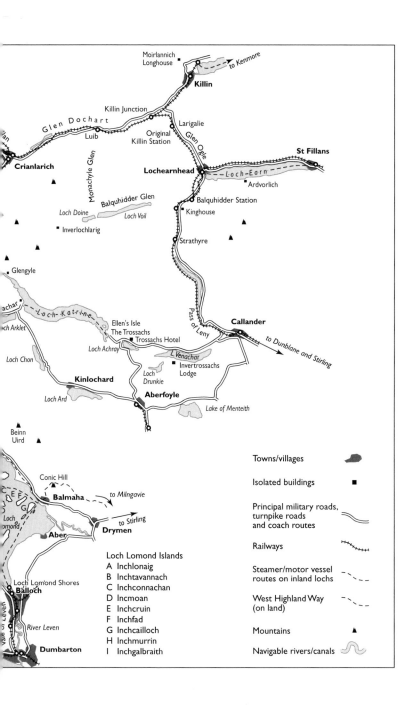

Moirlannich
Longhouse
to Kenmore
Killin

Killin Junction
Glen Dochart
Larigalie
Luib
Original
Killin Station
Glen Ogle
St Fillans
Crianlarich
Monachyle Glen
Lochearnhead
Loch Earn
Ardvorlich
Balquhidder Glen
Balquhidder Station
Loch Doine
Loch Voil
Kinghouse
Inverlochlarig

Glengyle
Strathyre

Loch Katrine
Ellen's Isle
The Trossachs
Trossachs Hotel
Pass of Leny
Callander
ch Arklet
Loch Achray
L. Venachar
to Dunblane and Stirling
Loch Chon
Invertrossachs
Lodge
Kinlochard
Loch
Drunkie
Aberfoyle
Loch Ard
Lake of Menteith

Beinn
Uird

Conic Hill
Balmaha
to Milngavie
Loch
omond
to Stirling
Aber
Drymen

Loch Lom'ond Shores
Balloch
River Leven
Dumbarton

Loch Lomond Islands
A Inchlonaig
B Inchtavannach
C Inchconnachan
D Incmoan
E Inchcruin
F Inchfad
G Inchcailloch
H Inchmurrin
I   Inchgalbraith

Towns/villages

Isolated buildings

Principal military roads,
turnpike roads
and coach routes

Railways

Steamer/motor vessel
routes on inland lochs

West Highland Way
(on land)

Mountains

Navigable rivers/canals

1

INVERSNAID: THE CROSSROADS AT THE END OF THE ROAD

Famous visitors

'No through road', indicates the sign as you drive westwards out of Aberfoyle. So it proves to be, but not immediately. There are fifteen long miles ahead, many of them single-track, winding to and fro, up hill and down dale, past Loch Ard and Loch Chon and Loch Arklet, past the fort that became a farm, past the church that became an outdoor centre. It is only then that the road eventually heads down the long steep hill to reach Inversnaid, a hotel beside a pier on Loch Lomond, with a handsome waterfall and a magnificent view to the Arrochar Alps across the water. Attractive, but there are many places equally so that are easier of access. And it is indeed the end of the road: for the motorist, the only way out is back.

Yet down the centuries a great many well-known people have come to Inversnaid. Gerard Manley Hopkins used the name *Inversnaid* itself as the title for one of his best known poems ('. . . What would the world be, once bereft/Of wet and of wilderness . . .'). William Wordsworth was inspired here to write 'To a Highland Girl'. Samuel Taylor Coleridge came here. So did Walter Scott and Hans Andersen and Jules Verne. So did Rob Roy and General Wolfe of Québec, early in his career. So too did Queen Victoria, and Thomas Cook and, in his wake, hordes of the queen's subjects.

Of these only Rob Roy was resident, and for him the ability to move around in any direction at short notice was vital. So what were he and all the others doing at Inversnaid?

It is a truism that, in the course of progress, for every two steps forward there is a step back. Our general acceptance of the motor car as the everyday means of personal transport has tended to blind us to

The waterfalls at Inversnaid fall directly into Loch Lomond (*Author*)

the former use, and present potential, of many other modes. In 1713, for instance, circumstances dictated that Rob Roy take up residence in Glen Dochart at a point some 5 miles east of Crianlarich. W.H. Murray, in *Rob Roy Macgregor: His Life and Times*, points out that he could still reach former haunts at Balquhidder and Inversnaid in 2½ and 6 hours respectively, walking along the hill paths which were the roads of those days. The distances as the crow flies are about 5 miles and 14 miles; by present-day motor roads they would be about 22 and 51 miles respectively, and I leave it to readers to calculate how long it might take to drive these: while we have gained much in speed, we have lost much in flexibility of route.

Far from being an isolated spot at the end of the road, Inversnaid has always been a nodal point of communications. The route westwards was and is formed by the ferry to the western shore of the loch, very old-established and still operating, even though it is no longer the practice to call it, as formerly, by blowing a coach horn or lighting a fire on the shore. The north/south route was formed by paths but also, more importantly, by the loch itself.

Since time immemorial and until very recently, Loch Lomond and other long, narrow Highland lochs were seen not as obstructions to movement but as aids to it. Travel ashore meant walking or riding along hill paths through forests and across moors. Travel by boat, paddled, rowed or sailed along a loch, was a pleasant alternative.

The principle reached its peak in Victorian times, with the development of steamer services on the lochs. They provided lochside residents with the same ease of movement as branch line railways. And as with branch lines, so development of more modern forms of transport saw their withdrawal in the twentieth century. The steamer services on Loch Lomond – in their day the most extensive of any on a freshwater loch – lasted until 1989 when the *Countess Fiona* (which was, to be accurate, a motor vessel rather than steamer) was withdrawn. It is to be hoped they will yet be revived, when restoration of the loch's last paddle steamer *Maid of the Loch* reaches fruition.

On the east shore of Loch Lomond there could be no direct replacement of the steamer by bus or car, for along much of it no suitable road has ever been built. This is no doubt a reflection of the former ease of travel along the loch itself. But there were rough footpaths, and in recent years Inversnaid has seen travellers passing northwards and southwards in increasing numbers. The revival of interest in travel on foot, from the 1930s onwards, led to the establishment of the first modern long-distance footpath in Scotland, the West Highland Way, completed in 1980. In its route from Milngavie at the edge of Glasgow to Fort William, it follows the east shore of Loch Lomond from Balmaha to the head of the loch, and on it Inversnaid forms an important staging point.

The Trossachs Tour

What really brought visitors in quantity to and through Inversnaid in days gone by was the Trossachs Tour. This is now almost

LOCH KATRINE.

Fares : E'burgh to G'gow, abt. 18s., 14s. Circular : E'burgh, 26s. 4d., 20s. 4d. G'gow, 20s. 4d., 16s. 4d. Available 7 days.

		a.m.	a.m.	a.m.	a.m.			a.m.	a.m.	a.m.	p.m.
Edinburgh { Princes Street ..		—	6.55	9.30	11.25	**Glasgow** (Qu.St. or Central) dep.	—	8.14	11.10	2.20*
{ Waverley		—	6.15	9. 5	—	Balloch (steamer) .... ,,	—	8.50	12.15	3.15*
Glasgow (Buchanan St.)......		—	7.15	10.10	12. 0	Inversnaid (steamer) ...... arr.	—	10.12	1.58	4.48*
Callander (coach) .... dep.		—	9. 0	11.35	2. 0					
						Oban (train) .... dep.	—	—	8.20	—
Glasgow (Queen Street) ,,		—	8. 5	10.32	1.40	Crianlarich (coach) .... ,,	—	—	11. 0	—
Aberfoyle (coach) ...... ,,		—	9.52	12.45	3.55	Ardlui (steamer) .... ,,	6.30	8.30	1.25	4.20
						Inversnaid (coach) .... ,,	7. 5	10.35	2. 5	4.50
Trossachs ....} Fare, { dep.	7.10	11.20	2.15	5.35	**Stronachlachar** } Fare, { dep.	8.10	12.30	3.40	6.30
Stronachlachar } 2s. 6d. { arr.	7.50	12. 5	3. 0	6.15	**Trossachs** ....} 2s. 6d. { arr.	8.40	1.15	4.25	7.15
Inversnaid (coach) .... arr.	6.50	1.10	4.10	7.30	Aberfoyle (coach) ..... arr.	—	2.50	6. 0	
Ardlui (steamer) .... ,,	10.35	2.20	6.50*		**Glasgow** (Queen Street) ,,	—	5.33	8.15	
Crianlarich (coach) .... ,,	—	4.15	—		Callander (coach) .... arr.	10.25	3.30	7. 0	
Oban (train) .... ,,	—	6.32	—		**Glasgow** (Buchanan St)... ,,	12.20	5.15	8.35	
Inversnaid (steamer) ...... dep.	6.55	1.50	4.45		**Edinburgh** { Princes Street ,,	12.36	5.22	9. 4	
Balloch (steamer) .... arr.	8.35	3.20	6.30		{ Waverley .. ,,	2.55	6.24	9. 1	
Glasgow (Q. St. or Cent.), approx.	9.26	4.20	7.25						

Single Fares : Length of Lake, 3s., 2s.   **LOCH LOMOND.**   Return Fares : 3s. 6d., 2s. 6d.

		a.m.	a.m.	p.m.	p.m.			a.m.	a.m.	a.m.	p.m.	p.m.
Glasgow (Q. St. or Cent.), approx.		8.20	11.20	2.20	4. 0	**Oban** (train) .... dep.	—	8.20	—	—	
Balloch .... dep.	8.50	12.15	3.15	4.50	Crianlarich (coach) .... ,,	—	11. 0	—	—	
Balmaha .... ,,	—	12.40	—	5.15	**Ardlui** .... dep.	6.30	8.30	1.20	4.20	6.30
Luss .... ,,	9.20	1. 0	3.50	5.35	**Edinburgh** (Princes St.) ... dep.	—	6.55	9.30	—	
Rowardennan .... ,,	9.37	1.18	4.10	5.50	Callander (coach) .... ,,	—	7.25	11.35	—	
Tarbet .... ,,	9.57	1.38	4.30	6.10	Trossachs (steamer) .... ,,	6. 0	8. 0	12.10	3.10	
Inversnaid .... ,,	10.12	1.58	4.48	6.25	**Inversnaid** .... dep.	6.55	8.55	1.50	4.45	6.55
Stronachlachar (coach) ...... arr.	11.35	3. 5	5.50	7.30	Tarbet .... ,,	7.10	9.10	2. 5	5. 5	7.10
Trossachs (steamer) .... ,,	1.15	4.25	7.15		Rowardennan .... ,,	7.30	9.28	2.25	5.25	7.30
Callander (coach) .... ,,	3.30	7. 0	—		Luss .... ,,	7.50	9.45	2 45	5.43	7.50
Edinburgh (Princes St.) .... ,,	5.40	9.52	—		Balmaha .... ,,	8. 5	10. 0	—	6. 0	—
Ardlui .... arr.	10.35	2.20	5.13	6.50	**Balloch** .... arr.	8.35	10.30	3.20	6.30	8.25
Crianlarich (coach) .... arr.	—	4.15	—		**Glasgow** (Q. St. or Cent.), approx.	9.30	11.20	4.20	7.30	9.20
Oban (train) .... ,,	—	6.40	—								

* Also **Waverley**, arr. 6.24 and 10.19 (via Forth Bridge).   † Also **Waverley**, 6.15 and 9.5 (via Forth Bridge).   ‡ Central, 9.11.

LOCH LONG.

Fares			a.m.			a.m.
	Glasgow (Qu-st., LowLevel) dep.	10. 0	**Glasgow** (Qu.-st. or Cent.) dep.		11.20
Glasgow to	Craigendoran Pier ...... dep.	10.40	Balloch (steamer) .... ,,		12.15
Arrochar,	**Glasgow** (St. Enoch) .... ,,	11. 5	Tarbet (coach) .... ,,		2. 0
2s. 6d., 2s.	Greenock (Princes Pier) ...... ,,	11.48	Arrochar............... dep.		2.25	2.40†
Ret., 4s., 3s.	**Glasgow** (Central) ...... ,,	—	Gourock .... ,,		4.40	—
Helensburgh	Gourock .... ,,	10.45	**Glasgow** (Central) .... arr.		5.25	—
or Greenock	Arrochar .... arr.	1.10	Greenock (Princes Pier) ...... ,,		—	4.10
to Arrochar,			**Glasgow** (St. Enoch) ...... ,,		5. 3	
1s. 6d., 1s.	Tarbet (coach) .... ,,	1.35	Craigendoran Pier............... ,,		4.35	—
Ret., 2s., 1s.6d.	Balloch (steamer) .... ,,	3.25	**Glasgow** (Queen-st.) ...... ,,		5.25	—
	Glasgow (Queen-st. or Cent.),,,	4.20				

Calling also at Dunoon, Kirn, Blairmore, and Ardentinny, etc.

* 1.58 on Sats.; Arrochar arr. 5.15.   † 5.15 p.m. on Sat.; Glasgow arr. 8.54.

Fares for the Round : From Glasgow to Glasgow by Loch Long and Loch Lomond, 7s., 5s.

LOCH TAY.

		a.m.	a.m.	noon			a.m.	a.m.	p.m.
Perth .... dep.	—	9.30	12.10	**Oban** .... dep.	7.55	9.30	3.20
Dunkeld .... ,,	—	10. 7	12.50	Callander ...... ,,	8.55	11.38	3.44
Blair Atholl ... ,,	—	10. 0	1.30	Killin Junc. ...... ,,	10. 3	1.40	5.10
Pitlochry ...... ,,	—	10.20	1.50	**Killin Pier** .... dep.	10.10	—	5.45
Aberfeldy (coach) ,,	—	11. 0	3. 5	Ardeonaig .... ,,	10.45	—	6.10
Kenmore Pier dep.	7.25	12.30	4. 0	Lawers .... ,,	11. 0	—	6.25
Fernan .... ,,	7.40	—	4.20	Ardtalnaig .... ,,	11. 5	—	6.30
Ardtalnaig ... ... ,,	8. 0	—	4.40	Fernan .... ,,	11.25	—	7. 0
Lawers .... ,,	8. 5	—	4.45	**Kenmore Pier**...... arr.	11.55	3.30	7.35
Ardeonaig ...... ,,	8.20	—	5. 0	Aberfeldy (coach) . arr.	1.10	4.40	*8.35
Killin Pier ... arr.	9. 5	1.50	5.40	Pitlochry .... ,,	—	5.23	9.22
Killin Junc. ...... arr.	9.34	2.37	6.58	Blair Atholl ... ,,	—	5.44	9.40
Callander ..... ,,	10.32	3.32	7.12	Dunkeld .... ,,	2.25	5.38	—
Oban............... ,,	11.45	4.50	9. 0	**Perth** .... ,,	2.58	6.30	—

Extra : Kenmore to Killin Pier, 1.30 M.W.F.; starting back, 3.40.   *6.50 (M.W.F.)

Summer 1912 timetables show how steamers on Loch Lomond and Loch Katrine fitted into a wider transport network, with connections as far afield as Edinburgh and Oban (*Author's collection*) forgotten, yet to generations of tourists in the latter part of the nineteenth century and the early part of the twentieth it was famous. It provided some with their introduction to the Highlands, others with a day or two out from the big cities.

In it the Inversnaid–Aberfoyle road played little part. What mattered was that, by keeping straight on at the T-junction four miles from Inversnaid, people would shortly afterwards reach Stronachlachar pier on Loch Katrine. And at the far end of Loch Katrine lay the Trossachs, the district of tangled woodland, hill and loch which, as if it were not attractive enough already, had been rendered world-famous by Sir Walter Scott, most notably in his narrative poem *The Lady of The Lake*.

Today we tend to think of loch cruising in terms of going for an out-and-back cruise, but it was not always so. Formerly, loch cruises formed integral parts of more extended travels. The essence of the Trossachs Tour was the approach to Inversnaid by Loch Lomond steamer (most probably from the railhead at Balloch Pier), the journey by four-in-hand coach from Inversnaid to Stronachlachar, the passage by Loch Katrine steamer to Trossachs Pier, and the onward journey by four-in-hand to a railhead, most commonly Callander. Or, of course, vice versa. Balloch Pier and Callander were easily accessible by train from both Glasgow and Edinburgh. So for some this was a round tour, a day trip; for others, it was the route taken between Glasgow and Edinburgh on a more ambitious tour of Scotland, or indeed of Britain. It could be extended over more than one day by staying at one of the hotels en route.

There were numerous other permutations, such as use of Aberfoyle as a railhead and coach over the Duke's Pass to Trossachs Pier; or taking the steamer from Inversnaid to the head of Loch Lomond, and continuing thence by coach or train into the West Highlands. Whatever the route, however, there were two things of which the tourist could be sure. Firstly, the different modes of transport – trains, steamers and coaches, with their different operators – would connect with one another. And they would do so both in time and in place, with no more than a short wait and a short walk between them. Secondly, purchase of but one ticket was all that was needed to see them though from start point to destination. Truly integrated transport, to which present-day planners and politicians pay lip-

One ticket, with several detachable coupons, covers the tour from Edinburgh to Glasgow via the Trossachs, Inversnaid and Loch Lomond (*BRB (Residuary) Ltd/National Archives of Scotland, BR/GEN/S/3/11*)

service to so little effect, is not in Scotland a dream for the future so much as something which we have had and lost. From that comment I must exclude, largely but not entirely (as we shall see in Chapter 7), the area served by Strathclyde Passenger Transport Executive. Even in Victorian and Edwardian times, there was an exception to integrated transport. Where two railway companies were competing to serve a district, or a destination, their trains were likely to do anything but connect. Of the effects of this, there is more in Chapters 7 and 12.

How did the Trossachs Tour come into being? Tourists in search of the picturesque had been coming to the district since the late eighteenth century; they were rowed or sailed on the lochs and walked, or rode on Highland ponies, over the path between Inversnaid and Stronachlachar.

Here is how the scene struck the writer of *Lumsden & Son's Steamboat Companion* of 1831 (steamboats were already familiar on the Clyde and on Loch Lomond):

> We shall not soon forget the picturesque appearance of a group of strangers with whom we once accidentally met on this route. The cavalcade was threading the narrow pass, which led to a rustic bridge . . . The gay attire of the female equestrians contrasted well with the *unhobby*-like garniture of their steeds – their gay gallants, shouldering fishing-rods and fowling-pieces, seemed their guard of honour – the Highland attendants, in their national costume, acted as men-at-arms – while a few kilted urchins, carrying bags and packages, and attended by at least half-a-dozen of sheep-dogs, made out a group, which, coupled with the wild and romantic scenery around, recalled the . . . pageant expeditions of former ages, when Scotland had her feudal chiefs and feudal dependants.

Hans Christian Andersen experienced an early version of the Trossachs Tour during his one and only visit to Britain. This was in August 1847. At that date the railway system was far from complete and the only line of use to him on this tour was from Glasgow to Edinburgh.

So when Andersen left Edinburgh, travelling in company with members of the Hambro family, who were bankers of Danish extraction, their mode of conveyance was the steamer up the Forth to Stirling. Here they stayed overnight, visited the castle, and continued to Callander for another overnight stop. The next day was a long one. They went by four-in-hand coach to Loch Katrine – the heather in full bloom – and up the loch on the little steamer which had been put into service only the year before.

At Stronachlachar, most of the tourists continued by walking or riding. But because Mrs Hambro and Andersen were exhausted, Hambro obtained the use of a little carriage for them. This is the earliest reference I have found to a carriage or coach on this section of the tour, and I suspect it may have originated at the same time as the steamer. Even so it cannot have been a comfortable journey: the day was misty and there was as yet no proper road. The coachman walked beside the horse and in attempting to follow the path the carriage jolted over clods and stones, was tugged uphill and reeled downhill, until they reached the top of the steep hill leading down to Inversnaid itself. This was too steep to be safe, and the party walked the rest of the way down to the inn.

After embarking on the steamer they went first to the head of the loch, waited for two hours or so in the rain, and then went down to Balloch and by coach to Dumbarton for the night. The following day Andersen travelled by steamer to Glasgow and thence by train to Edinburgh.

Andersen later related an incident which occured on this journey. He had with him a walking-stick which, during the journey over the heath between the two lochs, he had lent to a young son of the Hambros for a plaything. Pointing it at Ben Lomond when it appeared out of the mist, the boy asked of the stick, 'Can you see the highest hill in Scotland?', and in due course, 'Can you see the great lake?', and so on. Andersen promised him that when the stick went with him back to Naples, where he had purchased it, it would tell its friends of its visit to the land of mists and purple flowers. Then, in the bustle of going aboard the steamer at Inversnaid, the stick was left behind.

It caught up with Andersen at Waverley station, Edinburgh. He was on the point of catching the London train when a train from Glasgow arrived; the guard got out, came up to him, and handed him the stick with the remark, 'It has travelled quite well on its own.' Attached to it was a label reading 'Hans Christian Andersen, the Danish poet'; this had sufficed for the walking-stick to be passed from hand to hand over the same journey that Andersen himself had made. The story of the stick that went by itself seems to have all the essence of a fairy tale!

To matters more mundane: Thomas Cook brought a party through Inversnaid in 1850 for the first time. In 1856 his brochure stated that a new road had been made between Stronachlachar and Inversnaid; the old 'drosky' had been superseded by new carriages which were both larger and cheaper for the traveller. Jules Verne noted, at Inversnaid, the splendid coachman in scarlet livery who gathered up the reins of four horses in one hand before setting out up the hill.

By the end of the decade Cook's tours through the district were well established. Railways had reached Stirling in 1848, Balloch in 1850, and eventually Callander in 1859. However in 1862 the railway companies in Scotland decided to take over the excursion business for themselves, rather than charter trains to Cook.

Queen Victoria, staying at Invertrossachs Lodge in 1869 and wishing to visit Loch Lomond, took a similar route to that taken by her subjects: up Loch Katrine in the steamer and then by hired carriage to Inversnaid, where a steamer had been placed at her disposal for a tour of Loch Lomond – and home again by the same route in reverse in the evening.

On railway routes to the Trossachs, competition came in 1882 when the line to Aberfoyle was opened. Despite proposals, no railway was built nearer to the Trossachs than these. The railway companies were, however, assiduous in cultivating a booming tourist trade. To give but one example, when the North British Railway issued its 'Programme of Tourist Ticket Arrangements' for September 1887, the pamphlet described at least twenty-one circular tours which incorporated Loch Katrine, Inversnaid and Loch Lomond. Most of these originated at either Edinburgh or Glasgow, and incorporated other places as far afield as Inverary and even Inverness.

Among the crowds came Gerard Manley Hopkins in September 1881. During a brief month-long spell of working in Glasgow, he managed an even briefer two-day visit to the Highlands. In this the spectacle of the waterfall at Inversnaid evidently re-awoke the yearning for wildness, free from the marks of men, which had previously haunted him at Oxford, according to his biographer

Paddy Kitchen (*Gerard Manley Hopkins*, 1978). Since by 1881 there was something of a scrum at Inversnaid when passengers disembarked from the steamer and embarked on the coaches, I am inclined to guess that he stayed the night at the hotel and visited the waterfall when the crowds had dispersed.

Baedecker's *Great Britain* for 1910 stated that the tour from Glasgow to Edinburgh via Loch Lomond and Loch Katrine was 'in favourable weather one of the most delightful in the United Kingdom.' Baddeley & Ward in their guide *Scotland* for 1908 noted that when the steamer came to Inversnaid 'there is a great landing of passengers for Loch Katrine and the Trossachs.' Wordsworth, who just over a century before had described the scene: '. . . The cabin small,/The lake, the bay, the waterfall . . .,' would, they considered, prefer a more secluded locality. Ward & Lock's guide *The Complete Scotland* of the 1930s was blunter. Quoting the same words, it commented that those who landed at Inversnaid expecting to find nothing else would be disappointed, particularly if they arrived on a busy afternoon.

But by then things were changing. As early as 1908 Baddeley & Ward's guide had included a bound-in supplement on 'Cycling and Motoring' (my italics). One of the suggested cycle tours involves taking the bicycle up Loch Katrine on the steamer. For motorists comprehensive tours throughout Scotland are proposed. Certain roads in the vicinity of the Trossachs were initially closed to motors, but by 1931 the Callander-Trossachs and Stronachlachar-Inversnaid roads were both open, and about 1933 the Aberfoyle-Trossachs road, which had originally been a private toll road, was opened to them too. By this date Loch Lomond was the goal for motor-coach tours from as far afield as Oban, and it was being stated (with perhaps only a little exaggeration) that practically every clachan in Scotland was within hail of a motor service to and from the nearest town.

In these circumstances the horse-drawn coaches between Callander and the Trossachs were replaced by motor charabancs in 1923, and the same happened between Aberfoyle and the Trossachs in 1931. The public felt the loss of a link with the past: the auction sale of horses and coaches at Aberfoyle attracted more than 1,000 people and a lengthy report in the *Stirling Observer* (16 April 1931). Among those present was Peter McAlpine, who had driven the Duke

The Inversnaid Hotel, with Loch Lomond in the background and a coach leaving for Loch Katrine (*Collection J. Danielewski*)

of Montrose over the road when it was opened almost fifty years earlier, had driven coaches over it regularly ever since, and had now driven his last one.

Two of the four-in-hand coaches were bought for further use between Stronachlachar and Inversnaid. Here, convoys of five or so coaches, their passengers perched high up in the open air on forward-facing seats, continued to link the steamers of the two lochs. This was, I believe, the last horse-drawn coach service to operate in Scotland. It became an attaction for tourists in its own right.

In 1937 the London Midland & Scottish Railway publicised the Trossachs Tour by producing a film, *The Beautiful Trossachs*. This is, or was recently, available on video and, with the passing of the years, it has become a little time capsule. It opens with scenes, perhaps obligatory, of the LMS crack express *Coronation Scot* as it leaves Euston: streamlined steam locomotive and carriages with 'go-faster' stripes all down their length. This train was put on in 1937 to mark the coronation of King George VI and Queen Elizabeth, and it was taken off in 1939 at the outbreak of war. Later on in the film, tourists are seen emerging from Callander station past the sign reading 'Book Here for the Trossachs Tour' to join 1930s motor coaches for the ride to the Trossachs. There are references – also perhaps obligatory – to *The Lady of the Lake*. At Trossachs Pier tourists join the steamer *Sir Walter Scott*. Seemingly unchanged and unchanging, she had plied the loch since 1900 and continues to do so in 2003. At Stronachlachar the coaches wait for them, each with its four horses driven by a coachman clad in scarlet – or so we are informed, for the film of course is black-and-white. After the journey to Inversnaid, the tourists embark on one of Loch Lomond's paddle steamers for the cruise to the foot of the loch.

Despite this publicity, 1937 proved to be the last summer during which the horse-drawn coaches operated. They were replaced by buses. For some years these were run by the grandly-named Loch Lomond-Loch Katrine Services Ltd. By 1954 the reality, as recorded by Duncan Graham in *Sunset on the Clyde* (1993) was rather less grand: a handful of passengers were carried in a decrepit blue Bedford with a driver whose manner of driving depended on just how much he had imbibed beforehand. He never lost a passenger; bits of the bus, left behind on rocks or in ditches, were another matter. The potholed condition of the road between Inversnaid and Stronachlachar may also have had something to do with the condition of the bus; still private, the road was eventually taken over by the local authority only in 1959.

With the closure of Aberfoyle station to passengers in 1951 and Callander in 1965, the eastern railhead retreated to Stirling where it had been so long before. But the circular tour incorporating both lochs was still offered. If my memory of a cruise on *Sir Walter Scott* in the late 1970s serves correctly, as the ship approached Stronachlachar the announcement came over the public address system: 'Change here for Loch Lomond.' But the tour was no longer famous, and it faded out when CalMac withdrew PS *Maid of the Loch* from service on Loch Lomond at the end of the 1981 season. Earlier that year Jimmie Macgregor, experiencing the West Highland Way in its first season for the benefit of the BBC, had come to the Inversnaid Hotel; the proprietor proudly displayed a photograph of himself as a wee boy with coach and horses in the hotel yard. But in general the former importance of the Inversnaid–Stronachlachar road as part of a busy through-route was quickly forgotten. When the Loch Lomond Local (Subject) Plan was issued in 1982, the planners merely noted that the narrow road giving access to Inversnaid was a cul-de-sac, and considered that no improvements would be justified 'as part of the policy of maintaining the remote character of this area.'

Yet, with ingenuity, it is still entirely possible to take advantage of the region's potential for travel by routes which are far from obvious on a road atlas. Here is how a friend of the author's, resident in Edinburgh but needed in Balquhidder by lunch time, made the journey. Being both a cyclist and an early riser, he first made his way to Waverley station. There he embarked in the seating coach attached to the London-Fort William sleeper which departs at 04.50. Stowed safely in the brake van was his bicycle: his intention was to change at Dalmuir for Dumbarton, and thence to cycle up national cycle route 7 which, as it happens, would lead to his destination.

Heavy rain as the train approached Dalmuir through the dawn suggested a change of plan. Using his mobile phone, he contacted the Inversnaid Hotel to find out if the ferry across the loch would be running; having ascertained that this was so, he stayed on the train as far as Arrochar & Tarbet station. Thence he cycled to Inveruglas and crossed by ferry to Inversnaid. From there he continued by bike up the road to Stronachlachar, then along the private road (upon which bicycles and walkers are permitted, but not cars) which follows the north side of Loch Katrine as far as Trossachs Pier, and so almost to Callander before turning north on to route 7 for Balquhidder. He was in time for lunch.

The National Park

Nowadays Inversnaid lies centrally within the Loch Lomond & The Trossachs National Park. Some indication of the popularity of Loch Lomond and the Trossachs with visitors over the past two centuries will be evident from what I have already written. Much more will become apparent. Such popularity bears within it the seed of its own destruction, as the writers of those 1930s guide books appreciated.

The possibility of incorporating the region into a national park was being suggested even then, and designation was recommended in 1947. Subsequent decades saw much talk but little action. Tom Weir wrote wisely of Loch Lomond (in *The Scottish Lochs*, 1970) that recreation and conservation were not separate things, but depended on the balance of access and inaccessibility. The *Glasgow Herald* on 1 April 1977 included a two-part article about derelictions and dilapidations around the loch and headed it 'The Scandal of Loch Lomond'. One committee after another considered and reported. But this is scarcely the place for a blow-by-blow account of the area's progress towards the status of national park. That was eventually achieved in 2002 when the park authority for the Loch Lomond & The Trossachs National Park came into operation.

The aims of the national park, as defined in section 1 of the National Parks (Scotland) Act 2000, are:

- to conserve and enhance the natural and cultural heritage of the area
- to promote sustainable use of the natural resources of the area
- to promote understanding and enjoyment (including enjoyment in the form of recreation) of the special qualities of the area by the public
- to promote sustainable economic and social development of the area's communities

Shorn of jargon, the essence of this seems to be: 'Use it but don't spoil it.' That cannot be bad.

While this book has been in production, the national park authority has commenced publication of a public transport timetable – a praiseworthy venture in gathering together in a single volume information, which is otherwise widely dispersed, about routes and times for transport by bus, train, ferry and steamer to and within the national park.

2

INVERSNAID: THE WORDSWORTHS
AND WHAT THEY FOUND THERE

Across the Highland Line

To Loch Lomond and Inversnaid in 1803 came a party of three
visitors: William Wordsworth, his sister Dorothy, and their friend
Samuel Taylor Coleridge. Times were changing and they came
perhaps at a moment more interesting than they knew.
During the latter part of the eighteenth century travellers who
came to the Highlands – such as Thomas Pennant in 1769 and 1772,
and Dr Johnson in 1773 – had come in a spirit of discovery, even of
exploration, of what seemed to them a little-known and 'primitive'
country. Dr Johnson was particularly unimpressed by Loch Lomond.
Being there on a wet 27 October cannot have helped but the islands,
attractive at a distance, disgusted him because on closer approach
he found them lacking in the 'arts of embellishment', soft lawns
and shady thickets, and consisting of no more than uncultivated
ruggedness. By the time the Wordsworths and Coleridge came,
however, people were beginning to appreciate the picturesqueness
of the natural world; mountains, for instance, from being objects
of horror, had become objects of attraction. In this spirit the
Wordsworth party was heading for the Trossachs.
Dorothy Wordsworth was then in her early thirties, her brother
a year and a half older. As orphans, they had spent much of their
childhood apart, only to become close friends in adulthood and
share a house together. From a legacy William derived sufficient
income to support them, but they were far from wealthy. When
they went to Scotland with Coleridge their conveyance was a horse-
drawn car, something similar to an Irish jaunting car. William had
married in 1802, but his wife Mary was left at home with a young
baby while her husband and sister-in-law toured in Scotland.

It is to Dorothy that we owe most of our knowledge of this tour, for (as Louis Stott points out in *Literary Loch Lomond*) the journal that she kept is one of the finest pieces of literature not intended for publication ever written. It was eventually published in 1874. And it is abundantly clear from it that, whatever the picturesque attractions of woods, lochs and mountains, the compiler was just as interested in, and sympathetic to, the people she met – at all levels of society – and how they lived.

In 1803 passing from the Lowlands into the Highlands was marked by far more than the change in the landscape that marks it today. There was a huge cultural transition too, possibly even greater than in crossing the border from England into the Lowlands of Scotland. It was evident in style of dress, type of housing, way of life, language spoken and modes of travel.

Yet in the Highlands much was then undergoing a transformation, besides visitors' appreciation of the scenery. No change in the Wordsworth's mode of travel was immediately evident to them, for they were initially able to drive northwards along the military road built up the west shore of Loch Lomond half a century before. But a couple of miles short of Luss they saw for the first time boys wearing the Highland dress with 'philabeg' or kilt. At Luss itself they first saw thatched huts without glazed windows and smoke coming out of open window-places; the chimneys, Dorothy wrote, were like stools with four legs, with a hole in the roof for the smoke and a slate placed on four sticks over it.

At the inn at Tarbet the Wordsworth party at first thought the people coarse in their manners, for they stared when spoken to, and were slow to answer. Then they realised that the family who ran the inn had difficulty in understanding English: they were Gaelic speakers.

The Wordsworths were to meet many more people whose first language was Gaelic (or Erse, as Dorothy called it) for Gaelic was then generally spoken throughout the region. Most people evidently spoke some English too but, as Dorothy herself put it, 'very distinctly, as all Highlanders do who learn English as a foreign language; but in a long conversation they want words' – that is to say, they were restricted by a limited vocabulary.

In the *Statistical Account of Scotland* prepared in the early 1790s the sections for the parishes of Aberfoyle, Callander, Balquhidder, Comrie and Killin all refer to Gaelic as the language of the people. It would continue to be spoken for many years to come. Robert Southey, for instance, heard Gaelic spoken in Callander town when he passed through it en route for the Trossachs in 1819. By the date of the New Statistical Account (1837) both Gaelic and English were being taught in the schools in Balquhidder parish. In Comrie, Gaelic was still spoken, but English was more common. Queen Victoria noted in 1869 that all the people around Loch Ard and at Stronachlachar spoke Gaelic. Campbell Nairne, in *The Trossachs and the Rob Roy Country* (1961) wrote that there had been Gaelic speakers at Brig o' Turk and on Loch Katrineside within living memory, and Gaelic is said to have been common in Glen Lochay, near Killin, until the 1930s.

To The Trossachs

To revert to Tarbet, the Wordsworths did not find it easy to obtain directions for the route to the Trossachs, partly because of the difficulty of making themselves understood, but also because the people there just did not know. The information needed was eventually obtained from the maidservant who waited upon them, who had been born beside Loch Katrine. The Wordsworths seem to have been misdirected earlier, for most visitors to the Trossachs came by way of Callander. This proved however to be to their advantage (probably) and ours (certainly). The jaunting car was left behind for their return, and they were rowed over Loch Lomond. That was an adventure in itself during which William had the misfortune to drop into the water the two cold fowls intended as provisions – they were recovered. Then, landing at Inversnaid, they found themselves in a world where people continued to live and move as they had done since time immemorial. It was a world innocent of wheels: 'The manner of their travelling is on foot, on horseback and in boats across the waters – young and old, rich and poor', as Dorothy expressed it. Goods were carried on pack horses.

Inversnaid comprised a landing place in a small bay, the ferry house, which was 'a small hut under a steep wood', and, a few yards away, the waterfall, 'of no inconsiderable size' dropping directly into

the loch. Guided by a Highland woman who had crossed the loch
with them, the Wordsworths and Coleridge headed uphill by a path,
a short cut to the 'mountain horse-road', which they then followed
over the moors towards Loch Katrine.

After a couple of miles or so they came to several clusters of
houses: there was cultivated ground growing corn and potatoes
(even these were probably a fairly recent introduction to the district),
people busy making hay, and linen bleaching on the grass. Among
the cheerful sunny hills it was a pretty sight. If there were sheep
here, Dorothy does not mention them (she does elsewhere). Sheep-
farming, and all the changes it brought, had evidently still to reach
that particular corner of the Highlands. People continued to live
largely by subsistence agriculture, as they had always done.

The Highland woman had reached her destination, and left them.
The other three continued to Loch Katrine, but they found no
houses at its shore, only a path leading northwards towards the head
of the loch. The whole loch appeared a solitude. By now faint with
hunger, Dorothy and Coleridge ate one of the fowls between them;
William anxiously pressed on to see what might lie ahead. When
they caught him up, they found him sitting on a hillock whence he
could see further up the loch. There was some debate on whether
to go forward or back: going forward meant no inn nearer than
Callander. Enquiring from a bonnet-and-plaid clad Highlander
on horseback who had caught up with them, they learned that
there were two 'gentlemen's houses' near the head of the loch. They
determined to carry on and eventually rounded the head of the loch
and came to the first of these. This must have been Glengyle, and
after some negotiation they were made welcome for the night.

Dorothy noted in particular the contrast between the mistress
of the house, no different in appearance from an English country
lady (she was 'a tall fine-looking woman neatly dressed in a dark-
coloured gown with a white handkerchief tied round her head')
and her kitchen: roof, walls and floor of mud, all black alike. She
noted too that they had their groceries from Glasgow, which I
suspect meant salt and similar essentials delivered at rare intervals
by boat or packhorse, rather than the regular quick trip to the
supermarket that the expression now suggests. The Wordsworth
party was entertained with tales of Rob Roy, who had lived at the

The horse road from Inversnaid heads down to the west end of Loch Katrine, much as the Wordsworths must have seen it (*Trustees of the National Library of Scotland: Leighton, J.M.,* The Lakes of Scotland *1834*)

next farm and was dead only eighty years, and Dorothy was given a present of some precious eagle's feathers.

In the morning they continued, now along 'a horse-road, upon which narrow carts might travel.' After three miles they came to a ferry house more or less opposite the point at which the path from Inversnaid had reached the shore. Here they were able to persuade the ferryman to row them not across the loch but down it to their goal, and so embarked. At least Dorothy and William did: Coleridge preferred to walk. William wrapped himself in the boatman's plaid, as protection against heavy rain, lay down in the bottom of the boat, and fell asleep.

His sister eventually woke him when the scenery, initially rather bleak, gave way to rocky points and bays, islands and steep birchwoods on shore. At the end of the loch they met up with Coleridge and, with the ferryman as guide, walked through the pass of the Trossachs – rocks, knolls and hills all around, luxuriant heather everywhere, and birch trees scattered around. Dorothy was delighted: the perfection of loveliness and beauty, she wrote.

The Longhouse

Yet her delight at the Loch Katrine ferryman's house and household
was if anything greater. Here they had had a meal earlier and now,
retracing their route, they returned to enjoy his family's hospitality
for the night.

The house was 'the first genuine Highland hut we had been in.'
The entrance was through the byre, the house-door being within
at right-angles to the outer door. When they first came the fire had
been low, but the woman of the house heaped up dry peats and
heather to make a blaze; a small part of the smoke found its way
out of the chimney-hole, the rest through the open window-places.
Returning in the evening they arrived chilled and wet, yet the fire
was brighter and 'when I sate (sic) down in the chimney-corner,'
wrote Dorothy, 'I thought I had never been more comfortable in my
life.' Coleridge had been there long enough to get a pan of coffee
boiling; drams were provided, and sugar, butter, barley-bread and
milk. Dorothy continues:

> We caroused our cups of coffee, laughing like children at the strange
> atmosphere in which we were: the smoke came in gusts, and spread
> along the walls and above our heads in the chimney, where the hens
> were roosting like light clouds in the sky. We laughed and laughed
> again, in spite of the smarting of our eyes, yet had a quieter pleasure
> in observing the beauty of the beams and rafters gleaming between
> the clouds of smoke. They had been crusted over and varnished by
> many winters, till, where the firelight fell upon them, they were as
> glossy as black rocks on a sunny day cased in ice. When we had eaten
> our supper we sate about half an hour, and I think I had never felt so
> deeply the blessing of a hospitable welcome and a warm fire.

Wordsworth, Coleridge, and a third traveller who had accompanied
them back from the Trossachs – he was an Edinburgh drawing-
master on a walking tour – were to sleep in the barn on the hay. It
proved comfortable. Dorothy was offered a bed in the third section
of the house, an end room which served as both larder and bedroom.
But the partitions were not full height and once in bed she could
watch the light from the fire in the next room flickering overhead
among the beams and rafters which 'crossed each other in almost
as intricate and fantastic a manner as . . . the under-boughs of a

large beech tree'. Dorothy found it beautiful, fairyland even, as she lay looking up at the gradually fading firelight and listening to the waves of the loch beating against the shore: 'I was less occupied by remembrance of the Trossachs', she wrote, 'beautiful as they were, than by the vision of the Highland hut, which I could not get out of my head.'

In the morning, from the fireside, she could hear their hostess milking the cow in the byre beyond the partition ('I had seldom heard a sweeter fireside sound; in the evening . . . it would lull one like the purring of a cat' wrote Dorothy). Tea and sugar were provided for the visitors; the family breakfasted off curds and whey, taken from the pot in which cheese was being made. Dorothy tried some, and thought it exceedingly good; she said to herself 'that they lived nicely with their cow: she was meat [i.e., provided food], drink and company.'

The Wordsworths had clearly been visiting a longhouse, one with cruck frames: crucks being those roughly curved timbers which meet in pairs beneath the ridge of the roof but spring not from the tops of the walls but from the ground or a level close to it. The stonework of the walls serves mainly to fill in the spaces between the crucks: in earlier times it would probably have been turf. Since the crucks, and their associated roof timbers, are not far removed from their natural state as tree trunks and branches, Dorothy Wordsworth's description of them is indeed apt.

Such longhouses seem once to have been used throughout mainland Scotland, but to have died out as agricultural improvements made their way north. In the Lowlands they had largely died out by about 1800, but improvements had then scarely penetrated north of the Highland Line, so that it was at that point in their travels that the Wordsworths first encountered such a building.

The layout has proved persistent. Near Killin is Moirlannich Longhouse, the property of the National Trust for Scotland and open on certain days in summer. It was inhabited until the 1960s. There is evidence of gradual development of detail: separate entrances for man and beast, glass in the windows, corrugated iron to cover the thatch, ceilings to the rooms. Yet the fireplace is open (there is no kitchen range), there is access to the byre past the partition which separates it from the rest of the house, and in the byre the cruck frames and complex roof timbers are plain to see and wonder at.

The Highland Girl

English travellers – and indeed Lowland Scots – in the Highlands in the eighteenth and early nineteenth centuries were inclined to equate primitive housing with oppressive poverty or indolence or both. There is little sense of this in Dorothy Wordsworth's writing. Yet she does not go to the opposite extreme of suggesting any sort of rural idyll. The people she meets are happy, content with what they have, and neither more nor less industrious than anyone else. A nice example of this came as the little party, having been rowed across Loch Katrine by the ferryman, headed towards Inversnaid.

As they started down the hill in the rain, pouring as ever, they overtook two girls, of whom the older was about fourteen, both dressed in grey plaids. The Wordsworths fell into conversation with them. They could not go on the ferry over Loch Lomond until evening, they learned; as it was Sunday the boat had gone to the far side with people bound for church. The older girl was the sister of the ferryman, left in charge at the ferry house, and the younger his wife's sister. In the meantime the visitors might wait beside the fire. The older of the two girls, Dorothy noted, was extremely beautiful; Coleridge was smitten – 'O she was a divine creature!' he recorded in his notebook. William Wordsworth, not long after his return from Scotland, was moved to write:

Sweet Highland Girl, a very shower
Of beauty is thy earthly dower!
Twice seven consenting years have shed
Their utmost bounty on thy head:
And these grey rocks; this household lawn;
These trees, a veil just half withdrawn;
This fall of water, that doth make
A murmur near the silent Lake;
This little Bay, a quiet road
That holds in shelter thy abode;
In truth together ye do seem
Like something fashion'd in a dream; . . .

'To the Highland Girl of Inversnaid', l. 1–12

Only a few years after the Wordsworths' visit, a party of tourists heads up the hill behind Inversnaid. Just about here the Wordsworths encountered the two Highland girls. (*Trustees of the National Library of Scotland: Beattie, W., Scotland 1836*)

Dorothy's account, more down-to-earth, is yet if anything more vivid. In the ferry house the rough floor was wet from rain blowing beneath the door, so that the girls' bare feet were as wet, in walking from one room to another, as though they had been walking through puddles in the street. But while the fire burned up, and above it a fowl stewed in barley broth, and the visitors warmed their toes on the hearth stone, and the granny of the family rocked a crying baby in its cradle and tried in vain to sooth it with songs in Gaelic, then the two girls

> were both exceedingly desirous to get me what I wanted to make me comfortable. I was to have a gown and petticoat of the mistress's; so they turned out her whole wardrobe on the parlour floor, talking Erse to one another, and laughing all the time. It was long before they could decide which of the gowns I was to have; they chose at last . . . and one or the other, or both together, helped me to dress, repeating at least half a dozen times, 'You never had on the like of that before.' They held a consultation of several minutes over a pair of coarse woollen stockings, gabbling Erse as fast as their tongues

could move, and looked as if uncertain what to do: at last, with great diffidence, they offered them to me, adding, as before, that I had never worn 'the like of them'.

By the time the boat came back clothes had been dried and Dorothy had, presumably, changed back into her own. Eventual departure was hurried because the ferryman, having brought twenty passengers across, had to go back for more. The mistress of the house was amongst the first load and enquired of the Wordsworths how they had fared, solicitously but of necessity briefly. One somehow feels that it was as well that they were out of the way before she discovered just what her younger sister and sister-in-law had got up to with her wardrobe in her absence!

3

THE GARRISON, ROB ROY
AND THE JACOBITES

The Violent Highlands

When the Wordsworth party had first arrived at Inversnaid and climbed the hill to the moorland beyond, they had noticed near the top a very large stone building with a high wall around it. What this might be they could not guess. Since it appeared to have been strongly built for defence against storms, William supposed it might have been a spittal, a shelter for travellers, like those in the Alps.

The Highland woman in their company had insufficient English to enlighten them, and it was only at Glengyle that they discovered the building's purpose. It was, they learned, 'The Garrison', built at the request of the Duke of Montrose for the defence of his territories against Rob Roy, and for control of the Highlands in general; soldiers had been withdrawn from it only some thirteen or fourteen years previously.

Here was solid evidence both of recent pacification of the Highlands, which was enabling visitors such as the Wordsworths to move around freely, and of the former unruly nature of the region. For many centuries the pastoral tranquillity of the Highlands had all too often been disturbed by violence and bloodshed.

This had its roots in the nature of the clan system, and in changes or attempted changes to it. In the ancient Celtic system that obtained in the Highlands, tenure of land was based on the kinship of members of the clan which resided upon the land in question. The clan system also involved military allegiance between members of a clan and their chief. A typical clan chief might have at his command several hundred armed men. He in turn was bound to look to the interests of his clansmen.

Here is how this aspect of the clan system was described by Tobias Smollett – himself a native of the Vale of Leven – in *Humphry Clinker*, published in 1771:

> The connection between the clans and their chiefs is, without all doubt, patriarchal. It is founded on hereditary regard and affection, cherished through a long succession of ages. The clan consider the chief as their father, they bear his name, they believe themselves descended from his family, and they obey him as their lord . . .; while he, on his part, exerts a paternal authority, commanding, chastising, rewarding, protecting, and maintaining them as his own children.

Onto this patriarchal system the kings of Scots had, from the twelfth century onwards, attempted to superimpose the feudal system of land tenure, in which land was held by vassals from their superiors and ultimately from the king. They had been only partially successful.

Clan chiefs differed one from another in the extent of their willingness to accept the feudal system, and indeed to exploit it. They jockeyed for power. There were intrigues between chiefs, feuds between clans, and a central authority willing to exploit these in attempts to extend its own power. Fighting between the clans led to repeated revenge attacks which degenerated into appalling atrocities.

In all the Highlands no area was more unruly than that which lay just to the north of the Highland Line, around Loch Lomond and the Trossachs – or so the Lowlanders believed. The mere expression 'Highland' was used by them as a term of abuse, encompassing all the supposed worst qualities of Highlanders from aggressiveness to stupidity. Yet that apparent stupidity was no more than a consequence of limited ability to understand Scots or English rather than Gaelic.

Of the barbarities which Highlanders could inflict on one another, one particular occasion gave ample evidence: the Battle of Glen Fruin. Glen Fruin lies in Dunbartonshire, to the west of the southern part of Loch Lomond. There had been a long history of feuding between MacGregors and Colquhouns when, during the winter of 1602–3, two young MacGregors, laden with goods, were heading home from Dumbarton up the west shore of Loch Lomond. They intended to cross the loch to reach MacGregor lands around

Inversnaid, but became benighted near Luss. They were refused shelter by the Colquhoun inhabitants, so they took shelter in a hut and killed a sheep for food. For this they were arrested next day by Luss men, taken before their chief and sentenced to hang, which sentence was carried out.

Such provocation might have provoked instant retaliation, but in fact an attempt seems to have been made at conciliation: MacGregor and Colquhoun chiefs were to meet in Glen Fruin to discuss compensation. Both, by way of security, were to be accompanied by a band of a hundred men. Both took more, and kept them out of sight. But not for long, for a pitched battle erupted; many Colquhouns were killed, some MacGregors, and probably some bystanders too, who may or may not have been armed.

Accounts of Glen Fruin vary greatly. Indeed accounts of clan warfare in general vary greatly, according even now to the allegiance of the teller. Folk memories linger long, too. In *Wild Drumalbain*, published in 1927, Alasdair Alpin MacGregor recalled enjoying the hospitality of the Colquhoun chief of the day, at his home at Rossdhu near Luss. But when he was introduced by name to the chief's young son, the little boy looked up at his father and nervously inquired, 'Daddy, will he kill us all?'

The Jacobites

By the seventeenth century clan battles were being fought against a background of constitutional changes. These were to have lasting effects at local level, although they may at first have seemed remote. At the union of crowns in 1603, James VI inherited the throne of England to become known as James VI & I. In 1688 came the revolution in which the Catholic James VII & II was replaced by Protestant joint sovereigns, William of Orange and his wife Mary. Both were of Stuart descent: William was descended from Charles I and Mary was the eldest daughter of James VII & II. Until a few months earlier she had been James's heir presumptive, but then his second wife had borne a son, Prince James Edward, who would be brought up abroad as a Catholic. In England this 'Glorious Revolution' of 1688 was in effect bloodless. In Scotland (and also in Ireland) it was not.

To many in the Highlands, William and Mary appeared as usurpers. The Scottish throne had been occupied by Stuart kings (with a few interruptions) for more than three centuries. Highlanders rose to fight for James at Killiecrankie, and many retained their Jacobite allegiance during the uncertain times which followed. These saw Scotland and England united as Great Britain in 1707, and in 1714 the death of Queen Anne, Mary's younger sister. Without a direct heir, she was replaced on the throne by the Hanoverian King George I: Protestant, German, descended very remotely from the House of Stuart, and scarcely able to speak English let alone Gaelic. He and his immediate predecessors found their support among the progressive whigs in the increasingly commercial and mercantile world of the Lowlands, and of England. The Highlands, to them, were a primitive, backward region. The Stuarts on the other hand, for all their faults, understood the Highlands and the Highland way of life. Indeed they understood them so well that they were able to exploit the military aspect of the clan system in their attempts to regain the throne.

In 1714 there was a real possibility that George could be replaced by the exiled Prince James Edward. His claim was much stronger and only his Catholic faith stood in the way. Or so it seemed to Jacobites, and they were many. The Jacobite clans rose in 1715. But although Jacobites enjoyed much general popularity, they lacked good military leadership. At the crucial battle of Sherriffmuir the right wings of the opposing forces each routed their immediate opponents and the battle ended in indecision. James came to Scotland, stayed briefly, and went again. By 1716 the rising had fizzled out. There would be further risings in 1719 and 1745.

Rob Roy

Enter Rob Roy MacGregor (1671–1734). His story has received much attention from Daniel Defoe's day down to our own. A good recent account is W.H. Murray's *Rob Roy MacGregor: His Life and Times* (1982). MacGregors had a long history of violence, in aggression or self-defence according once again to the inclination of the teller. The present author is trying, rather desperately, to steer a middle course! Both aspects are of course true, at different times and on different occasions. During much of the seventeenth century, savage attempts were made to eliminate the clan, and the very name MacGregor was proscribed.

So for much of his life Rob Roy himself went by his mother's name of Campbell. He was the son of the chieftain of the MacGregors of Glengyle, and he built up a flourishing business in cattle droving and dealing: these were the days when cattle were the one great marketable export of the Highlands. But the skills of cattle droving were closely allied to cattle rieving, the traditional stealing of the cattle of a neighbouring clan, sometimes accompanied by a fight but not regarded as a crime. He played his part in this. Close to the Highland Line there was a further temptation, the cattle of Lowland farms, owned by Lowlanders of Saxon stock and so, to Celtic Highlanders, legitimate booty.

Sometimes, too, a gang of Highlanders would lift from a Lowland farm not merely the cattle, but a wife for one of themselves. Even this practice, remarkable as it now seems, was far from meeting with universal condemnation. It was indeed a compliment to the looks of the girl concerned. Perhaps to many a bored young girl growing up on a Lowland farm, the thought that one dark night a handsome Highlander might appear at the door to bear her away may have seemed quite a romantic notion!

Lowland farmers did not take the loss of their cattle as philosophically as Highland clansmen did. The result was the 'Watch', an arrangement by which clansmen – such as, at times, Rob Roy – would guarantee to Lowland farmers, in return for payment called 'blackmail', that their cattle would not be lifted or, if they were, then they would be recovered. This, though a thinly disguised protection racket, had official sanction in the absence of anything better.

In any event it did, at least sometimes, work as intended. This we can tell from a personal reminiscence which Scott was able to include in the introduction to his novel *Rob Roy* (1817). Its immediacy lifts, briefly, the mist of time which otherwise clouds our vision of those days, when viewed from almost three centuries on.

In Scott's day, Rob Roy and his activities were within the memory of old men still living. One such recalled to Scott that when fifteen years old he had lived with his father, who was cowherd on a

Lowland estate, close to the Highland Line. On a morning in late October it was found that a dozen cattle had been lifted during the night. Rob Roy was sent for, and arrived with seven or eight armed men; after hearing all the circumstances he expressed confidence that the cattle could not have been taken far, and that he should be able to recover them. Scott's informant and his father were sent off along with Rob Roy and his men, to drive the recovered cattle. There ensued a long day's march towards Ben Vorlich, a night in a ruined bothy, and a further morning during which the cattle were tracked by Rob Roy himself from signs and marks he observed of their passing.

Scott continued:

About noon, Rob commanded the armed party to halt, and to lie couched in the heather where it was thickest. 'Do you and your son,' he said to the oldest Lowlander, 'go boldly over the hill. You will see beneath you, in a glen on the other side, your master's cattle feeding, it may be with others; gather your own together, taking care to disturb no one else, and drive them to this place. If any one speak to, or threaten you, tell them that I am here, at the head of twenty men.' [One notes the exaggeration!] – 'But what if they abuse us, or kill us?' said the Lowland peasant, by no means delighted at finding the embassy imposed on him and his son. 'If they do you any wrong,' said Rob, 'I will never forgive them as long as I live.' The Lowlander was by no means content with this security, but did not think it safe to dispute Rob's injunctions.

He and his son climbed the hill, therefore, found a deep valley, where there grazed, as Rob had predicted, a large herd of cattle. They cautiously selected those which their master had lost, and took measures to drive them over the hill. As soon as they began to remove them, they were surprised by hearing cries and screams; and looking around in fear and trembling, they saw a woman, seeming to have started out of the earth, who *flyted* at them, that is, scolded them, in Gaelic. When they contrived, however, in the best Gaelic they could muster, to deliver the message Rob Roy told them, she became silent, and disappeared without offering them any further annoyance. The chief heard their story on their return, and spoke with great complacency of the art which he possessed of putting such things to rights without any unpleasant bustle. The party were now on their road home, and the danger, though not the fatigue, of the expedition was at an end.

The overnight halt, on the homeward journey, was made on a wide moor across which whistled the cold north-east wind. The Highlanders lay down among the heather comfortably enough, wrapped in their plaids; the Lowlanders lacked such protection. 'Rob Roy' wrote Scott 'observing this, directed one of his followers to afford the old man a portion of his plaid; "for the callant (boy), he may" said the freebooter, "keep himself warm by walking about and watching the cattle."'

But as the night wore on, colder and colder, the boy decided to lie down in the shelter of the largest of the Highlanders, who acted as Rob's second-in-command. Having done so he found a corner of the man's plaid close by, and by imperceptible degrees drew more and more of it around him. He then slept soundly until daybreak. But on waking up he found to his horror that his neighbour's neck and shoulders, no longer protected by the plaid, were covered with hoar frost. He crept away, expected a beating at least. But the big man merely arose, shook himself, rubbed the hoar frost off with his plaid and muttered something about a 'cauld night'. The cattle were then driven home.

Even recalling this adventure decades later, Scott noted, his informant bore a look which was 'half-frightened, half-bewildered'.

This story probably dates from the later stages of Rob Roy's life, and in telling it I have diverged far from any sort of chronological summary of his career. This was left at the stage of a flourishing business in cattle dealing. Earlier, Rob Roy had fought on the Jacobite side at Killiecrankie, and subsequently took part in lifting cattle from Lowland estates owned by whigs, which to a Jacobite doubtless seemed entirely justified. But by the early 1700s his legal cattle dealing business was in the ascendant and he was indeed flourishing, the owner of nearly 7,000 acres to the north-east of Loch Lomond. Further land purchases followed, for his own benefit and that of relatives. Yet that successful business was leaving him beholden to whig grandees who at one and the same time trusted him as an honest and reliable dealer yet distrusted him as a Jacobite.

The climax came in 1712 when Rob Roy's head drover, despatched to the north to purchase cattle, absconded with the funds. These were perhaps as much as £1,000 sterling, a colossal sum. He proved

Rob Roy's territory: the east side of Loch Lomond as it is today, showing the Inversnaid Hotel, and Ben Lomond to the right (*Author*)

impossible to trace, and in the meantime the Duke of Montrose, who had advanced much of it, decided to foreclose without giving Rob Roy time to attempt to repay.

Montrose was young and ambitious – 'of good understanding', says his entry in the *Dictionary of National Biography*, yet 'easily led by the nose'. He had become fourth Marquis of Montrose in 1684 while still a minor; in 1702 he purchased the property of the Duke of Lennox, south-east of Loch Lomond, and in 1707 he was created Duke of Montrose for his support of the Union. He became one of the sixteen Scottish representative peers. As a prominent Whig his distrust of Rob Roy as a Jacobite and a MacGregor had perhaps overcome his trust in him as a cattle dealer. Or perhaps, in those complex times, there was more to it; Murray, despite extensive and painstaking research, seems to have been unable to unravel these crucial events to the full. What is clear is that within weeks if not days Rob Roy's prosperity had collapsed. He was not only bankrupted but also, since Montrose had influence with Government, outlawed early in 1713.

The immediate effect was that Montrose as sherriff was able to dispatch troops, led by his own factor, to evict Rob Roy's family from their home at Craigroyston (he himself was away) and to render it uninhabitable. In that unstable period their solution was for Rob to place himself under the protection of his mother's cousin the Earl of Breadalbane, who was elderly, wily, powerful, Campbell and Jacobite. Breadalbane provided the house in Glen Dochart, mentioned earlier, where Montrose's men dared not venture.

Deprived as an outlaw of land and rent, tenants' services, cattle and work, Rob Roy still had to support himself and his family. He determined to do so off Montrose's lands. He could still find many to assist him in this, starting with his former drovers. They began to raid Montrose's principal tenants for cattle, grain, and, by arriving shortly before the factor was due, rent money. This was collected at pistol point in exchange for a receipt. Small tenants were unmolested and at times assisted. For example, Murray notes the instance of a cottar near Balfron due to be evicted: Rob Roy arrived early on the day appointed with sufficient money for her to pay off the bailiffs – and advised her to make sure of getting a full receipt. Of course the bailiffs were later ambushed and the money recovered. It was for actions such as this that Rob Roy came to be regarded as a popular hero.

Outlawry certainly did not prevent Rob Roy and his men from taking an active part in the rising of 1715, and an instance of this is recounted in a later chapter. After the rising an amnesty was offered to Jacobite clansmen in response for surrender of arms. But to whom was Rob Roy to surrender? Scarcely to Montrose, who was now high in government – he became a Privy Counsellor in 1717. Breadalbane was Jacobite and dying; Swiss mercenaries in government employ had already burned the house Breadalbane had provided. Rob Roy's solution was to surrender to the Duke of Argyll – Campbell and less wholeheartedly pro-government than many – or rather to one of his aides, at Inverary. Rob Roy may earlier have been providing Argyll with intelligence. Or he may not. Or if he did, it may have been of little or no value. We cannot now tell. At any rate, he was now under Argyll's protection, and was able to build a house in Glen Shira, in the hills to the north of Inverary, to which he retreated from time to time when things got too hot elsewhere.

For Rob Roy now resumed his harrying of the Duke of Montrose's lands in Lennox. His exploits became ever more audacious, Montrose's responses ever more heavy handed, Rob Roy's escapes, when occasionally captured, ever more daring if not miraculous. I shall return to one of the most outrageous exploits in a moment. One gets the impression that to Montrose's rivals for power this thorn in his side cannot have been entirely unwelcome! Eventually, perhaps, Montrose realised this and eased off.

Others did not: there were to be many more attempts, by government forces and others, to capture Rob Roy. All ended in fiasco or daring escape or both. His popularity in the country was too great. These attempts too eventually died down. Rob Roy fought in the brief Jacobite rising of 1719, but subsequently most of his time was spent on his farm at the head of Balquhidder glen, with some droving, a little discrete lifting of cattle and activities with the Watch. He died eventually in his bed.

In today's terms Rob Roy MacGregor would probably be hailed as a freedom fighter by his friends, and stigmatised as a terrorist by his enemies. Somehow 'outlaw' seems happier, with its overtones of Robin Hood and Just William!

'Happy' indeed, for Rob Roy was of cheerful disposition and, in a violent age, seemingly disinclined to use violence when he could achieve his ends merely by its threat. A remarkable example of this came in 1716, by which date his house at Craigroyston had twice been burned by troops, and that in Glen Dochart too. For these, he felt that Montrose owed him compensation.

It was customary for Montrose's factor, John Graham of Killearn, to collect rents in cash at the end of November each year. For this purpose he met the tenants at a farmhouse at Chapelarroch, near Gartmore – in the Lowlands but temptingly close to the hills. It was on this occasion, about 9 p.m. as business was drawing to a close, that Rob Roy burst into the room with a gang of armed men. He meticulously wrote out receipts to tenants in the duke's name, and then made off with money, rent books and the factor too.

Yet, notwithstanding that Graham had led the troops who had burned Rob Roy's Craigroyston house three years before, he does not seem to have been treated over-harshly, at least by the standards of the day. Rather, the kidnapped factor was taken to Loch Katrine, and held on the island which to this day bears the name 'Factor's Island' – it lies immediately off the pier at Stronachlachar. First, however, he was made to write to his employer:

'MAY IT PLEASE YOUR GRACE, – I am obliged to give your Grace the trouble of this, by Robert Roy's commands, being so unfortunate at present as to be his prisoner . . .'

A ransom demand followed, with promise of 'hard usage' for Graham if an attempt was made at reprisal. Montrose's reaction seems to have been to write furiously to the highest civil and military authorities, recounting in detail, from his point of view, all the sins against him of 'that very notorious rogue, Rob Roy'. He expected military assistance. This was not immediately forthcoming – the military authorities were probably all too well aware of their impotence against one such as Rob Roy on his home ground – but neither, so far as Rob Roy was concerned, was there any sign of any ransom money. After about a week, therefore, he had Graham of Killearn taken to Kirkintilloch and there released. His books and accounts were returned to him: the money was not. Montrose was then in the position of having to write a further letter to his earlier correspondents, explaining that his factor had now been released unharmed. It can have done little for his prestige (and much, perhaps, for Rob Roy's!).

The Garrison at Inversnaid

It was this incident which seems to have crystalised in Montrose's mind the desirability of a barracks to enable troops to be stationed in Clan Gregor territory: he pointed this out in his earlier letter and he had already discussed it with General Carpenter, commander of government troops in Scotland. The proposal for a barracks at Inversnaid was taken up by the Board of Ordnance, which was equally considering the construction of barracks at Fort Augustus, Bernera (Glenelg) and Ruthven (Strathspey), as part of a general plan for controlling the Highlands. Sites for all four were agreed in August 1717, as the *Inventory of the Ancient and Historical Monuments of Stirlingshire* makes clear.

Yet the origins of the barracks, or Garrison, at Inversnaid are not clear at all: in gathering the material for this chapter I have time and again come across references new and old which suggest an earlier date. F.J. Evans in *The Trossachs Report*, which he prepared for the Countryside Commission for Scotland in 1972, dates the Garrison

The Garrison of Inversnaid. The engraving, after a drawing by Alexander Nasmyth, was included in the autobiography of his son, James Nasmyth. (*Author's collection*)

prior to the rising of 1715, and specifically to 1713. *Lumsden & Son's Steamboat Companion* of 1831 equally dates the Garrison to 1713. In *The Islands of Loch Lomond* published by the Friends of Loch Lomond about 2001, we read that Rob Roy blew up the duke's fort at Inversnaid in 1713.

The earliest suggested date which I have come across is 1703. It appears in *James Nasmyth Engineer*, an autobiography published in 1883. Nasmyth was a prominent nineteenth-century engineer and son of Alexander Nasmyth, the artist noted for his iconic portraits of Robert Burns. The Nasmyths were a family of strong practical bent, and James Nasmyth wrote thus of ancestor Michael Naesmyth, a builder and architect in Edinburgh:

> The last work that Michael Naesmyth was engaged in cost him his life. He had contracted with the Government to build a fort at Inversnaid, at the northern end of Loch Lomond. It was intended

to guard the Lowlands, and keep Rob Roy and his caterans within the Highland Border. A promise was given by the Government that during the progress of the work a suitable force of soldiers should be quartered close at hand to protect the builder and his workmen. Notwithstanding many whispered warnings . . . Michael Naesmyth and his men encamped upon the spot, though without the protection of the Government force. Having erected a temporary residence for their accommodation, he proceeded with the building of the fort. The work was well advanced by the end of 1703, although the Government had treated all Naesmyth's appeals for protection with evasion or contempt.

Winter set in with its usual force . . . One dark and snowy night, when Michael and his men had retired to rest, a loud knocking was heard at the door. 'Who's there?' asked Michael. A man outside replied, 'A benighted traveller overtaken by the storm.' He . . . begged for God's sake that he might have shelter for the night. Naesmyth . . . unbolted and unbarred the door, when in rushed Rob Roy and his desperate gang. The men, with the dirks of the Macgregors at their throats, begged hard for their lives. This was granted on condition that they should instantly depart, and take an oath that they should never venture within the Highland border again.

Michael Naesmyth and his men had no alternative but to submit, and they at once left the bothy with such scanty clothing as the Macgregors would permit them to carry away. They were marched under an armed escort through the snowstorm to the Highland border, and were there left with the murderous threat that, if they ever returned to the fort, certain death would meet them.

Poor Michael never recovered from the cold which he caught during his forced retreat from Inversnaid. The effects of this, together with the loss and distress of mind which he experienced from the Government's refusal to pay for his work . . . preyed upon his mind . . . One evening . . . a death-like faintness came over him; he . . . fell forward dead on his own hearthstone.

Thus ended the life of Michael Naesmyth in 1705 . . .

This story with its wealth of detail has a plausible ring to it except in two particulars. Firstly, the date 1703 is uncomfortably early in Rob Roy's career, although by no means impossible. Secondly, the *Inventory* mentioned above names the principal contractors for the barracks (in 1718) as Gilbert Smith, mason, Robert Mowbray, carpenter, and James Syme, slater, this being derived from records at the Public Record Office. Other names are mentioned, but Naesmyth is absent.

I am inclined to think the essence of the story true, and to relate to an early and unsuccessful attempt to build a barracks at Inversnaid, perhaps in 1713, with Nasmyth incorrect about either the date or the ancestor. But it remains an enigma.

The Garrison, as Built

There is no doubt, however, that work began on construction of Inversnaid Garrison in 1718 – the building contracts were signed on 14 June, and a quarry was opened nearby to provide stone. There was an interruption to the work on 8 August when eight masons and quarriers were abducted by 'armed Highlanders' – one may guess who these were. But the work went ahead. Two three-storey barrack blocks were built along the north and south sides of a courtyard which was presumably used as a parade ground; ramparts linked these along the east and west sides, and towers extending outwards from north-east and south-west corners provided for flanking fire along the outer walls in the event of attack. The building was similar to Ruthven Barracks near Kingussie, which are still prominently in view to motorists on the A9; Bernera and Fort Augustus were larger.

Of the four, Inversnaid was completed first. The building was probably garrisoned by 1720, although the earliest indication that it was in use appears to come not from military records but, surprisingly, from the Register of Baptisms for the Parish of Buchanan: on 19 March 1721 this recorded the birth of a son to the wife of a soldier stationed there.

Rob Roy is said to have gained entry to the barracks by arranging for a MacGregor lassie to ply the soldiers with so much whisky that the sentinel became intoxicated and she was able to open the gate. He and his men then rushed in and set the buildings on fire; the soldiers were lucky to escape with their lives. But the barracks do seem to have had some effect, for it was about the date that they were first garrisoned that Rob Roy started to make his base at a distance from Inversnaid, at Inverlochlarig at the head of Balquhidder glen, where it remained for the rest of his life.

Meanwhile wider attempts were being made by the government to bring the Highlands under control. General Wade reported to George I in 1724 that there were in the Highlands 22,000 men capable of bearing arms, of whom 10,000 were 'well affected' to the government. The remainder 'have been engaged in Rebellion against Your Majesty, and are ready, whenever encouraged by their Superiors or Chiefs of Clans, to create new Troubles and rise in Arms in favour of the Pretender.' He also reported on cattle thieving, and how it led to blackmail, and to revenge attacks in which people's cattle, houses and lives were at risk.

The Disarming Act of 1716 had been less than wholly effective: clans which favoured the government had surrendered their arms, but Jacobite clans had surrendered only arms which were old or useless – as indeed had Rob Roy and his MacGregors at Inveraray – and had retained those which might be of further service. This had left clans which were loyal to the government at the mercy of those which were not.

Efforts were intensified to enforce the disarming of the clansmen; to that end, further barracks were built, and construction of the military road network commenced, to enable government forces to move more easily about the country.

In this, the place of the road from Aberfoyle to Inversnaid is unclear. It certainly did not form part of the main system of military roads, and gets little if any mention in either William Taylor's *The Military Roads in Scotland* (1976) or J.B. Salmond's *Wade in Scotland* (1934). Yet the old *Statistical Account* for Aberfoyle (1793), having mentioned the barracks at Inversnaid, adds that 'a very tolerable road [was] carried through the whole length of this parish, by which alone Inversnaid is accessible.' F.J. Evans in *The Trossachs Report* specifically describes this road as a military road and mentions military bridges and culverts such as the bridge over a burn beside the former Tea Pot cottage.

I am doubtful: one of the characteristics of the early military roads is their tendency to run as straight as possible, and the road in question certainly does not do that. The straight lengths at its northern end were the nineteenth-century work of Glasgow Corporation in connection with its Loch Katrine Waterworks. Maybe the eighteenth-century soldiers merely widened and improved an existing horse road, without realigning it. Suprisingly, I have found no reference to taking supplies to Inversnaid by boat up Loch Lomond – for on Loch Ness at the same period the 'Government Galley' was put into service to take supplies to Fort Augustus.

The '45 and After

The steady pacification of the Highlands came to an abrupt halt in 1745 when, with Britain and France at war, Prince Charles Edward Stuart took the opportunity to come to Scotland and raise the Jacobite clans in yet another attempt by the Stuarts to regain the throne. Inversnaid was at this time garrisoned by a force of eighty-nine men. But these were employed building roads, and all but nine were away when a troop of MacGregors, commanded by Rob Roy's nephew Gregor MacGregor, took their opportunity. They descended upon the barracks, overpowered those soldiers who were there and made prisoners of the remaining detachments as they returned. They then occupied the barracks until ordered to garrison Doune for Prince Charles, at which point they left with their prisoners, having first set fire to the buildings.

In the immediate aftermath of the '45, therefore, there were no troops stationed at Inversnaid, and in their absence gangs of MacGregors, MacLarens and MacFarlanes, who had kept their arms after the collapse of the rising, resumed their former habits. There were constant reports from the adjoining Lowlands of cattle stolen and houses plundered. Plans were made for new buildings at the barracks, but it seems they were not built, perhaps because of the cost, and the old ones were repaired. Nevertheless, the article in the *Dictionary of National Biography* for Major-General James Watson, RE, c.1713–61 states that he remained in the Highlands after Culloden, at which date his rank was Lieutenant-Colonel, to design and superintend the erection of barracks at Inversnaid. The facts once again remain elusive.

James Wolfe too may have had some responsibility for work at Inversnaid, for according to some accounts he was stationed there in 1746: only nineteen years old, he had already seen action at Dettingen and Culloden. He was certainly in the district during the years 1749 to 1753, this time on the less adrenalin-rousing task of road-making, while his regiment manned the Garrison. Subsequently he would become famous as General Wolfe for the capture of Québec from the French in 1759, the action in which he himself was killed.

Troops from Inversnaid were instrumental in the capture of Rob Roy's son Robin Oig in 1753. Robin Oig, in company with his elder brother James Mohr, had attempted to follow the tradition of lifting a wife from the Lowlands. Unfortunately, as tends to happen when sons attempt to follow in the footsteps of a father who was an exceptionally strong character, they got it all wrong. Robin was in it for the money, and they chose to abduct twenty-year-old Jean Key, recently widowed, to whom being carried off to the Highlands by a MacGregor offered no solace at all. The ponderous legal processes of the period eventually concluded with his execution for the crime.

Soldiers did not man Inversnaid without complaint, particularly in winter: according to William Taylor the buildings leaked like a sieve and the peats cut by unskilled soldiers would not burn. There must have been consolations. In 1803 on Loch Katrineside an elderly woman, partly disabled, told Dorothy Wordsworth that she had travelled far in her time, for she had married an English soldier stationed at the Garrison. In old age she had returned to her native place.

Yet the need for the Garrison of Inversnaid was to evaporate with surprising speed, not that this was obvious in 1746. Defeat of the Jacobite army by the Hanoverians at Culloden was followed by reprisals. This is the period to which the well-known traditional song 'The Bonnie Banks o' Loch Lomond' appears to refer. It is supposed to be the farewell, to his sweetheart or his comrade in arms, of a captured Jacobite soldier awaiting execution at Carlisle. Of the refrain 'O, ye'll tak' the high road, and I'll tak' the low road,/ And I'll be in Scotland afore ye; . . .' the 'low road' is said to refer to the grave, from which the speaker's spirit would return to Loch Lomond quicker than the listener. Yet for so well-known a song, it is surprisingly difficult to find out much about its origins, and many questions remain. One wonders, for a start, about a Jacobite from Loch Lomondside speaking in Scots dialect rather than Gaelic.

Of the severity of the reprisals in the Highlands themselves there is, regrettably, little doubt. Perpetrated under the authority of the Hanoverian commander the Duke of Cumberland – son of George II – they were so harsh, and carried out with such Teutonic efficiency, as to earn for him the nickname 'Butcher'. Such actions perhaps generate as much defiance as defeatism. But they were followed by government measures designed to destroy armed Jacobite support at its source – the clan system itself. A further disarming Act of 1746 prohibited not only carrying and possessing arms, but also such encouragements to military action as the wearing of tartan and the playing of bagpipes. The act was enforced with the construction of an expanded network of forts and roads. The military characteristics of Highlanders – their liking for a fight, their loyalty to their superiors and to each other – were deflected into newly-formed Highland regiments in the British army. Wolfe, at Québec, had under him men who had fought on the Jacobite side in the '45, and were now keen to avenge themselves on the French for their lack of support when needed.

Clan chiefs found their military power broken and took on the role of landlord rather than patriarch, some of them with more enthusiasm than others. In that lay the seeds of problems which persist even now. Tartan and the pipes were in due course permitted and then popularised; the warlike aspects of the clan system were not. Harsh though they undoubtedly were, the measures taken after the '45 do seem to have had the long-term benefit of stamping out the violence which had been endemic in the Highlands for centuries. The Highlands soon became the peaceable region we take for granted today.

Against that background the value of Inversnaid barracks rapidly declined. By 1768 the numbers stationed there were down to twenty-four, and at the time of the American wars in the 1770s they were reduced still further, to five men, all of them 'invalids', i.e., men disabled by injury. Young Walter Scott, passing that way in 1792, found only one old man, reaping his barley, who told him that he would find the key to the fort under the door.

Yet it seems to have been only a little before this that Scott himself had been provided with an armed military escort of a sergeant and six men from Stirling when as an apprentice lawyer he needed to serve a legal document in Balquhidder. On that occasion the particular place concerned was Invernenty, near the head of the glen, where

Robin Oig had once, in pursuit of a dispute over land, shot and killed the occupant MacLaren in cold blood. Since Scott's document was an eviction order on MacLarens then still present, it seems that trouble was anticipated even as late as 1790 or thereabouts. It did not materialise, but the visit did provide Scott with his introduction to the district, and to tales of Rob Roy recounted by his sergeant.

To return to Inversnaid: the Garrison seems last to have been occupied in 1796. Subsequently the building became ruinous, and today its site is occupied by Garrison Farm. This is a working farm and the farm buildings incorporate what little remains of the original structures.

4

LOCH LOMOND: ISLANDS AND ISLANDERS

Tarbet and the Norsemen

As with Inversnaid on the east bank of Loch Lomond, so Tarbet on the west bank gives access to a pass leading between the hills to another navigable loch. In this case it is a sea loch, and no steep hills intervene in the couple of miles to Arrochar at the head of Loch Long. Like the Inversnaid-Stronachlachar road, the road from Tarbet to Arrochar formed a link between steamer services and so formed part of a round trip. This was the popular Loch Lomond-Loch Long tour, Glasgow back to Glasgow incorporating the steamers on Loch Lomond and on the Firth of Clyde. It was on offer by Cooks as early as 1856, and it lasted until the early 1970s. Between Tarbet and Arrochar most participants seem to have walked, although a coach was available at times.

The very large Tarbet Hotel was provided for steamer passengers. Today it sits incongruously in the Y of dividing main roads, with its back to the more important of the two, but it is neatly aligned on the steamer pier. Its facade is prominent in the view from far away down the water, as I recall noting from the deck of *Maid of the Loch* as she approached.

Some earlier travellers between Loch Long and Loch Lomond were less welcome than those who came on the steamers. The name Tarbet or Tarbert, as is well known, signifies a portage between two waterways, where cargoes or complete boats could be dragged over a narrow neck of land. It was via this particular Tarbet that Norsemen dragged their vessels in 1263 to ravage Loch Lomond, its islands and the Lennox shore. This may not have been quite as astonishing an achievement as it at first appears, for in those days harbours were few and Norse ships were regularly hauled out of the water on rollers onto the beach. Probably, too, these were not large longships which had come from Norway, but smaller vessels used around the Hebrides.

The event came, as things turned out, close to the end of several centuries of Norwegian rule of the Hebrides. Scots had been increasingly raiding Norwegian territory there, and it was to re-assert his dominance that King Hakon (or Haco) of Norway set sail from Bergen that June with a vast fleet. Aged about sixty, he was getting old for such activities, but he had the largest ship, with a gilded dragon's head on the prow.

Sailing via Shetland and Orkney, King Hakon reached the Outer Hebrides to rendezvous with King Magnus of Man and his ships; a further rendezvous off Kerera in the Firth of Lorne added still more ships. The fleet continued southwards, King Hakon all the while accepting submissions from chiefs and petty kings, and sending his forces to ravage the lands of those who would not submit. There were not many of the latter.

Having rounded the Mull of Kintyre he was in the Firth of Clyde with 120 ships by early September: sovereignty over the islands of the firth was a particular bone of contention between the Norwegian and Scottish kings. But by now the two were in negotiation to confirm what was Norwegian and what was Scottish: emissaries were going to and fro. And they continued to go to and fro while the Scottish King Alexander III procrastinated, knowing that the summer would soon end and worsening weather would relieve the Norwegian threat.

Hakon evidently knew that too and lost patience: if it could not be peace, it would be war. It was at this point that he detached forty or more ships from the fleet and sent them, under the command of King Magnus, on an expedition to ravage far into Scottish territory. They went up Loch Long creating havoc on the shores as they went. Once at the head of the loch the small vessels from the detachment were hauled overland to Loch Lomond.

The principal islands of Loch Lomond were then well populated, the population perhaps increased by people who had thought them safe. If so they were rudely disillusioned: the Norsemen slaughtered the inhabitants, plundered their goods and burned their houses. This was repeated down the islands, along the shores, and far into Lennox, whence the Norsemen drove back to their ships several hundred cattle. Many – perhaps most – of these Norsemen, so-called, had evidently come from no further away than the Hebrides.

Their work done, the Norsemen hauled their ships back overland to Loch Long to rejoin the larger vessels waiting there. But now the weather changed. Before they could move off to rejoin the main fleet, a tremendous gale blew up; no fewer than ten ships were wrecked, and the departure of the others was delayed. Meanwhile the main fleet, anchored off the Cumbraes, was faring even worse. The storm here on 30 to 31 September (a belated equinoctial gale, no doubt) was so fierce that several ships were driven ashore on the mainland and even the king's ship went adrift despite having no fewer than eight anchors out.

When the Norwegians went ashore to their stranded ships they were set upon by the army of the Scots which was waiting. The ensuing Battle of Largs was looked upon by the Scots as a great victory, and by the Norwegians as a tactical withdrawal. They were at least able to rescue some of the ships. The Loch Long contingent subsequently rejoined the main body, and the fleet which until recently had seemed so powerful limped away up the west coast. At Orkney King Hakon himself was taken ill and died; and at the Treaty of Perth in 1266 the Hebrides were ceded to the Scots.

The Islands of the Loch

How many islands are there in Loch Lomond? The eighth-century historian Nennius was of the opinion that there were sixty islands, and in the twelfth century Geoffrey of Monmouth followed him. Hector Boece in his sixteenth-century history of Scotland wrote of Loch Lomond that 'there are XXX Ilis, weil biggit with kirkis, templis, and houses . . .' Boece was credulous enough to repeat as fact all sorts of strange legends, but in the number of islands he evidently seemed about right and subsequent writers tended also to plump for thirty.

Yet although the question is simple, to give a definitive answer is almost impossible. How is 'island' to be defined? Even in the absence of tides the water level fluctuates and what are usually islands may at times be peninsulas. How large does a rock or shoal

From the Conic Hill in the foreground, the islands of Inchcailloch, Creinch and Inchmurrin stretch out across Loch Lomond following the straight line of the Highland Boundary Fault (*Author*)

which breaks the surface have to be, and how much vegetation has to grow on it, before it deserves the appelation 'island'? Should one include crannogs, man-made islands? And so forth.

The best thing when confronted with such a difficulty seems to be to refer to the official chart: to the chart, that is, which forms the major part of *A Guide to Navigation* published by the Loch Lomond Park Authority. This was the consortium of local authorities which preceded the National Park. The chart marks twenty-two islands substantial enough to be given names. Confirming the border nature of the loch, some of the names include the English words 'island' or 'isle', and two include the Gaelic equivalent 'eilean', but most include 'inch', the Scots/Middle English derivative of the Gaelic word 'inis', for 'island'. The chart also marks at least twenty-seven small, un-named islands, making the total forty-nine or more, which suggests that Nennius was not so far out as he seemed.

Despite Dr Johnson's jaundiced view, which was mentioned in Chapter 2, the islands of Loch Lomond have long been noted for their natural beauty. Even Lord Cockburn, whose capacity for the caustic comment approached the doctor's, noted in *Circuit Journeys* that 'the islands scattered over the broad part of . . . [the loch] are delightful'. Smollett, in *Humphry Clinker*, waxed eloquent. After listing a series of well-known lakes on the Continent, he wrote (attributing the words to one of his characters) '. . . upon my honour, I prefer Loch Lomond to them all; a preference which is certainly owing to the verdant islands that seem to float upon its surface, affording the most enchanting objects of repose to the excursive view.'

Theodor Fontane, whose travels in Scotland in 1858 were published in translation as *Across the Tweed* (1965), wrote of Loch Lomond: 'the islands float on it like great water-lilies'. The expression is so similar to Smollett's that one wonders if Fontane was aware of it. Yet there is no mention of Smollett in the index, although it makes clear that Fontane was much influenced by Scott.

Yet it was scarcely their beauty that first led mankind to the islands. They were first inhabited in the Mesolithic period, and they have probably been inhabited continuously from pre-history to the present day. Eleven of the islands named on the chart seem to have been inhabited at one time or another during recorded history. The principal attraction they offered throughout most of this period, despite the events of 1263, was safety – safety from both hostile people and hostile animals on the mainland shores.

Crannogs

It was probably this consideration which caused Iron Age Celts, who seem to have arrived after 500 BC, to build defensive homes on small islets and, I presume subsequently, to construct islets of stone and timber which were wholly artificial.

Such structures are called crannogs. Typically they seem to have comprised a mass of tree trunks placed like piles in the bed of the loch to support a deck upon which a hut of wattle and thatch was built: or such is the construction of the replica crannog recently built on Loch Tay at Kenmore. Crannogs seem usually to have had a bridge or a causeway – perhaps slightly submerged – to the adjoining land where their inhabitants farmed during the day, retreating on board their crannog overnight.

Crannogs sometimes survive either as shoals below the surface, waiting to trap unwary boaters, or in some instances breaking the surface as mounds of boulders. The latter, if they rise high enough to be above the highest usual water level, are covered in undergrowth and sometimes trees.

There are at least ten crannog sites in Loch Lomond and possibly more. All of them lie in the southern part of the loch and most adjacent to its gently shelving shores. One, however, called The Kitchen, is almost half-a-mile from the nearest mainland shore at Balmaha, but close to Clairinsh island. It appears as a small wooded island. Other substantial crannogs are close to Strathcashel Point on the East Shore, and the islet called Swan Island in Aldochlay Bay on the West.

Several of the other lochs in the National Park contain crannogs, or islets which are probably crannogs. Loch Ard has two, the Lake of Menteith four, Loch Achray two, Loch Lubnaig possibly two, Loch Venachar one, and Loch Earn two or possibly more. Some crannogs were still being used, because of the security they offered, well into historical times.

Early Christian Settlements

The security offered by natural islands was particularly attractive to the saints of the Celtic church, and there are many islands in Scottish lochs and Irish loughs which are associated with them. Loch Lomond is no exception. Saint Kessog, whose father was King of Munster, made his home on Inchtavannach, off Luss, in the sixth century. This was no retreat from the world, but rather a base from which he set out on expeditions to spread the Gospel. These took him not just to Loch Lomondside around Lennox but as far east as Callander and Auchterarder, and perhaps even as far north as Inverness and as far south as Girvan.

In Inchtavannach Kessog founded a monastery and trained his helpers. The principal hill on the island is Tom-na-Clag, the knoll of the bell, which is attributed variously to the saint's having tolled his bell, summoning his flock to worship, from its summit – or alternatively to a resemblance between its shape and such a bell. Island safety was re-emphasised in 560 when war between the Picts and the Scots swept through the district. Kessog was caught up in this and killed. This may have happened a mile or so south of Luss, or it may have happened at a distance. In that case, the legend says, his body was embalmed in sweet herbs to be brought home for burial. The herbs in due course germinated and, the Gaelic for herb being *lus*, gave their name to the district.

Inchmurrin is named after sixth-century St Mirren. He was based mainly at Paisley where he built a monastery, but worked far and wide among the Picts and the Britons. On Inchmurrin he built a chapel near the south end of the island. The ruins of this were still visible in the early eighteenth century, but have since disappeared.

On the island of Inchcailloch off Balmaha, on the other hand, there survive substantial ecclesiastical remains. In this case the saint concerned was Kentigerna, a daughter of the King of Leinster. Widowed, she left Ireland for Scotland about 717, in the company of her brother St Comgan and her family, one of whom became St Fillan. For some years they laboured, evangelising successively in Galloway, in Islay, and up the west coast in Lochalsh. Eventually Comgan moved east to Turriff, but Kentigerna and Fillan came south to Loch Lomond. Kentigerna was now elderly and the island upon which they settled became called Inchcailloch, the island of old women. She founded a nunnery on the island, and there she lived until her death in 734. Saint Fillan went on to do great work in Strath Fillan and elsewhere.

The religious institution on Inchcailloch eventually became the parish church with its burial ground. Indeed the island gave its name to the parish. By the seventeenth century the walls of the church were in bad repair and the congregation was finding it increasingly inconvenient to cross to the island every Sabbath, particularly if the weather was bad. Worship was moved to a church at Buchanan, and the name of the parish eventually followed suit.

The burial ground on Inchcailloch continued in use, and many MacFarlanes and MacGregors lie buried there. Murray describes the state funeral of Gregor, chief of the MacGregors, in 1693. Corpse and mourners were brought down the loch from Inversnaid by a fleet of galleys while the pipes played a lament.

Smollett in *Humphry Clinker* suggests that on the island with a churchyard the bell rings of its own accord before a person dies. The novel takes the form of letters written by his characters, and this suggestion is attributed to the most credulous of them, so it is not clear whether the idea is Smollett's invention or a genuine local tradition.

In 1904 the remains of Archie Davie were buried on Inchcailloch. He had lived and died on Inchcruin: the funeral service was held there and the coffin was then placed on a large boat, more usually employed in ferrying cattle, which was towed to Inchcailloch where the interment took place. Burials continued on Inchcailloch until the mid-twentieth century. But whether any bells rang spontaneously I do not know.

Island Castles

While the security offered by islands appealed to men – and women – of peace, it appealed equally to men of war. As early as the sixth century the Picts and Scots had been harassing the Britons of Strathclyde so severely that King Arthur himself, according to legend, came to the aid of the Britons. After three battles, the Picts and Scots retired to the islands of Loch Lomond, supposing they would there find safety.

They were wrong. King Arthur brought a fleet to the loch and besieged the Picts and Scots on their islands. Pausing long enough to beat off a force from Ireland which had come to the aid of the besieged, he resumed the siege until many of the Picts and Scots died from starvation. The situation was eventually relieved by the bishops and clergy of the district. They waited on the king barefoot bearing relics of the saints and other consecrated objects before them; once in his presence they knelt down and begged for mercy for the small number who survived. They were successful: the king granted them a pardon.

In 1360 war and pestilence on the mainland caused the Earls of Lennox to remove themselves to Inchmurrin where they built a castle. One of its early residents was the tragic figure of Isabella Duchess of Albany, daughter of an Earl of Lennox. She became enmeshed in events which were ferocious even by the standards of the time.

The once substantial castle that Clan Galbraith built on Inchgalbraith has long since deteriorated into a ruin (*Collection J. Danielewski*)

King James I had been brought up as, in effect, a prisoner at the English court. In Scotland his uncle the Duke of Albany acted as regent, to be succeeded in 1420 by his son Murdoch, King James's cousin. Isabella was Murdoch's wife. In 1425 the king was eventually released and came north convinced, probably with good reason, that his uncle and cousin had been false friends and had been enjoying the benefits of regency far too much to worry about seeking his early release. One of his first acts on his return was to have his cousin Murdoch Duke of Albany beheaded – and not only the duke but his two sons and father-in-law the Earl of Lennox also. The duchess therefore suffered the execution on the same day of father, husband and two sons.

She was on Inchmurrin but her garrison was outnumbered and without provisions; it surrendered and she was removed. Later she was allowed to return, and on Inchmurrin she eventually died in 1460.

There are other island castles in Loch Lomond. Ellan Rhosdhu near the west shore is a crannog upon which a fortified keep was eventually built. Upon Inchgalbraith, not far away off Inchmoan,

Clan Galbraith built a substantial castle. Towards the north end of the loch are two island castles formerly used as refuges by Clan MacFarlane, on Inveruglas Isle and Island I Vow (I use the Ordnance Survey's spelling, which probably makes Gaelic purists wince). The latter, during the nineteenth century, was occupied by a hermit.

Deer Parks and Illicit Stills

Other uses to which Loch Lomond's islands have been put are numerous. In former times, of course, inhabitation of any island – other than those so small as to offer a defensive location for a castle and little more – implied subsistence agriculture; more recently, islands have been farmed and Inchmurrin is still. Among those formerly but no longer farmed are Inchcruin and Inchcailloch.

In the latter case it is now some two centuries since farming ceased and the island was planted with oak trees, there being then a market for both the wood and the bark. Inchtavannach likewise supported a commercial oakwood at the same period. Yew trees were planted long ago on Inchlonaig to provide a source of the wood used in archers' bows. Inchmoan, though seemingly never permanently inhabited, must have been regularly visited, for it provided the residents of Luss with peat.

Two islands were for long periods maintained as deer parks – and sources of venison – by their proprietors: Inchlonaig by the Colquhouns of Luss, and Inchmurrin by the Dukes of Montrose. Deer, however, can swim, and from time to time deer on one or other island would band together in a herd and set off swimming across the loch in search of greener grass. Their keeper then had the tedious task of rounding them up and driving them home. Both islands also had illicit stills hidden away upon them in the eighteenth century, as also did Inchconnachan and probably Inchfad. Their activities became so extensive that a revenue cutter was placed on the loch. Inchfad had a legal distillery early in the nineteenth century, with a short canal to link it to the loch. By contrast Inchlonaig and Inchtavannach were both used as retreats by alcoholics attempting to dry out. Sadly, Inchcruin was used in the early nineteenth century for confining the insane, and a little earlier Fraoch Eilean off Luss seems to have been used as a prison.

Three Wonders

As is only to be expected, Loch Lomond was formerly supposed to support an island which floated, and indeed moved around too. The credulous Boece wrote thus, with the spelling of his time: 'in this loch ar thre notable thingis, fische swomand but [i.e., without] ony fin, ane richt dangerous and stormy wal [i.e., wave] but ony wind, and ane Ile that fletis [i.e., floats] heir and their as the wind servis.' Loch Lomond became famous for its three wonders – fish without fins, waves without wind, and a floating island – and much thought has been put into explaining them.

It is possible that an island which appeared to move – and so, logically, to float – could have been the consequence of falling and rising water levels, which mean that an island is closer to or further away from the shoreline. It seems more probable that the floating island originated in large clumps of floating sedge and turf, broken away from the shore. Perhaps there was an element of both. It does seem that in the late eighteenth century a substantial clump did break loose and float out into the loch; having become known as the floating island, it evidently went aground and settled (but retained its name) off the south-west corner of Inchconnachan.

Eels and swimming snakes have been suggested as explanations for 'fish without fins', but these were convincingly identified as lampreys by Henry Lamond in *Loch Lomond: A Study in Angling Conditions* (1931). Lampreys, he wrote, though superficially not unlike eels were strikingly different in that they lacked pectoral fins, and the loch swarmed with them.

'Waves without wind' are more difficult. Lamond made a suggestion in the light of a phenomenon which, he said, is well-known to anglers. When the wind gets up on a previously calm day across a loch lying in a basin, as does much of Loch Lomond, the wind moves slowly across the water for it has to clear away the 'dead air' before it; this means that waves generated by the approaching wind spread across the surface of the water more quickly than the wind itself. So they become evident while the air is still calm. Another possibility is production of waves on a calm day by earth movements, a consequence of the Highland Boundary Fault, which runs across the loch. These might or might not also be associated

'Remains of the Floating Island' appear to be a large piece of floating sedge beside the rowing boat (*Collection J. Danielewski*)

with the phenomenon known as seiches, to which I will return in the chapter on Loch Earn.

A Boating Tragedy

Loch Lomond has always been a busy waterway, and so has had its share of disasters. One of the most tragic, partly because its cause has never been fully explained, is associated with Inchlonaig.

On 18 December 1873 Sir James Colquhoun had had a good day's pre-Christmas shooting on his island – nine deer had been killed – when he set off for Rossdhu and home some time after 4 p.m. He was in a large rowing boat with four of his gillies, two of whom had little or no experience of the loch. They were seen to head straight for the channel between Inchtavannach and Inchconnachan. They were never again seen alive.

At about 8 p.m., two other gillies, who had left the island later and taken a course to the east of Inchconnachan, returned to the island and told the resident keeper that Sir James and his men had not arrived at Rossdhu. An all-night search followed among the islands and on the east shore. The next day Sir John's boat was found, bottom up, on a gravel bank off Strathcashel Point on the far side of the loch.

It now seemed that the boat's occupants must have drowned, and there followed an intensive search for the bodies. The paddle steamer *Prince Consort* came with members of the Vale of Leven Humane Society equipped with grappling irons. Nevertheless it was several days before the body of one of the gillies was found north of Inchconnachan. Sir James's body was found nearby, and that of another gillie. The bodies of the remaining two gillies were never found.

The night of the accident was not stormy: there was a slight breeze from the north-west, no more. Darkness must have been falling, however, when Sir James set off. The boat was 22 ft long, with a beam of 4 ft 6 in. On board as well as the five men were the carcasses of five deer; it was said that the boat was not overloaded, but it must have been low in the water. The beam was not particularly great in proportion to the length, and the boat may well have had a tendency to roll. It is conceivable that if people – particularly inexperienced people – attempted for some reason or other to move around in it, when low in the water, that it would capsize. But that is no more than conjecture. The church at Luss was built in 1875 in Sir James's memory.

5

LOCH LOMOND AND THE RIVER LEVEN: A WATERWAY FOR COMMERCE

Galleys and Birlinns

Islands imply the presence of boats, but in former times boats were common on lochs whether there were islands or not. Travel by water along a loch was an attractive alternative to travel by land, in the days when paths led through dense forests which were home to animals and people, both equally fierce and hostile to intruders.

In prehistory people used logboats, or dug-out canoes – examples have been discovered submerged beside crannogs – and skin-covered boats. Logboats of necessity can only be small, and skin-covered boats not much larger. Writing in 1789, William Gilpin stated that formerly large rafts had been used on Loch Lomond. Made from several pine trunks fastened together, they carried cattle, hay and bulky loads. He believed they had gone out of use by his day, for boats were more manageable. Boats made from multiple timbers had emerged early, clinker built; by the time of the Vikings, great expertise in building such boats and ships was already evident. From these developments came the first boats we know of that were specifically associated with the west Highlands, the galleys and birlinns of mediaeval times.

They were not, in fact, very different from Norse ships, the main improvement being the stern-mounted rudder to replace the steering oar. Like Norse ships they were propelled when the wind was fair by single square sails, and otherwise by oars. Galleys were long and slender, fast ships for war; birlinns were shorter and beamier, merchant vessels for carrying goods, livestock and people. Probably there was no clear division between the two. To help keep time, their crews sang *iorrams*, rowing songs in Gaelic; galleys, being longer, had more oars than birlinns.

Such vessels were used not only on the west coast but also on many inland lochs, Loch Lomond among them. Those used inland may have been smaller than those used at sea, though probably not very much. They would have had to be almost as seaworthy. Fresh water, being less dense than salt, becomes rougher for the same windspeed – nor does there need to be any great fetch of water for the surface to become remarkably choppy, as many boaters have found to their surprise.

The key to commercial navigation of Loch Lomond lay at its southern extremity, at Balloch. Here the broad expanse of the deep loch gave way to the shallow fast-flowing course of the River Leven, and here vessels from settlements on the loch shores, and on the islands, converged for the short but difficult passage down the river to the Clyde. Or, of course, vice versa. Not only was the Leven narrow and winding, but it was and is subject to extreme fluctuations in flow and depth. It was said to have a mean depth of 3 feet in summer, but to rise by as much as 8 feet in winter. Such is to be expected of the outfall from a large and mountainous region subject to intermittent but frequently heavy rainfall. Only when there was neither too much water, nor too little, could it be navigated successfully. Fortunately the distance is not great – some seven-and-a-half miles from Balloch to the Clyde at Dumbarton, of which the lowest three or so are tidal. The fall, in the non-tidal length, is about twenty-six feet. Despite the difficulties, the Leven was for many centuries an important trade route.

One early traffic did not require boats for its carriage: timber was being felled in the forest around Luss in the late thirteenth century. It was floated in rafts down the loch and down the Leven to the Clyde; and it was used, notably, to build Glasgow Cathedral. A century or so later, timber was felled on Loch Lomondside to provide the material needed to build King James IV's navy: it was probably moved in the same manner.

In medieval times the chiefs of clans along the lochside probably all had their galleys with crews of sturdy clansmen to row them in state over the loch. The MacGregors used such means to take deceased chiefs to Inchcailloch, as mentioned in the last chapter. They also, on occasion, used their galleys for access to Lennox when setting out to raid cattle, navigating the lower part of the Endrick Water for the purpose.

Murray paints a nice picture of the young Rob Roy accompanying older members of his clan on their annual visit to Glasgow. Their object was to sell their surplus of corn, butter, cheese and poultry, and to return with essential salt and much else from ammunition to fish hooks and tobacco. They travelled, of course, by water – from Inversnaid to Balloch, down the Leven, and up the Clyde – and returned the same way, using sail or oar, or towing from the bank, according to vagaries of wind, current and tide.

Scott, clearly, was well aware of the MacGregors' use of the loch. In the closing stages of his novel *Rob Roy* the eponymous hero, finding government forces too close for comfort for travel from Inversnaid to Glasgow via Drymen, sends his fictional companions Frank Osbaldistone and Bailie Nicol Jarvie by boat down to Balloch. So, at Inversnaid, 'A boat waited for us in a creek beneath a huge rock, manned by four lusty Highland rowers . . .' and after cordial farewells, 'we bore away from the shore, and took our course for the south-western angle of the lake . . .' The voyage was enlivened by 'the Gaelic chant which one of the rowers sung in low irregular measure, rising occasionally into a wild chorus, in which the others joined.'

The Loch Lomond Expedition of 1715

The importance of Loch Lomond as a waterway at this period was well demonstrated in the opening stages of the 1715 rising. The Jacobites still had the assets of mobility and surprise, and on Michaelmas Day, 29 September, shortly after the Earl of Mar had proclaimed James as king, a large party of MacGregors raided into Lennox. Some came by land into Menteith where they made their presence felt from Drymen across to Callander; others came down the loch by water. These raided Luss, captured all the boats they could find along the west and east shores of the loch and on the Endrick Water, and took them to Inchmurrin, where they encamped. From there they set off again by night for the Leven, and landed near Bonhill. By then, however, their presence was known: church bells were rung and guns were fired from Dumbarton Castle to warn the populace. The MacGregors returned to Inchmurrin, again taking with them all the boats they could find. From there they retired to Inversnaid with the captured boats, taking the opportunity to relieve the Duke of Montrose not only of some of the cattle on Inchmurrin, but also of some of his deer.

This raid was far more than the opportunistic occurrence that it may have seemed to those affected by it. It had been ordered by the Jacobite leader, the Earl of Mar, as a preliminary to the landing of 'King' James, who was expected to come from France to arrive on the north shore of the Clyde early in October. The land operation in Lennox – whither James was expected to proceed – resulted in the capture of twenty-two Hanoverian guns. The water operation was intended to deny to the Hanoverians the use of the loch.

It was not wholly successful, prompting a remarkable mixed naval and military action in response, An account of this survives as a pamphlet, *The Loch Lomond Expedition*, written only a few days afterwards. There was already a large party of volunteers from Paisley stationed at Dumbarton, and they were joined by several hundred more from north and south of the Clyde. There were at the time several naval ships lying in the Clyde, and from these came about one hundred seamen in four pinnaces and three long boats. They were armed with four pateraroes, guns for firing a mixed charge of stones or old iron. Another boat came from Port Glasgow with two 'screw guns' which seem to have been a type more likely to prove effective; Murray defines them as having rifled barrels. Three more large boats were obtained in Dumbarton and the entire fleet of eleven vessels was then drawn by horses up the Leven despite its being, in the words of the pamphlet, 'next to the *Spey* . . . reckon'd the most rapid River in *Scotland*'.

At the entry to the loch, as many men as possible went on board the boats. The others marched up the west shore, followed on horseback by John Campbell of Mamore (uncle to the Hanoverian leader the Duke of Argyll) and a group of local gentlemen of Dunbartonshire. Many of these were also Commissioners of Supply, upon whom the cost of this expedition seems to have fallen. While those on shore marched 'with ardour and alacrity' the pinnaces and boats set their sails to take advantage of the favourable wind; they discharged their pateraroes, and the men on shore their small arms, though whether for practice or to show they meant business is not clear – perhaps both. At any rate they 'made so very dreadful a Noise thro' the multiply'd rebounding Echoes of the vast Mountains on both Sides of the Loch, that perhaps there was never a more lively Resemblance of Thunder.' At Luss they were joined by Sir Humphrey Colquhoun and forty or fifty clansmen, each of them well armed with gun, targe, claymore and pistols.

There they spent the night, while rumour-mongers spread propaganda among them. MacDonald of Glengarry had joined the MacGregors, they said and was in Strathfillan with fifteen hundred men, far more than the expedition's four hundred. The loch at Inversnaid was so narrow that MacGregors hidden among the rocks and trees on shore could pepper the boats with shot without danger to themselves: it was a desperate project. And so forth.

The men of the expedition were not disheartened. They set out again in the morning, and reached Inversnaid about noon. To rouse the enemy, one of the screw guns was used to put a cannonball through the roof of a house on the hillside. Says the pamphlet: 'An Old Wife or Two came crawling out, and scrambled up the Hill . . .' and otherwise there were only a few men atop distant crags. The men of the expedition could not be sure of it, but the MacGregor clansmen were indeed away with the Jacobite force in Strathfillan, preparing to attack Inveraray.

At Inversnaid, about a hundred of the volunteers went ashore and up the hill. They included some Dumbarton men under the command of two of the magistrates. At the top they fell in and paraded for an hour, with their drums beating. No enemy appeared to challenge them. They then went in search of the boats captured by the MacGregors. They first found some ropes, anchors and oars hidden in the bushes, and then some boats themselves, drawn well up from the shore. These they either destroyed or eventually took with them. It seems unlikely that all the boats which the MacGregors had brought up the loch were discovered; maybe they had used the others to go to the head of the loch en route for Strathfillan. Remarkably for the period, the men of the expedition made no attempt to loot or destroy the houses. Then, the wind having fortuitously veered, the expedition sailed swiftly back down the loch, gathering up en route any boats discovered along the shores or on the islands, and descended the Leven to Dumbarton where the captured boats were moored under the cannon of Dumbarton Castle. The Colquhoun clansmen of Luss, one fears, may have thought it all rather tame, but perhaps for the good volunteers of Paisley it was adventurous enough.

The writer of the pamphlet concludes, rather improbably, 'And thus in a short Time, and with little Expence, the *Mc greigours* (sic) were cow'd, and a Way pointed out how the Government may easily keep them in Awe.' Indeed the whole tenor of the pamphlet reads almost as a justification for the expedition, perhaps to pre-empt criticism that it had not achieved much, and to present it as a valuable show of force.

At any rate it is clear that neither the Jacobite nor the Hanoverian attempt to clear Loch Lomond of boats was wholly successful, for by December a group of MacGregors commanded by Rob Roy himself was at large on the loch, raiding places on its shores. This time it was the Duke of Montrose who called in the navy and the militia. Once again, by the time they reached Inversnaid the bird had flown, although Rob Roy soon afterwards had a narrow escape in Glen Falloch.

The 1715 Loch Lomond expeditions remained unique in scope and scale as operations of war on inland waterways in Britain. On the lakes of North America, however, such actions had already taken place, and would do so again on an increasing scale during the Franco-British wars of the eighteenth century.

Gabbarts and Scows

The late eighteenth and early nineteenth centuries were the great era of inland waterway transport – the canal age throughout much of Britain – and Loch Lomond and the River Leven were no exception.

By then the vessels most used there were called 'gabbarts' and 'scows'. The word gabbart was derived from the french *gabarre*; it was evidently used, in various spellings, in the south of England in the seventeenth century, but subsequently died out. It continued to be used in the west of Scotland. Sailing gabbarts were the coasters used on the Firth of Clyde and connecting waterways. Those which

A gabbart is towed up the River Leven, its mast lowered for the passage of
Bonhill bridge (*West Dunbartonshire Libraries and Museums Service*)

worked up the Leven and on to Loch Lomond were small, carrying
only 30 to 40 tons of cargo, compared with the 70 to 80 tons carried
by the gabbarts used on the Clyde and on the Forth & Clyde Canal.
Their masts could be lowered to enable them to pass beneath the
bridges; they were towed up the Leven by horses – sometimes
several horses were needed for a single vessel – and went down with
the current.

On Loch Lomond they sailed. Some sailing gabbarts were sloop-
rigged, with a single mast, a forestaysail and a gaff mainsail. Others,
as a few surviving photographs make clear, were two-masted with
a foremast and a mainmast. Both were rigged fore-and-aft, the
foremast carrying a sail almost as large as the mainsail. Such a
gabbart is shown at Luss in the illustration accompanying my
article about the loch in *Waterways World* (June 2000, p. 56). On
the top of the mast, or the mainmast, gabbarts carried a prominent
weather vane.

There are also numerous contemporary references to use of
the Leven and the loch by vessels called 'scows'. The word scow
is derived from the Dutch *schouw* and is perhaps related to the

A gabbart heads across Loch Lomond under sail (*West Dunbartonshire Libraries and Museums Service*)

Gaelic *sgoth*. The *Oxford English Dictionary* defines it as 'a large flat-bottomed lighter or punt'. On Scottish canals such as the Forth & Clyde, the term 'scow' was applied to the vessels used to carry goods; usually, at least in recent times, they were round-bilged and of iron or steel construction. They were hauled by horses and were not rigged for sailing.

Scows used on Loch Lomond must have been sailed. However what I have been unable to establish as yet, despite much delving, is whether in this context the terms gabbart and scow (which sometimes appear in the same sentence) referred to two distinct types of vessel, or whether they were used more or less indiscriminately for vessels of the same type.

At any rate these vessels, according to the old *Statistical Account* (1791) for Bonhill parish,

> are chiefly employed in bringing coals and lime, and other heavy articles, to the manufacturers, and to the gentlemen who reside upon the banks of the Leven and of the lake; and in carrying down the wood and barks that grow upon the banks, with slates from the slate quarries in the parish of Luss.

Coal was carried as far as the head of the loch, for it was needed to smelt lead ore. This was mined at Tyndrum between 1741 and 1790, and again between 1838 and 1866. In the early years transport north of the loch was by pack pony; at Tyndrum the coal was mixed with peat in an effort to keep costs down. At one stage, too, it seems that a smelter was built at the head of the loch and the ore brought to it; either way it was expensive and the mines never prospered greatly.

After the Forth & Clyde Canal had been completed to Bowling on the Clyde in 1790, gabbarts were able to load coal on the canal and carry it through to destinations on the Leven and on the shores of Loch Lomond. Those who obtained their coal supplies in this way had to keep large stocks as a precaution against interruption: in summer the river was likely to be un-navigable through drought, and in winter the canal was likely to be frozen over.

Slates were quarried at Luss and Camstradden over several centuries, and by the 1830s more than 800,000 were being produced annually with some 50 men employed. They were dispatched by water not only to places around the loch but also to Dumbarton, Glasgow, Paisley and Greenock. Sandstone was quarried near Aber, at the south-eastern extremity of Loch Lomond, and boated to Balloch en route for Glasgow.

The traffic in timber ranged from trees floated down loch and river in rafts to birchwood from the shore and the islands, which was carried to Paisley to be made into bobbins for the cotton industry. Nor was all the timber local: Lord Cockburn, in 1843, encountered a large depot of sawn timber and cut trees in Glen Falloch, and learned that it had been cut around Taymouth – the Breadalbane seat at Kenmore – and was on its way to the Clyde.

By that date scows had for many years navigated up the River Falloch for rather more than a mile beyond the head of Loch Lomond, to a landing place called Garabal. They brought coal and lime for use in the country to the north, and took out its products such as wool and, evidently, timber. At this period the Marquis of Breadalbane was extending the navigation even further, by construction of the Inverarnan Canal, described in Chapter 7.

Even the tributary Endrick Water was used for trade – in the 1830s scows regularly carried coal and other goods almost to Drymen bridge, and returned with wood and agricultural produce.

There were also numerous small boats on the water. Many were equipped for sailing as well as rowing. William Gilpin, describing the view of the islands from Tom-na-Clag on Inchtavannach, wrote that:

> the little barks, which navigated the lake, and plied among the several channels, appeared and disappeared by turns; dividing portions of land into islands, which to the eye seemed united.

Some of the little barks were used as ferry boats: there were long-established ferries from Inveruglas to Inversnaid, Inverbeg to Rowardennan, Balmaha to Luss, Aber to Balmaha, and across the River Leven at Balloch and Bonhill. The latter two were eventually replaced by bridges.

By the early nineteenth century use of the water by tourists was increasing; the story of boating for pleasure will be told in Chapter 6. It was probably the increasing popularity of Loch Lomond with tourists that prompted the introduction of a paddle steamer as early as 1818. Yet although initially aimed at the early tourist market, the steamer service became, as I have pointed out, an integral part of the passenger transport network of the area. Eventually the steamers carried not only passengers but mails, merchandise and livestock too. Their story is told in Chapter 7.

A steamer primarily for freight was built about 1840 at Pollochro, according to Mike Trubridge in *The Inversnaid Hotel and its Surroundings*. Pollochro is on the east shore a couple of miles north of Inversnaid, a remote spot where formerly there seems to have been a boatbuilding yard, now long since deserted. The steamer was used, apparently, to carry timber to Paisley, returning with coal. One would like to know more. It must, at that date, have been a paddle steamer for the successful screw propeller had yet to be developed.

The Leven: Change and Proposals for Change

The snag to all this bustling commerce was the state of the River Leven. Even the old *Statistical Account* for Bonhill had commented that it was 'navigable for one half of the year'. The *New Statistical Account* for Luss (1839) noted:

The only direct water-carriage is by Loch Lomond. This lake renders the different districts around its extended margin easily accessible by boats of different descriptions; but although the river Leven is also navigable,it is only by very small vessels; so that communication this way is limited to the towns along the banks of the Clyde.

In other ways, the Leven, and its vale, were changing. Smollett in the 1770s had written thus of the river:

Pure stream! in whose transparent wave
My youthful limbs I wont to lave;
No torrents stain thy limpid source;
No rocks impede thy dimpling course,
That sweetly warbles o'er its bed,
With white, round, polish'd pebbles spread;
While, lightly pois'd, the scaly brood
In myriads cleave thy crystal flood:
The springing trout in speckled pride;
The salmon, monarch of the tide;
The ruthless pike, intent on war;
The silver eel, and mottled par . . .

(Ode to the Leven Water lines 5 to 16; included in *Humphry Clinker*)

[The par, or parr, is a young salmon.]

Sadly, here is how Lord Cockburn found the Leven in 1843:

And oh! how abominable is the whole course of the Leven! Pure enough, I suppose, in Smollett's time, but now a nearly unbroken track of manufactories, which seem to unite the whole pollutions of smoke, chemistry, hot water, and squalid population, and blight a valley which nature meant to be extremely beautiful. No 'mottled parr' now, unless they are mottled by the refuse of dyes.

The River Leven, unfortunately, had held within it the seeds of its own disaster. The extreme purity of the water, flowing down from the Highlands, had encouraged the establishment of bleachfields – already present in Smollett's day – where linen was washed and bleached. These had led in turn to the building of dyeworks and printing works for cotton. They were fed with water by lades from the river, and returned waste water to it. Nor, despite Cockburn's horror, had the industry then reached its peak, which came in

The River Leven in the mid-nineteenth century with, presumably, Leven lighters. The lighter in the foreground may be going downstream with the current, or alternatively the absence of a towline may be artist's licence. (*Trustees of the National Library of Scotland:* Measom, G., *Official Illustrated Guide to the Lancaster & Carlisle, Edinburgh & Glasgow and Caledonian Railways 1859*)

late Victorian times. Even in the early 1930s the river was still badly polluted – although salmon still ran – and today, in this post-industrial era, it has regained much of its former clarity.

The establishment of numerous industries along the Leven had increased the demand for transport. By the 1840s, in times of low water, goods were being transhipped into small 'Leven lighters' for the passage of the river. More and more traders were avoiding the river altogether and sending goods to Glasgow by cart.

This was not for want of schemes to improve the Leven for navigation. Probably the earliest was prepared by John Golborne. Golborne, an engineer, accompanied Thomas Pennant during part of his 1772 tour and Pennant describes his proposals. Pennant came from Flint and Golborne originally from Chester, which must have given them something in common. Golborne's recent work, however, had been around Glasgow, and his scheme for deepening the Clyde up to that city – where it was then only inches deep at low tide – had been accepted. He proposed a combination of dredging, and confining the current to the dredged channel by means of jetties. This work was eventually carried out with great success.

The level of Loch Lomond was considered at that time to be rising, which it may have been if the entrance to the Leven was silting up. Some low-lying land around the southern shores was also subject to floods in winter. Golborne had been consulted by the landowners and what he proposed was to deepen the channel of the Leven and also to shorten it by cutting across the extremities of two great oxbow loops. This, it was considered, would make navigation more reliable and at the same time lower the water level of the loch, enabling land to be recovered for agriculture.

No physical progress was made with such a scheme, then or later. Henry Bell, who introduced commercial steam navigation to the Clyde in 1812 and was at the same time working on one of the calico-printing works in the vale, was involved in some similar proposals for deepening the river and lowering the loch. Sir Walter Scott too must have been aware of such ideas, which were reflected in his *Rob Roy*. During the journey down the loch to which I have already alluded, Frank Osbaldistone (who narrates the tale) observes that Bailie Nichol Jarvie after a long silence:

> . . . during which he had been mentally engaged in the calculations necessary, . . . undertook to prove the possibility of draining the lake, and 'giving to plough and harrow many hundred, ay, many a thousand acres, from whilk no man could get earthly gude e'enow, unless it were a gedd, [which, a footnote in the original explains, was a pike] or a dish of perch now and then.'
>
> Amidst a long discussion, which he 'crammed into mine ear against the stomach of my sense,' I only remember that it was part of his project to preserve a portion of the lake just deep enough and broad enough for the purposes of water-carriage, so that coal-barges and gabbards [sic] should pass as easily between Dumbarton and Glenfalloch as between Glasgow and Greenock.

Clearly Scott did not rate the credibility of such schemes very highly. More prosaically, the writer of the *New Statistical Account* for Luss parish (1839) pointed out that however feasible such a proposal might have been many years earlier, the vested rights – in, I presume, water extraction – of the proprietors of works along the Leven meant that all idea of it had been abandoned.

There were other means by which the object of improving navigation might have been achieved. Hugh Baird, of the noted family of Scottish canal engineers, produced a *Report on the Improvements of the River Leven and Loch Lomond* in 1824. At that time he had recently completed the Edinburgh & Glasgow Union Canal. He proposed that weirs should be constructed at intervals to maintain the water levels, with locks for boats to pass the weirs. The river would thus be made safe and accessible at all seasons for vessels able to ply on the Firth of Forth, the Firth of Clyde and through the Forth and Clyde Canal. They would include large steam vessels. There were thoughts too of a link between Loch Lomond and Loch Tay. Once again nothing came of it all; Baird himself died in 1827.

By the end of the 1830s the second Marquis of Breadalbane was thinking of a water link from Kenmore to the Clyde, which meant artificial waterways between Loch Tay at Killin and the head of Loch Lomond, and from the foot of Loch Lomond through the Vale of Leven to Bowling. At this period the famously large Breadalbane estates extended from near Kenmore west towards the sea. The second marquis comes across as a man greatly concerned to improve communications to and within his estates: he re-appears in this role in Chapters 7, 11 and 12.

The northern section of the proposed waterway would probably have been part-canal, part the River Dochart made navigable; the southern one, wholly canal. Both schemes were surveyed, but the northern one made less progress – apart from the short canal at Inverarnan described in Chapter 7 – than the southern. This would have been connected not only with the Clyde but also with the Forth & Clyde Canal. Detailed plans were drawn up and costed for the Vale of Leven Canal, 5 ft 6 in. deep and 33 ft 6 in. wide; the Forth & Clyde company promised its support.

The promoters were overtaken by events, for the railway age burst upon them. The Edinburgh & Glasgow Railway, the most important early main line railway in Scotland, was opened in 1842. Between Balloch Pier and Bowling it was a railway which was built, and opened in 1850. Its story, however, is closely associated with the steamer services on Loch Lomond, and I shall return to it in Chapter 7.

Waterways in the Railway Age

Clearly a waterway navigable only with difficulty was in no position to compete with a railway, and after the railway was opened use of the River Leven declined. Yet records are so few, and so sketchy, that it is almost impossible to say how quickly, and how much.

In *The Story of the Vale of Leven* J. Agnew states that the last record of a gabbart passing up the Leven to Balloch was in 1874. It was sufficiently unusual to arouse curiosity. Youths on Bonhill Bridge shouted insults at the crew, and the crewmen evidently gave as good as they got, until the gabbart was towed away out of sight.

That is a convincing picture, yet three years later, in 1877, there was a big legal case over navigation on the Leven. Orr Ewing & Co. had built a bridge over the river to link two of their works, and two of its piers were founded in the bed of the river. Colquhoun's Trustees felt strongly enough about this apparent obstruction to navigation to take Orr Ewing to court. The case went as far as the House of Lords. The eventual decision was confused: the Court of Session held that as the river was a public navigable river no-one had a right to execute works in its bed, but the Lords reversed this on the ground that it had been plainly established that there was no interference with the right of navigation. On one vital point there was no difference of opinion: the river was a public navigable river, proved to have been constantly navigated by scows or gabbarts.

Even though use of gabbarts on the Leven may have died out about then, the river was still used from time to time for delivery of newly-built paddle steamers to the loch – often with great difficulty. It was also used by pleasure craft. Gabbarts under sail on Loch Lomond appear in photographs, which seem unlikely to have been taken before the 1880s, given the rate of progress of photographic techniques.

By then, cargo-carrying sailing craft on the loch had been joined by steam lighters. Such vessels had first been developed on the Forth & Clyde Canal in the 1850s, following the invention of a satisfactory screw propeller a few years earlier. They rapidly became popular on

Photographs of steam lighters on Loch Lomond are rare, but George Washington Wilson's photographer caught the steam lighter *Mary* moored to the slate wharf in Camstradden Bay. Her funnel and the top of her vertical boiler can be seen; her layout appears similar to contemporary steam lighters on the Forth & Clyde Canal. (*Aberdeen University Library*)

the Clyde, leading to the emergence of the familiar Clyde Puffer of *Para Handy* fame. On Loch Lomond one of their regular trades was in slates from Luss.

We know this because on 22 March 1877 the *Dumbarton Herald* carried a melancholy news item:

SAD DISASTER ON LOCHLOMOND
THREE MEN DROWNED

On the afternoon of Wednesday, 14th inst., about two o'clock, while a screw-lighter, belonging to Mr M.C. Templeton, the lessee of Luss Slate Quarry, was proceeding from Luss to Balloch, laden with a cargo of slates, and when a short distance from the mouth of the river Fruin – a strong north-westerly gale blowing – she was struck by two heavy waves, when she foundered, and in a few minutes went down stern foremost in deep water . . .

There were eight men on board, one of whom 'managed to get into the small boat' and with great difficulty rescued four of the others. The remaining three were drowned. They included the lighter's engineer; the other two were described as being in the employ of a wood merchant of Larbert who had men working at Rossdhu. That sounds as though, sadly, they had hitched a ride. The small boat was driven across the loch by the gale, and its exhausted occupants eventually landed on the far shore.

Steam lighters must have plied the loch over many years, for Mary B. Bruce and Alison Brown's *Drymen and Buchanan in Old Photographs* contains an interesting illustration of one at Balmaha in 1901. It is moored at the 'liquor works' where pyroligneous acid was prepared from local timber, for use in the manufacture of dyes used to print cotton. It was, says the caption, one of many scows used to carry timber, mostly oak, from lochside woodlands to the works, and acid in barrels from Balmaha to Millburn Works on the Leven.

The liquor works at Balamaha operated until 1920 and Millburn Works was located between Alexandria and Renton, so it appears that at the turn of the century there was regular trade by steam lighter that far down the river at least. Even as late as 1931 Lamond in *Loch Lomond: A Study in Angling Conditions* was able to describe the Leven as having an easy course unbroken by natural falls and unimpeded by artificial obstructions – a navigable river up which vessels of considerable size, but light draught, might be taken to the loch.

However, in the earlier story of the lighter bringing slates from Luss there is nothing to suggest it had intended going further than Balloch, and I am inclined to suppose that the cargo of slates would have been trans-shipped to rail at Balloch. Certainly on other inland lochs and lakes with rail-served piers – Tay, Awe, Windermere – there was regular traffic in freight trans-shipped in this way, and it seems likely that the same thing happened on Loch Lomond. That could mean that coal, for instance, brought by rail to Balloch would be distributed up the loch by gabbart and steam-lighter long after they had ceased to bring it up the Leven. Unfortunately so far as Loch Lomond is concerned other historians seem to have concentrated on the passenger steamers. C.L.D. Duckworth and

G.E. Langmuir in *Clyde River and Other Steamers* note only that there have been several 'cargo steamers' on this loch, two of which belonged to the owners of Luss slate quarries, and one, called *Glen Sloy*, which made general cargo runs. One day, I hope, I may find the right bundle of dusty, pink-tape-bound papers which will tell the whole story.

The continuing presence on Loch Lomond at the turn of the century of vessels able to carry substantial cargoes, and of their trans-shipment from rail, is however confirmed by two traffics which were intensive though temporary. The first of these was materials for construction of the West Highland Railway in the early 1890s. One of the construction depots was established at Inveruglas. A pier was built there, and materials delivered to it up the loch. These included the metalwork for the very substantial Dubh Eas viaduct in Glen Falloch.

The second came in 1910, when Glasgow Corporation, which had been drawing water from Loch Katrine for many decades, was expanding its scheme. It was necessary to raise the level of Loch Arklet, in the pass between Inversnaid and Stronachlachar. Materials for the dam were brought by rail to Balloch and thence up the loch to Inversnaid. An aerial ropeway then conveyed them uphill to Loch Arklet.

A Ship Canal Through Loch Lomond?

In the late 1880s there was the first of a series of proposals which, if they had come to fruition, would have brought large sea-going ships to Loch Lomond. At that period there was a reaction to the overwhelming ascendancy of rail transport, and it took the form of campaigns for improved waterways. It was reaching its zenith with the construction of the Manchester Ship Canal, then well on the way to completion. The proposal for this had drawn much of its inspiration from the example of the Clyde, successive improvements to which had enabled large ships to come right up to Glasgow, and in turn the example of the MSC suggested the possibilities of a ship canal to cross the central belt of Scotland from sea to sea.

The first firm proposal came in 1889. The canal was to be in two parts: the first to run from Loch Long at Arrochar to enter Loch

Lomond at Tarbet, and the second to leave Loch Lomond near Balmaha and follow the valley of the River Forth to enter the Firth of Forth opposite Alloa. Remarkably, this line was considered to need no more than two locks at each end, to raise ships to the level of Loch Lomond.

Almost immediately a rival scheme emerged for a more direct route, running from Yoker to Grangemouth and so passing much closer to Glasgow. The campaigns for a ship canal over one route or the other gathered momentum over the next few years; the increasing likelihood of war with Germany drew attention to the value of such a canal to the Royal Navy, and the option of following the Vale of Leven from the Clyde to Loch Lomond was considered.

In 1906 a Royal Commission considered inland waterways throughout the British Isles; so far as this proposal was concerned, it concluded that the Loch Lomond route offered strategic advantages, but not so great as to justify large government expenditure. Nonetheless the possibilities attracted much attention during and immediately after the First World War, and again during and after the Second. On each occasion, however, the enthusiasm of admirals, members of parliament, individuals and local authorities for the scheme was exceeded only the by reluctance of governments to find the funding. There have been lesser proposals since then, but at the present time the mid-Scotland ship canal seems to have entered the category of fascinating might-have-beens: a might-have-been which would have seen the battleships of the Grand Fleet slipping through Loch Lomond on their way from the Clyde to the North Sea – and, at a more recent date, Polaris submarines doing likewise.

Recent Commercial Traffic

To return to reality, by the late 1940s it is evident that there were no vessels left on Loch Lomond able to carry cargo in bulk, and recourse had to be made to bringing in such vessels when they were needed. The main occasion was the construction of the Loch Sloy Hydro-Electric Scheme by the North of Scotland Hydro-Electric Board between 1945 and 1950. Sand in large amounts was needed for mixing into concrete; it was obtained from a natural deposit at Balloch. To have delivered it by road would have required one hundred or more return lorry journeys every day over 22 miles of the narrow, winding road up the west shore of the loch. Instead, two tugs and six 50-ton capacity dumb – i.e. unpowered – lighters were brought in. At least one of the tugs, *Dart* by name, and four of the lighters were brought all the way from the Thames by road in 1947. This being soon after the end of the Second World War, they were carried on war surplus vehicles: former United States Army tank transporters. They were launched into the loch at Luss.

To move the sand, each tug towed three barges at a time. A total of 117,000 tons of sand was carried up to Inveruglas over three years, during which the tugs covered 34,000 miles – which was equivalent, as the commemorative book published by the board to mark completion of the scheme proudly pointed out, to a voyage one-and-a-half times round the world.

Other commercial traffic in recent years has largely been in connection with movements to and from the islands. In 1946, for instance, according to Calder & Lindsay's *The Islands of Loch Lomond*, the then owner of Inchconnachan brought a twin-engined landing craft up the Leven in order to transport an electricity generator to his island.

The island mailboat service dates from 1948. Prior to that date islanders had to collect their mail from post offices on the mainland, but then Alec MacFarlane, whose family had a long connection with Loch Lomond, was awarded a contract to run a mailboat out of Balmaha, delivering mail to the inhabited islands – usually four of them – and collecting mail from them.

The boat he used was a teak-hulled, Norwegian-built launch which he purchased on the Clyde and rebuilt; she was named *Marion*, either after the first steamer on the loch or, it has been written, after one of Mr MacFarlane's relatives. Both may well be true. As well as the mails, the mailboat carried passengers, and operated year-round.

Two further wooden-hulled launches, *Margaret* and *Lady Jean*, were added to the fleet. Sometimes they were used, I believe, on the mailboat run, but more often on passenger tripping work, on towing boats laden with hay or fertiliser out to island farms, and on ferrying people to Inchcailloch. This little fleet still functions, the launches having with the passage of time become fine examples of

The *Marion* calls at Inchmurrin in 1978, and boatman-postman Alec
MacFarlane comes ashore with the mails (*Author*)

vintage craft serving their intended purpose. The mailboat service
continues to be a pleasant and unique feature of Loch Lomond;
control has passed to the third generation.

Several passenger ferries using motor boats continue to operate
across the loch between Inverbeg and Rowardennan, Tarbet and
Inversnaid, Inveruglas and Inversnaid, and Ardlui and Ardleish;
and to the islands of Inchcailloch from Balmaha (as just mentioned),
and Inchmurrin from Midross on the western shore. At the north
end of the loch, boats based on Ardlui are used to carry materials,
equipment and people to otherwise isolated sections of the West
Highland Way, when maintenance is required.

6

LOCH LOMOND AND THE RIVER LEVEN: A WATERWAY FOR PLEASURE

The Earliest Pleasure-boaters

People have been boating for pleasure on Loch Lomond since at least the eighteenth century and possibly earlier. Smollett in *Humphry Clinker* refers to an elderly eccentric whom he called 'The Admiral' because 'he insists upon steering his pleasure-boat upon the lake'. Smollett may have been facetious but real admirals were concerned in a document quoted by Alasdair Alpin MacGregor in *Wild Drumalbain*. It was a letter or *laissez-passer* which read thus:

> Suffer the Pleasure-Rowing-Boat called the Monmouth (the Property of the Marquis of Graham) . . . built to row with Six Oars to pass without any Lett, Hindrance, Seizure or Molestation, to and in Loch Lomond in the West of Scotland; the said Marquis of Graham, the Owner of the said Boat . . . having entered into a Bond to His Majesty that the same shall not be made use of in the Clandestine running of uncustomed and prohibited Goods. Given under our hands and Seal of the Office of Admiralty, the 18th day of July 1778
> To all persons whom these may concern
> By command of their Lordships.

The letter bore the Admiralty Seal, wrote MacGregor, and was signed by no less than four admirals. It dates, presumably, from the days of the revenue cutter.

Over a long period, a boating excursion among the beauties of Loch Lomond's islands was popular with visitors. One of the earliest was Thomas Gray the poet in 1764. Gray had been attracted by the Alps while on the Grand Tour; he enthused about the Highlands and before long would help to make the Lake District famous. He

In the 1780s Col. Thornton shoots a Mallard off Inchmurrin and good dog 'Pero' leaps overboard to retrieve it. Some of the resident deer can be discerned on the island, and their keeper's house. *(credit: Trustees of the National Library of Scotland: Thornton, Col. T.,* A Sporting Tour . . . through the Highlands . . .)

liked wild places, ahead of his time, perhaps; Dr Johnson, whose excursion upon the loch in 1773 I have already mentioned, did not. He would soon be in a minority.

Colonel Thomas Thornton hired a boat from Balloch to take him to the island of Inchmerin (sic) sometime in the 1780s. The precise date is unknown for the chronology of his eventual description of his visits to Scotland is confused; as *A Sporting Tour through the Northern Parts of England and great part of the Highlands of Scotland* . . . it was published only in 1804. The boat was an 'awkward large incommodious vessel', but its inconvenience was soon forgotten 'blessed as we were with two fair ladies, a beautiful day, and sailing on the finest lake in the universe.' Thornton then spent several days among the islands, fishing and shooting – he was a man whose hunting instinct was somewhat overdeveloped, to judge from the frequency with which birds are shot, beasts killed and fishes caught throughout his narrative.

The Wordsworths and Coleridge took the opportunity of an excursion from Luss among the islands when they were travelling up the west shore of the loch in 1803. The weather was threatening but 'We had two rowers and a strong boat; so I felt myself bold, though there was a great chance of a high wind' wrote Dorothy. They landed on Inchtavannach and she was suitably enchanted by the scene; but afterwards, when they had left the shelter of the islands, they found 'the main lake very stormy'. Dorothy had earlier spotted an islet on which stood an ivy-covered ruin – Inchgalbraith, perhaps – and wished to visit it but, unsurprisingly, 'the boatmen were in a hurry to be at home'.

Felix Mendelssohn and his friend Carl Klingemann had an experience of the same sort in August 1829. They were on the return leg of the tour of the Highlands and Islands which had extended to Staffa and Iona and provided the inspiration for the Fingal's Cave overture. Their experience of Loch Lomond was regrettably more prosaic. They were out in the twilight in a small rowing boat, when they were struck by a sudden squall which came down off the hills. The boat pitched violently, everything on board was thrown about, and Mendelssohn started getting ready to swim. But the squall evidently subsided as quickly as it had arisen; at any rate Mendelssohn noted that they got safely through with what he described as their usual luck.

Despite the hazards of their calling, at least one professional boatman was long-lived, and kept his memory too. When Lord Cockburn was taken out to Inchtavannach in 1845, the boatman said he had rowed him forty-one years earlier, and again a mere sixteen years earlier. His lordship, who must have been about sixty-six years of age, then offered to hire him again in sixteen years' time – and was impressed by the ingenuity of the man's response, that as soon as he saw him there he would be sure to appear.

Races and Regattas

Competitive rowing came early to the loch – the first regatta was organised in 1828, a year before the first Oxford & Cambridge Boat Race and eleven before the first Henley Regatta. The first Loch Lomond regatta was organised by the local gentry, but by the middle of the century substantial sums were on offer to professional rowers. I.M.M. MacPhail in his brief but fascinating history of the subject, *Rowing on Loch Lomond*, records that in 1857, when the average weekly wage was about £1 5s 0d, Robert Campbell of Alexandria won the sculling championship of Scotland and more than £150 in prize money. The course of two miles ended at Balloch Pier, which he reached more than 100 yards ahead of the runner-up.

Remarkably, as it seems to us now, the popularity of professional rowing was not due entirely to the prize money, but to an element of snobbery in the definition of 'amateur'. In those days the authorities at Oxford and Cambridge, who framed the rules, defined 'amateur' to exclude not only those who competed for money, but also those engaged in manual labour – which, it was considered, would have given them an unfair advantage over the young gentlemen of the universities. This situation persisted, according to MacPhail, until as recently as the Second World War.

The effect on the pragmatic oarsmen of Loch Lomond and district was that regattas included races for both professionals and amateurs – and indeed crews from local works and local estates. The latter rowed in pleasure boats, More serious oarsmen used four-oared 'jolly-boats', longer and narrower than pleasure boats, and sculling boats. Regattas on Loch Lomond became popular and successful events. Even the depression years of the early 1930s produced a 'silver lining' benefit to rowing, for a great many oarsmen were unemployed and so had all the more time to train.

Touring by Oar and Paddle

Touring by water, and particularly by canoe, received an immense boost with the creation of the Rob Roy canoe by John MacGregor. MacGregor was a London barrister and a wealthy man; rather than legal practice, he preferred philanthropic pursuits and foreign travel. He had also since childhood enjoyed what would later be defined as 'messing about in boats'. He was forty before he had a canoe built for him in Lambeth in about 1865 : cedar on oak, 15 ft long, 28 in. beam, drawing 3 in. of water, equipped with sails as well as a paddle and with the name *Rob Roy* painted on the stern.

It would be nice to be able to record that MacGregor came to Loch Lomond and the Trossachs with the *Rob Roy*. In fact he seems to have headed in the opposite direction, to explore the Meuse, the Rhine, the Danube, and further afield. The books he wrote, however, and the lectures he gave resulted in instant popularity for the new form of adventurous recreation. The *Rob Roy* gave her name to the type of canoe that was used. The Canoe Club was formed and the Prince of Wales became its first commodore. Cruising by canoe and indeed also by rowing boat proved to have a lasting popularity.

Something of what this meant for Loch Lomond can be gleaned from F.E. Prothero's and W.A. Clark's *A New Oarsman's Guide to the Rivers and Canals of Great Britain and Ireland* published in 1896. Loch Lomond, we read, is a 'paddler's paradise' – and they mean 'paddle' as in canoe, rather than with bucket and spade, or indeed steamship. To the paddler and camper the loch offers an ideal cruising ground, which for size, beauty, safety, and accessibility is unequalled by any other British fresh-water lake.

At the foot of the loch, they wrote, are two railway stations; Balloch and Balloch Pier: but since there are few facilities at the pier for lowering boats into the water, boats arriving by rail are best consigned to Balloch. There they can be launched into the River Leven, which the local boatbuilder, Mr Lynn, will attend to 'if communicated with'. Once on the water, Inchmurrin is the first place at which the 'cruiser' may land and pitch his tent – always with permission first from the resident keeper, who can also usually supply milk and 'any little necessities the camper may have forgotten'. North of Inchmurrin and as far as Ross Point is a splendid sailing stretch: the loch being open and the islands low, the wind is steady. Beyond Ross Point the 'sylvan beauty' of the lower part gives way to the 'gloomy grandeur of a typical Highland loch'.

At Tarbet there is the possibility of a portage to Arrochar and Loch Long; for this, the hotel-keeper at Arrochar can provide a 'horse and lorry' for a charge of 3s 6d. Those wanting a round trip, however, are recommended to come up Loch Long and portage to Loch Lomond, eventually descending the River Leven.

To ascend the Leven, though troublesome, was entirely practicable. The river gets a section of the guide to itself. A good volume of water passes down the river, we are told, and even after dry weather there is plenty of water for canoes and boats of light draught; the stream is generally strong and after rains it is almost impossible to paddle or row against it. But there is a good towpath on the west bank, and boats ascending the river are usually towed up.

The attractions of Loch Lomond were evidently sufficient to encourage the Clyde Canoe Club, which had been formed in 1873, to move its base to the loch in 1898. The base was at first located in the vicinity of Balloch, and then in 1932 was moved to Millarochy Bay where it remains. It was only in 1998 that the club, with change going on all around, decided that its name should reflect what had become its members' principal interest, and it re-named itself the Loch Lomond Sailing Club.

The Voyage of the Kelpie

Something of what people achieved in the 1890s is to be found in T. Ratcliffe Barnett's *The Road to Rannoch and the Summer Isles*, first published in 1924. Barnett was a prolific author, most of his books being either on religious themes or of the 'tours amongst the Highland heather' genre. Most of *The Road to Rannoch* is of the latter variety, but Chapter XI 'The Voyage of the *Kelpie*' is different. It describes a canoe cruise made long before, in 1890, by two young men. They are described only as 'the skipper' and 'the cook' – but clearly the latter is the author and the former his elder brother.

First they had to build the canoe, which was designed by the skipper and built in the family coachhouse. The *Kelpie* was 14 ft long, wooden, flat-bottomed with watertight compartments and a centre-board – for she was fitted with masts bearing lug sails fore and aft. She also had a pair of wheels and an adjustable axle so that she could be portaged; these in turn could be stowed away forward when not in use.

Early one June morning the *Kelpie* was trundled on her wheels out of the front gate and to a point on the River Cart in Renfrewshire, where she was launched. Without previous practice the two young men set off down the Cart, down the Clyde, and into the Leven at Dumbarton. They were late for the tide and, after struggling against it for a while, found themselves towing, with the cook wading through water stained dark red by the outflow from calico printing works. Then, by good fortune, they encountered a launch being towed up to Balloch by a horse. The owner of the launch threw them a line, and like that they progressed easily up to the loch.

Several days of cruising the lower part of the loch ensued, racing along under sail when the breeze was favourable and paddling when it was not, and visiting the islands. It was idyllic, rain or shine, with the cook from time to time serenading ladies on the bank with his banjo. They came to Inversnaid, and commenced to portage, hiring a cart to get them to the top of the hill and then trundling the canoe along on its own wheels. Half-way to Loch Katrine they stopped for a rest, the cook sitting astride the *Kelpie*, twanging his guitar and singing a favourite ditty – to the astonishment of members of a shooting party who chose that moment to appear across the heather!

This had a happy consequence. While the *Kelpie* was being paddled down Loch Katrine, she was overtaken by the steam launch *Goblin* with the shooting party aboard. Then, when the cook and the skipper landed at Brenachoile Lodge on the north shore, where they had been advised to spend the night at the keeper's cottage, the skipper of the *Goblin* appeared with a letter addressed 'To the Gentlemen in the Canoe': an invitation to spend the evening as guests at the lodge with the shooting party. It was a happy evening, in a room full of Eastern rugs and hangings, the hosts an old gentleman in a velvet coat and his son in blue evening jacket and trousers with a blue silk cummerbund, the talk of South African rivers and Indian canoes.

But the *Kelpie* still had far to go. From the foot of Loch Katrine she was trundled through the Trossachs to Loch Achray. Down this loch she raced, the lug-sails drawing well. She navigated the river and its rapids down to Loch Venachar, with the cook astride the bow and the skipper the stern, both of them fending off from the rocks with their bare feet, and so continued down Loch Venachar to its eastern extremity.

Here she was left briefly while the two young men repaired to Callander for the night. The following day, oilskinned and sou'westered against torrential rain, they struggled with the canoe for a portage of five weary miles to Loch Lubnaig. Happily the weather then cleared for the sail up the loch to Strathyre.

Having reached Strathyre, the problem arose of how to get away again. This was solved by the decision to go by train, which meant ordering from Oban a special truck of the type normally used to carry horse-drawn carriages. Upon this the *Kelpie* was mounted, and the train carried the canoe and her crew to Stirling. There it was back into the water and down the River Forth: with a strong breeze and the tide both favourable, they were carried past the canal entrance at Grangemouth and eventually made landfall at Bo'ness. That meant back up to Grangemouth when the tide turned, through the Forth & Clyde Canal and all its locks to Bowling, and so home. To the cook in later life the cruise evidently seemed the experience of a golden age.

Steam Launches, Motor Boats and Houseboats

Those of the wealthy who were also energetic had followed in John MacGregor's wake and taken to oar and paddle. During the same period others, less energetic, had adopted the steam launch as their favoured means of waterborne travel. The owner of the *Goblin* on Loch Katrine was one of them. On Loch Lomond, the Duke of Montrose had a steam launch by the 1890s. In 1894 it had a melancholy task to perform in connection with the funeral of Walter MacGregor, who had been keeper of Inchmurrin for forty-three years. From the island to Balloch the steam launch towed a small boat carrying the coffin, which was en route for Alexandria Cemetery. Relatives of the deceased travelled in the steam launch itself.

This launch may or may not have been the *Violet*, but by the 1900s the duke did own a steam launch of this name. She was named after the duchess. The launch was elegant with a clipper bow, counter stern, and raked funnel and masts – all of which gave her a 'big-ship' look – and was a familiar sight on her mooring at Balmaha. Her master was the father of Alec MacFarlane, who eventually started the island mailboat service, and who in conversation with the author in the 1970s recalled sailing in the *Violet* as a child. Sadly, the launch was broken up between the wars.

The internal combustion engine for small craft was introduced at the turn of the century, and motor boats had become commonplace by the 1920s. They were not instantly popular with everyone. Writing

The Duke of Montrose's steam launch *Violet* was regularly moored at Balmaha. In the background are piles of timber brought in by water for the liquor works. (*Collection J. Danielewski*)

at that period, Alasdair Alpin MacGregor expressed a preference for a light rowing boat, with a sail for use when conditions were right, as a means to get around the loch. This preference survived a bad experience. He had rowed, with a friend, the length of the loch from Ardlui to Balloch against a fresh wind – only to have to pay, in the tea room at Balloch Castle (then owned by Glasgow Corporation), the extortionate sum of tenpence for a pot of tea for two!

MacGregor conceded, however, that the most comfortable and expeditious manner of visiting the islands was by motor boat. Many agreed with him on that. The 'boating stations' at Balloch, which had been established in the 1880s to hire out rowing boats, had expanded into offering trips by steam launch and then, even before the First World War, by motor launch. In the 1920s they became busy centres for powered craft which were based there for cruising on the loch. Moored craft thronged both sides of the river for the half-mile reach downstream from its entrance.

Many of these craft, however, were houseboats. Such vessels became popular at this time, not only at Balloch but elsewhere on Loch Lomond. Balloch, however, saw the greatest concentration of them; Henry Lamond called it a 'veritable floating village' and

THE HOUSE BOATS, ALDOCHLAY, LUSS, LOCH LOMOND.

Houseboats became a feature of Loch Lomond between the wars (*Author's collection*)

arranged for the local authority to take a census in July 1925. This found 126 houseboats on that short stretch of water occupied, it was estimated, by 350 people.

Doubtless such developments were indeed, as Lamond put it, 'not altogether sheer gain to the nature lover'. Yet at the time of the Depression the houseboats must have provided many people with an enjoyable holiday at an affordable price. Nor was their appearance any great blot on the landscape, to judge from the enthusiasm with which the Scottish Colourist G. Leslie Hunter set about depicting them. They stand out from his paintings in contrasting hues – yellow and green, or blue, white and red – bright but not garish.

After that burst of expansion, the use of Loch Lomond for pleasure seems to have settled down during the years preceding and following the Second World War. Small clinker-built boats were used by anglers, larger motor cruisers were based on the loch by people living within range and wanting to be afloat at weekends or for longer periods. Ship-breaking yards in the vicinity provided a ready source of former ships' lifeboats; with the addition of a cabin, these could be converted economically into cruisers for the loch. Boats based on the loch have evidently been long-lived, and vintage

HIGHLAND   MARINE   CHARTERS   LTD.

Cruising on Loch Lomond

SELF DRIVE

CABIN CRUISERS

GENERAL BOOKING AGENTS—

TRAVEL TRIPS LTD.

22 RENFIELD STREET, GLASGOW, C·2

Telephone: CITY 7871 (3 Lines)

Brochure for an early attempt to hire out motor cruisers on Loch Lomond, probably in the late 1950s. Six fine vessels were on offer, ranging in length from 28 ft to 37 ft, and in price from £20 to £50 per week. (*Collection R.N. Forsythe*) motor cruisers remain a feature of it. Hire cruisers on the other hand are not, so far as I am aware, although there have been several attempts since the Second World War to establish fleets of hire craft. Some of these were in operation for more than a decade. Despite its extent, the loch is perhaps small for a whole week's holiday, with the added complication that bad weather may restrict movement upon it for several days at a time.

The trip boats continued to be popular, with a partial hiatus during wartime. When Thomas Lynn & Sons purchased a further boat in 1949, a former Royal Navy harbour launch, it was delivered to Balloch up the River Leven, having reached there from the Isle of Wight via the east coast and the Forth & Clyde Canal.

The Leven Barrage

Such voyages would later become scarcely practicable, with the closure of the canal in 1963 and construction of the barrage across the Leven below Balloch. This was completed in 1971. It was built under powers given by The Loch Lomond Water Board Order of 1966. The order, a statutory instrument, incorporated the board and gave it powers to extract drinking water from Loch Lomond and to distribute it to local authorities in the central belt. The construction of new towns, on top of a general increase in demand, had made it evident since the early 1960s that additional water supplies were needed.

The purpose of the barrage is to control the flow of water out of Loch Lomond and down the river. It comprises gates, hinged along their lower edges, which remain lowered against the bed of the river while the water level of the loch is more than 26 ft above ordnance datum, but are raised when the level falls to this point. A specified flow of 'compensation water' has to be allowed down the river.

Use of the River Leven by boats was tacitly accepted by those planning the works needed for the water supply scheme. A press release issued by the Scottish Office on 10 April 1963 announced the scheme. It promised that the 'control works' in the Leven would incorporate 'a system for the passage of small craft', and that the anchorage in the river, between Lomond Bridge, Balloch, and the loch would be unaffected, with boats continuing to have free access to and from the loch.

The 1966 order made no specific reference to navigation on the River Leven. However, it did give the board powers to make slipways upstream and downstream of the barrage, by which small boats could be hauled out of the water, taken past the barrage and re-launched. These slipways were constructed. No lock was provided for boats to pass the barrage. The 1960s were a low point in waterway history, when many waterways had been closed but few re-opened, and I am inclined to the opinion that, had this scheme been promoted at almost any other period, a lock would have been built.

The River Leven continued to be a navigable river. Evidence about this was given to a fatal accident inquiry at Dumbarton in 1994. This tragic accident was an after-dark collision between boats on Loch Lomond. One of the points at issue was whether the loch had a navigable connection with the sea – in which case the international collision regulations applied (in full, The Merchant Shipping (Distress Signals and Prevention of Collisions) Regulations 1989). The Deputy Director of the Central Scotland Water Development Board – by that date the operator of the barrage – gave evidence that he knew of ten boats which had been taken out of the water to pass the barrage, though none of them had been within the previous four years. The enquiry determination makes references to the presence of a 12-tonne crane, and it may well be that some of these boats had been craned past the barrage. Another witness, a professional boatman, gave evidence that he had sailed a flat-bottomed assault boat through the barrage when the gates were lowered, en route for Bowling on the Clyde, and through the barrage again when he returned.

Sheriff Principal Robert Colquhoun Hay WS, who held the enquiry, considered the evidence and the precedents – notably the 1877 case – and gave his opinion that Loch Lomond is a public navigable loch, that the River Leven is a public navigable river, and that construction of the barrage, with the provision of slipways and a crane, had not changed the character of the river in that respect.

Crowded Waters

While use of the Leven declined, Loch Lomond was becoming more and more busy with boats. The increasing prosperity which enabled people – often inexperienced – to buy powered boats, the ease with which small boats could be carried on trailers to the loch and launched, the establishment of marinas with floating jetties from which boaters could walk onto their craft – all played a part. Once, visitors had been happy to throng the decks of the paddle steamers; now, it seemed, everyone wanted their own boat. By the early 1990s it was estimated that 1,200 to 1,400 boats were based at moorings on Loch Lomond, and many more were being launched temporarily by visitors.

By then it had long been recognised that such numbers were producing conflicts. There were conflicts between users of boats of different types and differing needs – sailing boats, motor cruisers, speed boats, ski boats, jetskis, rowing boats, canoes. There were conflicts, caused principally by noise, pollution, and excessive wash, between users of boats and other users of the loch – anglers, divers, swimmers, and picnickers on shore. There were similar conflicts between the interests of boating on the one hand and the interests of conservation, water supply, and lochside residents on the other.

There were successive official enquiries, reports and plans. There was talk of by-laws. The Loch Lomond Association was formed in 1981, with representatives from all with an interest in use of the loch. It looked toward voluntary regulation, rather than by-laws. The association produced an excellent code of conduct, full of good advice, which was widely circulated.

Such a code could only be successful where there was a concensus of boaters in its favour. On Loch Lomond there was always a minority of boaters who, from either wilfulness or ignorance, were not. A recommended speed limit of 5 mph among the islands was regularly and persistently ignored. According to the determination of the 1994 fatal accident enquiry, the steerer of one of the boats involved had never seen the code, and was unaware of its provisions. The code of conduct was eventually considered to have failed.

The Loch Lomond Park Authority had been formed in 1985 as a joint committee of local authorities. It was by then working towards regulation by by-laws, with the support of local organisations including the Loch Lomond Association. To draw up by-laws, and to reconcile so far as possible all conflicting interests, proved a long, tortuous and bureaucratic task.

A general welcome for the proposals was demonstrated in 1995: at a point when bureaucratic delays threatened formal introduction of the by-laws, the owners of no less than 760 boats registered them voluntarily under a pilot scheme. The by-laws eventually came into effect in 1996. Inadequate enabling legislation meant, however, that they were no more than a step in the right direction. They failed to require third party insurance, for instance, and it was estimated in 1998 that 60 per cent of boats on the loch lacked this insurance. The by-laws apply, too, only to pleasure craft. However, 3,880 powered boats were registered in the first year, and in the year 2003 there were 5,403. The figures of course include both resident and visiting boats. Administration of the by-laws has been inherited by the National Park authority.

Despite the popularity of privately owned boats, there continue to be some twenty or so tripping boats on the loch. The operators, in 2003, are Sweeney's Cruises at Balloch, Campbell McKirdy at Luss, Cruise Loch Lomond at Tarbet and A. MacFarlane & Son at Balmaha, together with Loch Lomond Leisure Scotland offering speedboat tours from Luss.

The Leven Link?

The rapid growth of interest in pleasure boating since the 1960s has been matched by the increasing frequency with which inland waterways, which had been closed or obstructed to navigation, have been restored. The most notable instance in Scotland has been the Millennium Link, that is the re-opening of the Forth & Clyde and Union Canals, from sea to sea and from Edinburgh to Glasgow, from 2000 to 2002. The possibility of making the Leven fully navigable between Loch Lomond and the Clyde has been talked of for some time. The proposal got official approval – or at least an investigation into its viability did – in *Scotland's Canals: an asset for the future*, a paper issued by the Scottish Executive in 2002.

The existence of the right of navigation over the River Leven gives the scheme a head start over many comparable schemes where such a right was or is absent. Physically the task seems likely to require the construction of four or five weirs, to hold back sufficient depth of water in the reaches above, with locks and fish passes to enable boats and fish to pass the weirs; a further lock past the barrage where there is already a fish pass; and dredging and moorings where necessary. This would be a small undertaking compared with the Millennium Link, or even compared with the Ribble Link. The latter was opened in 2002 and performs the very similar function of linking the Lancaster Canal with the tidal River Ribble and so with the rest of the English inland waterway system. It requires nine locks to rise 59 feet.

To make the Leven fully navigable would mean that Loch Lomond would become an attractive destination for those boating on the Millennium Link canals, with only a few miles of tideway to traverse – the prospect of a holiday which combined the canals with Loch Lomond would be enticing indeed. It would also make the loch accessible to yachtsmen on the Clyde, and enable those whose boats are based on the loch to travel further afield – to Edinburgh, if they wished, or out to sea. It would clearly have great recreational benefit, and local economic benefit to match.

It could, I hope, be done without too much disturbance to those living nearby, and the end-product would be a pleasanter amenity for them. The interests of fisheries would have to be taken fully into account. However, the concern expressed in newspapers in autumn 2002 that such a link would enable alien species of fish, at present in the canals, to enter Loch Lomond is evidently something of a red herring, if I may say so! They could not, unless able to survive several miles of salt water between Bowling and the tidal limit of the Leven; and if they can do that, there is little to prevent them moving to the loch right now.

At any rate, I look forward to setting out to cruise from Edinburgh to Ardlui.

7

LOCH LOMOND: THE STEAMER SERVICE AND ITS RAILWAY CONNECTIONS

The Missing Heritage

If there is one aspect of Loch Lomond's heritage which is, above all else, conspicuous by its absence it is the steamer service up and down the loch. Such services appear to flourish elsewhere – on Windermere, Ullswater, the Lake of Geneva, on lakes in Sweden, New Zealand, North America. But on Loch Lomond restoration of the paddle steamer *Maid of the Loch* proceeds only as fast as funds can be raised. Meanwhile the steamer piers up the loch stand waiting for the steamer which never comes, and at Balloch the multi-million pound gateway development, Loch Lomond Shores, remains – despite its many other attractions – a gateway through which one cannot pass: one can look up the loch, but not travel up it. Boat trips from Balloch are enjoyable but short.

Nor is this solely a matter of heritage. There is no single action which would better enable people in quantity to enjoy the scenery of Loch Lomond, without detriment to it, than reinstating the steamer service.

Steamers came early to Loch Lomond. Robert Fulton started the world's first commercially successful steamer service in 1807, on the Hudson River. Henry Bell did the same for the Old World when he put his *Comet* into service on the Clyde between Glasgow and Helensburgh in 1812. In 1818, the little paddle steamer *Marion* was taken up the River Leven and entered service on Loch Lomond.

From that start, three years after the battle of Waterloo, successive paddle steamers plied Loch Lomond until 1981, and the service continued for another eight years with MV *Countess Fiona*. It is an astonishing record.

The Marion

The *Marion* was a venture by the noted Glasgow engineer David Napier, who had built the boiler for the *Comet*; she was his first venture into shipowning, but would not be the last. In 1814–5 Napier had established the Camlachie Foundry in Glasgow, and completed his first marine engine there in 1816. The *Marion's* wooden hull was built at Dumbarton, measuring probably 60 ft in length by 13 ft beam, and the engine was installed in it; the little ship was named after Mrs Napier. She spent the 1817 season at work on the Clyde, and then she was taken up to Loch Lomond. Her master was Daniel McPhail, who had for a time been master of the *Comet*.

One of the passengers that first summer was Francis Jeffrey, who would later become Lord Advocate. He travelled five or six miles on board, but was not over-impressed: 'it was certainly very strange and striking to hear it and see it hissing and roaring past the headlands of our little bay, foaming and shouting like an angry whale.'

For Dorothy Wordsworth the *Marion* provided the means, on 20 September 1822, to re-visit scenes of happy memories from her earlier tour. This time she was travelling in the company of Joanna Hutchinson, who was sister to her brother William's wife. They came, as most passengers did at that time, by early steamboat from Glasgow to Dumbarton, and thence by coach to Balloch. On that particular occasion, four coaches were insufficient to carry all the passengers, and some of them walked the five miles. Once on board, she wrote:

> We pass at once from the calm river to the gently-stirring wide Lake. Ben Lomond with a shrouded head, and silvery lights on his sides. Opposite hills clear – to the top. A large hilly island . . . reminds me of the Island on Windermere, though much larger and higher. We pass another large island spotted in every part with fine old Yew trees . . . The wind soon blew cold and fierce – and waves so large we might have fancied ourselves at sea. Sheltered in the Cabin, and took a breakfast a la fourchette – not at the gentry end – for we had learned . . . that the other was quite as good, and only half the price . . . When I returned upon deck we were in calm water. Alas! steam-boats are always in a hurry, and take noise and commotion along with them; otherwise we might have sweetly glided among the beautiful Islands . . . No more islands after Luss. We halted in

David Napier's paddle steamer *Marion* heads up Loch Lomond in the 1820s (*Author's collection*)

the Bay to send out passengers, and again at Tarbet, then (rounding the promonotory) pass into the narrower part of the Lake. Ferry house at Inversneyde (sic) just the same, but there is now a glass window. A girl standing on the threshold. We are not near enough to distinguish whether her person be awkward or graceful, or her face pretty; but I cannot fancy her so fair as our Highland Girl . . . The white waterfall drops into the lake as before . . . Back to Tarbet, where a crazy Boat came out to meet us at 3 o'clock. I thought of our coffee and fowls dropped into the water when poor C. was with us, and of our coasting the Bay in a vessel, even more crazy than this. Quiet, warm, beautiful was now our approach to Tarbet – up the green field – lasses washing their linen beside the shady Burn, their kettle hung from a bough, fire smoking among the trees.

Rough in open water, calm and warm in shelter – it sounds like a typical September day on the loch. There were no piers at that time, and at boarding points the steamer lay at anchor off-shore – passengers were taken to and fro in small boats or scows.

Success breeds competition and in 1825 this came to Loch Lomond in the form of PS *Lady of The Lake*, owned by the Lochlomond Steamboat Company which had been formed in Dumbarton. A period of cut-throat competition followed, during which it seems that *Marion* at one point collided with her rival. The precise course of events, then and over the next couple of decades, is by no means easy to disentangle from sources which tend to contradict one another. But Napier seems to have had the feeder services buttoned up, so that neither the Dumbarton steamer nor the Balloch coaches would carry at the same terms for the new company, and the immediate competition collapsed. In 1828, however, Napier did bring a larger steamer up to the loch. This had been plying on the Clyde with the name *Post Boy*; on Loch Lomond she was re-named *Euphrosyne*. Euphrosyne was one of the three graces, the daughters of Zeus in Greek mythology; just what Mrs Napier may have thought about being replaced in this way is not recorded!

There were further outbreaks of competition from time to time, which Napier seems to have resisted successfully, although in the 1830s he entered into partnership with John McMurrich. McMurrich had been one of the proprietors of the Lochlomond Steamboat Company and the partners now traded under that name. In the late 1830s they put into service the *Lochlomond*, the first steamer on the loch to have its hull made of iron.

To Inverarnan and Beyond

By about 1840 improvements to the road up Glen Falloch encouraged the establishment of stage coach services to Killin and Fort William. A couple of miles above the head of Loch Lomond was the old-established inn at Inverarnan. McMurrich and Napier had an examination made of the lowest part of the River Falloch, which enters the loch at its head, to see if steamers could use it. After some work, they could: the river was dredged and a short canal cut to avoid sharp curves. Steamers could then, from 1844, reach a new basin close to the Inverarnan Inn, where they could connect with the coaches.

The canal was built, and the inn improved substantially, at the expense of the Marquis of Breadalbane, who leased the land from the proprietor, Campbell of Glenfalloch, for the purpose. So it was not McMurrich and Napier's vessel which first made regular use of the canal, but the steamer of a new rival company, in which Breadalbane was the largest investor. Advertisments for the *Lochlomond* subsequently made much of the fact that tourists who travelled on her were not detained by being taken up the Falloch where there was nothing to be seen!

The rival company was the New Lochlomond Steamboat Company, which was formed in April 1844 by a group of partners who bought the steamer *Water Witch* at public roup in Glasgow for £634 and brought her to the loch. The Marquis of Breadalbane had four £50 shares; John Bell, flesher of Dumbarton, had two and there were fourteen other partners. Bell, like McMurrich, had been one of the original shareholders in *Lady of the Lake*.

It looks as though McMurrich and Napier had fallen out with Breadalbane, although this is conjecture. Breadalbane was a power in the land and, as mentioned in Chapter 5, was at this period considering the construction of canals that would complete a waterway from Kenmore to the Clyde. What he did specifically require was that the new steamer should run in winter as well as summer to carry cattle, sheep and country produce – such a proposal might, perhaps, have caused friction with Napier whose long experience was of summer-only operation for the tourist trade.

At any rate the new company arranged to run its steamer at least once a week through the winter as well as daily in summer. It also arranged with Mr Ainslie of Fort William that passengers travelling by his coach, between Inverarnan and Fort William, would be carried at a cheap rate on the steamer, and made a similar arrangement with proprietors of a coach to and from Killin.

There had evidently been a coach connection to and from Fort William since the previous year at least, as the following extract from Lord Cockburn's *Circuit Journeys* makes clear. Of the summer of 1843 he wrote:

> There is a passage, I think, in one of Scott's novels in which he makes somebody, who is lamenting the encroachments of civilisation on Highland solitudes say . . . that he should not wonder if the mail-coach horn should one day be heard in Glencoe. Alas, alas! it has been heard all this summer. A romantic tourist pinched for time can now be hurried from Fort William to Edinburgh in one hot long day. A coach left Fort William all this season at about six in the morning, and after blowing away to Ballachulish, up Glencoe to

Kingshouse, and from thence to Tyndrum, and down Glenfalloch to Tarbet, which it reached about two, its passengers could get into a steamer there and reach Glasgow in time for the five o'clock train, which landed them at Edinburgh about seven. Spirits of Fingal and of Rob Roy! what say ye to this?

Whatever Fingal and Rob Roy might have said, tourists evidently liked it, and the connecting steamer and coach services became a lasting feature of travel in the Highlands. Reverting to the *Water Witch*, there were further inducements to travel on her. She departed from a pier near Balloch bridge, at least when the water was high enough, rather than having her passengers ferried out to her. Her owners had also obtained the services of D. McGregor, lately head waiter at one of the best hotels in Glasgow, as steward to serve breakfasts, lunches and dinners in the ship's deck saloon. That was an innovation which enabled passengers to enjoy the view while they ate.

All this evidently made the *Water Witch* successful enough to encourage the two sets of proprietors to settle their diffences. In 1845 they amalgamated, as the Lochlomond Steamboat Company, which had a long and successful career ahead of it. One of its earliest moves was to arrange with landowners around the loch for the erection of piers at the places where the steamers called. This was more than a matter of convenience: there had been a disaster at Tarbet a few years earlier. An overcrowded ferry boat, going to or from the steamer, capsized and about eleven of its occupants were drowned. Horrifyingly, from the deck of the steamer bodies could be seen on the bed of the loch. The piers were built over the next few years at Balmaha, Luss, Rowardennan, Tarbet, Inversnaid and Ardlui. The origin of Balloch Pier is mentioned below.

The Railway Arrives

Scarcely had the new company been formed, however, than it found its services in a further state of flux. Early in 1850 David Napier severed his interest with Loch Lomond after some thirty-two years' involvement. Having offered his shareholding to existing shareholders and been refused, he then sold to Messrs J. & G. Burns of Glasgow. Burns were prominent shipowners in the Clyde and west Highland trades, but now had another string to their bow. The Caledonian & Dumbartonshire Railway had been proposed as early as 1844, to run from Glasgow to Dumbarton and thence to both Balloch and Helensburgh. But funds proved hard to raise, and the promoters decided to concentrate on the section between Bowling and Balloch; this would be isolated from other railways, but would connect at Bowling with the Clyde steamers and the Forth & Clyde Canal, and at Balloch with the Loch Lomond steamers. It would in effect be a portage railway between the waterways.

Just about the time Messrs Burns were buying out David Napier, they also entered into an agreement to operate the new railway when it was completed that summer. They had a pier built at Balloch, which extended some 300 feet out into the loch, so that the steamers would no longer be affected by varying depths in the river, and there the railway terminus was placed. They also – despite protestations from their co-proprietors in the Lochlomond Steamboat Company, which already had one steamer on the loch and another one building – brought a further steamer of their own, the *Pilot*, up the Leven to ply on the loch as well.

The railway was complete enough by 5 July for a special train to bring the directors to Balloch Pier, where they embarked on the *Pilot* for a cruise up the loch and back. The public opening followed on 15 July and was an immediate success, with Burns providing a special steamer service on the Clyde to bring passengers from Glasgow. Suddenly there was enough traffic on the loch for all three steamers.

There was however a setback only a few days later when on 19 July the *Pilot*, failing to live up to her name, ran onto a submerged rock near Ross Point. She had to be beached. The passengers fortunately were rescued, and the ship was eventually recovered and repaired, but not for several weeks. The rock between the two Ross Islands still bears the name Pilot Rock.

Despite the general success of these operations, Burns sold their interest in the Loch Lomond steamers the following year, to concentrate on routes over longer distances. Perhaps they had seen that their combined water/rail route could not last indefinitely. Balloch obtained a link to the main railway system in 1856 with the opening of a line from Stirling – which offered a route to and from Edinburgh; direct connection with Glasgow followed in 1858 with the opening of a line between Glasgow and Bowling. All these lines, during the following decade, became part of the North British Railway. The Lochlomond Steamboat Company settled down to providing a service of steamers connecting with NBR trains at Balloch Pier.

The Admiralty Chart

There was a further instance of a ship striking a rock in September 1860. PS *Prince of Wales*, which had been built a couple of years earlier to meet the increase in traffic when the railway from Glasgow was completed, ran onto a rock in dense fog, north-east of Inchmurrin and not far off Creinch. Once again no-one was seriously injured but the ship had to be beached, and subsequently taken down the Leven to Bowling for her hull to be repaired. The rock too continues to be known as 'Prince of Wales Rock'.

The outcome of this accident was that the whole loch was sounded the following year by a survey party from the Admiralty under Captain Otter RN. Part at least of the costs were defrayed by some of the local landowners, by the steamer company and by the Dumbartonshire and Edinburgh & Glasgow Railways. Buoys and beacons were installed to mark the principal hazards and the results of the survey published as Admiralty Chart no. 2021.

The only other inland lochs in Scotland to be charted by the Admiralty were Loch Awe and the lochs of the Caledonian Canal; several of the large inland loughs in Ireland were also surveyed. The Loch Lomond chart was available for many decades subsequently, and Stanford's chart of Loch Lomond published in 1976 was based on it. My own copy of the Admiralty Chart is endorsed 're-published 22nd April 1930' and 'Small corrections 1953'. The chart was later re-numbered 5077. It was still available as recently as 1997, but seems now to have disappeared from the list.

Royal Visits

The Prince and Princess of Wales travelled from Balloch to Inversnaid by steamer in 1864, and their visit was followed by that of Queen

Victoria herself on 4 September 1869. The steamer made available
for her use was the *Prince Consort*, a name which she thought 'a
pleasant idea', perhaps fortunately in view of the extent to which she
still mourned her husband's death eight years before. The ship itself
she thought 'a fine large vessel'. The royal party was accompanied
by some local notables and officials of the steamboat company. They
boarded at Inversnaid and the ship at first headed south down the
east shore to start a circumnavigation of the loch.

Early mist had cleared and the queen seems to have spent most
of her time on deck admiring the scene. Someone must have been
pointing out the features of the shore and islands, for she noted
all the important ones in her journal; the 'Cornick Hill' which
they passed is perhaps a phonetic rendering of a crew member's
pronunciation of 'conic'. This sight-seeing ceased for a time when
the ship stopped off Portnellan while the royal party lunched in 'the
handsome large cabin'. Afterwards the ship continued to Balloch
and then headed up the west shore: the queen duly noted the villas
on shore and the islands in the loch, but the northern parts of the
loch proved more to her liking – here were the 'finest mountains,
with splendid passes, richly wooded, and the highest mountains
rising behind.' She found them 'Alpine' for they reminded her of
the Lake of Lucerne (although the *Prince Consort* was larger than
the *Winkelried* in which she had cruised on that lake). At one stage
she and her daughter Princess Louise 'sketched as best we could,
but it is most difficult to do so when the steamer keeps moving on.'
Nevertheless it was rated a 'most successful, enjoyable day': 'How
dearest Albert would have enjoyed it!' she wrote.

Inverarnan or Ardlui?

Once the pier had been built at Ardlui it became simple for steamer
passengers to land there to join connecting road transport, and this
seems to have been done when water levels were low, rather than
have the steamer tackle the sand banks and shallows of the River
Falloch. Nevertheless Inverarnan was still in use as an interchange
point in the 1860s, as is confirmed by advertisments of the period
such as those which appeared in Alexander Murray's *Scotland
Described* (1866). That summer the *Earl of Breadalbane* coach ran

between Aberfeldy, Kenmore, Killin, Crianlarich and Inverarnan, where it arrived in time for the 1.15 p.m. steamer for Balloch, and set off on the return journey at 2.15 p.m. The fare from Aberfeldy to Inverarnan ranged from 12s 0d to 15s 0d – coach travel was only for the well-off. Passengers changed at Crianlarich for the Fort William and Oban coaches.

In 1870, however, the Callander & Oban Railway was opened as far as 'Killin' station (located in fact at Glenoglehead) and in 1873 it was extended to Tyndrum. These places became the railheads for long-distance coaches and the Loch Lomond steamers no longer needed to go up the Falloch to Inverarnan to connect with them. The canal fell into disuse. Subsequently, transfers between steamers and local coaches were made at Ardlui.

In due course Colquhoun of Luss, who owned land on both sides of the Falloch where it entered the loch, started to build a suspension footbridge across the river. The Earl of Breadalbane took Colquhoun's trustees to court. Breadalbane had earlier, in 1858, taken legal action against Colquhoun and had obtained the right to dredge the river and to remove the bar which developed at its mouth, so as to preserve the navigation. Going to court again in 1881, he successfully obtained an interdict against erection of the bridge. Although the steamer service to Inverarnan had ceased several years previously, there were then no railways in Glen Falloch itself. Breadalbane, or his advisers, evidently still attached importance to preventing obstruction of the navigable link between Breadalbane property and Loch Lomond. Today the lower part of the river continues to be navigated by small craft; the canal can still be traced, and so can the basin although it is partly filled with debris which appears to have been washed into it.

By the late Victorian period traffic on Loch Lomond required a fleet of three or four steamers. In 1874, for instance, these were recorded as:

Prince Consort   built 1860 valued at £4,400
Prince of Wales   built 1857 valued at £4,000
Princess of Wales built 1865 valued at £3,250.

Steamers were replaced from time to time. *Princess of Wales* for instance was sold in 1881 and a new steamer, *The Queen*, built in 1883. She was 165 ft long by 25 ft beam; she could achieve 14 knots,

PS *Prince of Wales* heads away from Luss, probably in the 1870s. Black
smoke pouring from the funnel suggests that complaints were justified!
Maybe the stoker had been building up his fire for a record run to Balloch.
(*Courtesy of St Andrews University Library*)

and carry 300 passengers. Fifty of these could dine at once in the
mahogony-panelled dining saloon, forward; the aft saloon was
panelled in walnut with gold-fluted pillars topped by Corinthian
capitals. Its seats were upholstered in gold plush velvet, and there
were writing tables, sideboards and mirrors.

Occasionally, all did not go well. In 1881 the *Prince Consort*,
coming down the loch, collided with the *Prince of Wales*, which was
on her way up, at Rowardennan; they had been contesting priority
at the pier and *Prince Consort* did not give way until too late. No-
one was injured, although some of the lady passengers fainted, but
damage to the ships was substantial. Another problem was excessive
smoke from the steamers, and in 1887 the company's manager was
authorised to pay premiums to engineers and firemen who were
successful in abating this nuisance.

Railway Takeover

At this period there was an increasing tendency for railway
companies to take full control of steamer services, such as those on
the Clyde, which extended their routes. In 1888 the North British

Railway – or, rather, its associate the North British Steam Packet Company – offered to buy the Lochlomond Steamboat Company for £30,000. The shareholders, after an unsuccessful attempt to get the offer raised, decided to accept. So the Loch Lomond steamers and associated property passed into North British ownership, and the local company was dissolved on 21 February 1889 – 'one of the oldest and most prosperous steamboat enterprizes in Europe,' as its chronicler Donald McLeod put it.

This takeover was the harbinger of further change. On land at this period, wherever railways ran they exercised almost complete superiority over other means of transport. Yet they were seldom monopolies, for the period was also one of intense competition between railway companies. Such competition was beneficial to the public where there was traffic sufficient, or more than sufficient, for two railways; where there was not, it could be ruinous to the railway companies, or harmful in other ways.

In the present case the chief protagonists were the two principal Scottish railway companies: the North British Railway and the Caledonian Railway. One of the few areas in the Central Belt where there was a near-monopoly was the north bank of the Clyde with its industries, and Loch Lomond beyond, served almost entirely by the North British. In 1889 there came a proposal to build a second railway up the Vale of Leven, following its east side from Dumbarton to reach Loch Lomond at Aber near its south-eastern corner. This was quickly followed by a proposal for a new line from Glasgow out past the shipyards and engineering works to Dumbarton. Both proposals were backed by the Caledonian, and the Caledonian also proposed to put its own fleet of steamers on Loch Lomond. Indeed these proposals came so hot on the heels of the North British purchase of the Lochlomond Steamboat Company that one can only infer that the NBR directorate had got wind of them and acted first.

Construction of new railways required private Acts of Parliament, the bills for which were often hotly contested before Parliamentary committees. That for the new line out to Dumbarton was passed. Beyond Dumbarton it was evident that traffic was insufficient for two railways, and for two steamer fleets. Unusually for the period – and for the protagonists – after arbitration a joint committee

Trains ran alongside steamers at Balloch Pier for passengers to change from one to the other (*Collection J. Danielewski*)

was formed, to be controlled fifty-fifty by the North British and the Caledonian, and to own and operate both the railway from Dumbarton to Balloch and the steamers on the loch. This, the Dumbarton and Balloch Joint Line, came into operation in 1896 at the same time as the new line out from Glasgow to Dumbarton.

Although the steamers were owned jointly, the trains on the joint line were not. The effect was that passengers coming off the steamer at Balloch had the choice of two trains – one of them a North British train for Glasgow Queen Street and the other a Caledonian train for Glasgow Central, one leaving shortly after or (as the case might be) slightly before the other. The joint committee survived the railway 'grouping' of 1923 because, while the North British Railway became part of the London & North Eastern, the Caledonian passed to the London, Midland & Scottish. It therefore lasted until nationalisation in 1948 when both LNER and LMS became part of British Railways. Yet more than twenty years later the author, on a winter visit to Balloch Pier, found access to the *Maid of the Loch* forbidden by a notice in the name of the Dumbarton & Balloch Joint Line, as the accompanying illustration shows.

Back in the 1890s, the steamers on Loch Lomond continued to be an everyday part of peoples' lives, whether resident or visitor. During the exceptionally severe winter of 1894–5 when the lower part of the

Dumbarton & Balloch Joint Line notice was still in use more than twenty years after nationalization (*Author*)

loch froze over, the dining saloon of the *Prince of Wales*, frozen in at Balloch Pier, became a stationary restaurant for the benefit of skaters and others who had come to enjoy the fun.

In more normal times passengers could book through-tickets between steamer piers and railway stations without distinction. As well as passengers, the steamers carried the ordinary traffic of the district – mails, parcels, livestock. One of the many fascinating old postcards of local interest framed and displayed in the foyer of the Inversnaid Hotel depicts a group of Blackface rams. They are penned up on Inversnaid Pier while they wait for the steamer. The hotel management has had the happy thought of framing, along with each card, a transcript of the message on the reverse – and, in case you are wondering just to whom this particular card might have appealed, its message reads 'I hope you have been successful this year with your crops.'

Steamers Meet Competition

Tourists, as I have indicated earlier, found the steamer service integrated with the much wider transport network of the western Highlands. From 1894 there was an important addition – with the opening of the West Highland Railway from Craigendoran to Fort William, passengers could change between train and steamer at Ardlui where the station was close to the pier. Yet although the steamer service benefitted from tourists who travelled that way, for the first time it lost traffic, in the form of local passengers, to a competitor. There was much more of this to come. By 1907 the Ardlui Hotel was advertising not only that 'passengers travelling South by the West Highland Railway change here for Loch Lomond and Loch Katrine' but also (in bold type) that it offered 'MOTOR GARAGE. PETROL.' Yet change came gradually, and not all changes were harmful.

From 1908 visitors heading for Balloch had a further option: the electric tramcar. Dumbarton Burgh and County Tramways Ltd opened its line that year. Since the company's system extended on the far side of Dumbarton as far as Dalmuir, to which point Glasgow cars already operated, it became possible to travel by tram all the way from the Glasgow area to Balloch. On the first Sunday after opening, thousands of people took the trams to Balloch. But the trams lasted only until 1928, overtaken in their turn by motor bus competition.

New steamers continued to be delivered to Loch Lomond by bringing them up the River Leven, and when they were sold off they departed the same way. As ships became bigger, the task of bringing them up the Leven became more and more difficult. When the *Empress* was delivered early in 1890 the assistance of a hundred men on each side of the river, and seven horses, was needed although she was in steam, and the task of bringing her up the non-tidal section took from Friday to Monday.

The *Prince Edward*, built in 1911, was 175 ft long and just over 22 ft beam. She fared even worse than the *Empress* when the attempt was made to bring her up the river that May. As well as the engines, horses were used, and two of them were pulled into the water. Ropes were secured to trees, and the ship inched forward until they could be moved on to the next. An attempt was made to raise the water level by damming one of the bridges: the dam gave way. After several days the ship was aground so hard, and the water level had fallen so much, that she had to be left where she was until the autumn rains brought the water level up again.

The winter service of steamers, which had run every weekday for many years past, was reduced to three days a week after the outbreak of the First World War in 1914. The development of motor vehicles was greatly encouraged by the war; soon after it was over, a motor bus service to Balmaha was inaugurated, and Luss also had a bus service by the early 1920s. Later in that decade, Alastair Alpin MacGregor was able to describe the road between Glasgow and Balloch as one of the busiest thoroughfares in Scotland. This may have helped steamer traffic on Loch Lomond in summer, but in winter it was a different matter, with buses taking local traffic for the villages; the winter steamer service was discontinued completely from 1933.

Summer traffic that year had had a boost, both in numbers and in publicity, with the arrival of the *Northern Belle* train at Balloch Pier. The *Northern Belle* was the LNER's newly established cruise train, forerunner of today's *Royal Scotsman*. With sleeping cars, dining cars and daytime coaches, not to mention a cocktail bar and a hairdresser, it set off from King's Cross for a fortnight's tour of the Highlands. When it reached Balloch Pier, tour participants embarked on a loch steamer for the cruise up to Ardlui. Meanwhile the train went round to collect them and continue the tour over the West Highland Line.

Nevertheless, with the general decline in traffic fewer steamers were needed; steamers were progressively withdrawn, but they were not replaced. By 1939 only two were left in service – the *Prince Edward*, and the *Princess May*, which dated back to 1899. Then came the Second World War. Suddenly, with Clyde cruising and motor coach excursions alike reduced almost to nothing, the two elderly Loch Lomond steamers found themselves busier than they had been for decades. They carried as many as 500,000 passengers a year.

Maid of the Loch

Numbers were almost halved in the first post-war season, 1946, although subsequent fine summers improved things a bit. Meanwhile British Railways, which had inherited the Dumbarton & Balloch Joint Line, had a problem. Clearly, both of the Loch Lomond steamers were fast approaching the ends of their useful

LOCH LOMOND
STEAMER SERVICES
EXCURSIONS and TOURS

P.S "MAID OF THE LOCH"

23rd MAY until
11th SEPTEMBER, 1955

BRITISH RAILWAYS

Almost new, paddle steamer *Maid of the Loch* steams proudly up Loch Lomond on the cover of BR pamphlet promoting her services (*Collection R.N. Forsythe, courtesy of British Railways Board*)

HOLIDAY
RUNABOUT TICKETS

ARE ISSUED ON ANY DAY OF THE WEEK
AND PROVIDE

UNLIMITED TRAVEL

FOR SEVEN CONSECUTIVE DAYS

(including day of issue)

WITHIN THE AREA

GLASGOW — GOUROCK — BALLOCH — HELENSBURGH —
ARDLUI — SAILINGS ON LOCH LOMOND AND BETWEEN
GOUROCK AND CRAIGENDORAN

STATIONS AND PIERS EMBRACED IN AREA

*Alexandria and	Craigendoran	Greenock (Princes Pr.)	Partick Hill
Bonhill	Crookston	Greenock (West)	Partick (Central)
Anderston Cross	Crow Road	Hawkhead	Partick (West)
Anniesland	Cumberland Street	Helensburgh (Cen.)	Port-Glasgow
Ardlui	*Dalmuir Park	Helensburgh (Upper)	Renton
Ardlui Pier	Dalmuir Riverside	Hillington (West)	Rhu
Arrochar & Tarbet	Dalreoch	Hillington (East)	Rowardennan Pier
*Balloch (Central)	Drumchapel	Houston & Crosslee	*Scotstoun (East)
Balloch Pier	Drumry	Ibrox	*Scotstoun (West)
Balmaha Pier	*Dumbarton (Central)	Inversnaid Pier	*Scotstounhill
Bishopton	Dumbarton (East)	Jordanhill	Shandon
Bogston	Elderslie	Kilbowie	Shields Road
Bowling	Fort Matilda	Kilmacolm	*Singer
Bridge of Weir	Garelochhead	Kilpatrick	Stobcross
Cardonald	Georgetown	Langbank	Tarbet Pier
Cardross	†Glasgow (Central)	Mosspark (West)	Westerton
Cartsdyke	†Glasgow (Queen St.)	Old Kilpatrick	Whistlefield
Charing Cross	*Glasgow (St. Enoch)	Paisley (Canal)	Whiteinch Riverside
Clydebank Riverside	*Gourock	*Paisley (Gilmour St.)	Woodhall Halt
Clydebank (East)	*Greenock (Central)	Paisley (St. James)	*Yoker Ferry
*Clydebank (Central)	Greenock (Lynedoch)	Paisley (West)	Yoker (High)
Corkerhill			

FIRST CLASS RAIL	THIRD CLASS RAIL
33/9	**22/6**

Children (3 and under 14 years) half-fare

Passengers taking out Holiday Runabout Tickets can also obtain the undernoted tickets which cover the same points and have the same validity. Dog 5/8. Bicycle 11/3, Tandem 16/11, Pram (Not Folded) 15/-, Invalid Chair (Not Folded and under 60 lbs.) 15/-.
† First Class and Third Class tickets may be obtained at these stations. * Third Class tickets may be obtained at these stations and on board Loch Lomond Steamers.

Tickets can be obtained at other stations in the area on 12 hours' notice.

No allowance or extension of date can be granted on these tickets in consequence of there being no Sunday service in certain areas.

TRAVEL   AS   OFTEN   AS   YOU   LIKE

Note.—Passengers holding Holiday Runabout Ticket No. 9 may undertake the Three Lochs Tour by purchasing on board the steamer a supplementary ticket for the journey from Gourock or Craigendoran to Arrochar or in the reverse direction at a charge of 3/6.

The Arrochar sailing operates on Tuesdays, Thursdays and Saturdays commencing 28th May.

ASK FOR TICKET FOR AREA No. 9

B.R. 35020/1—FL—May. 1955   Printed in Great Britain by Munro Press Ltd., Perth

Back cover of BR 1955 pamphlet shows that holiday runabout ticket, area no. 9, included Loch Lomond piers equally with railway stations (*Collection R.N. Forsythe, courtesy British Railways Board*)

lives. Passengers were still coming and, it seems, on occasion in sufficient quantity to need more than one ship – particularly when the circular tour incorporating Loch Long and Loch Lomond was operating. Evidently there was a choice between building two ships of traditional size, or one very large one able to take all the traffic which might offer. That was the course which was chosen – presumably one large ship is less expensive than two medium-sized ones. No doubt it seemed a good idea at the time.

The new ship was ordered in 1950, brought to Balloch in sections and assembled there in 1953: the *Maid of the Loch*. Driven by a steam engine and paddle wheels, her machinery was conventional, even old fashioned: her superstructure by contrast was in part constructed of aluminium. This was to minimise her weight, and therefore draught, so that she could negotiate the shallows near Luss. She was built 191 ft long, with a beam of 28 ft, by far the largest ship ever to sail Loch Lomond, or indeed any other inland waterway in Britain.

She was launched in May 1953 and could carry up to 1,000 passengers. *Princess May* was withdrawn immediately; *Prince Edward* ran for two seasons more. Then she too was withdrawn and *Maid of the Loch* continued alone. Some years her passenger figures went down, and some years they went up, according to changes in holidaymaking habits, and the publicity effort put in to counteract these – but she was always large for the traffic on offer.

In 1971 Queen Elizabeth followed the example of her ancestor a century before and cruised Loch Lomond by paddle steamer. With her were the Duke of Edinburgh and Princess Anne.

By then *Maid of the Loch* had passed out of railway ownership. First, in 1957, she had become part of the fleet of the Caledonian Steam Packet Company – the company which was controlled by British Railways but perpetuated a familiar name and operated all the former railway steamer services on the Clyde. Then in 1969 the Government-owned Scottish Transport Group was established and CSP transferred to it along with the nationalised Scottish bus companies. A few years later David MacBrayne was absorbed and the shipping line became Caledonian MacBrayne, 'CalMac'.

The consequence of the 1969 transfer on coastal shipping routes was dramatic: they ceased to be treated primarily as extensions of rail routes, and became instead roll-on, roll-off ferries making the shortest practicable sea crossings in the interest of road transport. In this scenario, within a few years *Maid of the Loch* had become a unique survivor, a traditional steamer which continued to paddle up and down the loch with passengers who came by train to Balloch Pier – the line had been modernised and electrified in 1960–1. Some passengers, too, found their way there by car or by coach tour. Little attempt seems to have been made to link the steamer with local bus services, or to encourage round trips from piers up the loch.

Certainly, in this author's experience at Tarbet in June 1974, no sign indicated the presence of a pier to passers-by on the main road, and at the pier itself the only poster on display gave the times of departures for Balloch, with train connections for Glasgow. Yet the ship's progress up the loch was accompanied by a queue of cars which crawled along the lochside road while their occupants watched her, and many would doubtless have joined her had they known how. Unannounced at Tarbet were the possibilities of two short round trips daily to the head of the loch and one longer one to its foot. It is noteworthy that some years later the Cruise Loch Lomond tripping boat operation was based on Tarbet pier, with apparent great success.

That is not to denigrate the efforts that were made to build up traffic on *Maid of the Loch* – such as the presence of the 'Maid of the Loch' in person as a hostess on board, the 'swinging showboat' evening cabaret cruises operated from the 1960s onwards, and the many attractive flyers that were published to advertise the ship.

Piers and Their Problems

Despite all these efforts, a further threat to the loch steamer services came with successive closures of piers. Only Balloch pier belonged to the steamer operator; the others were owned locally. The days when Loch Lomond steamer passengers represented a valuable flow of revenue to pier owners were doubtless long past, while the costs of maintaining timber piers increased. In these circumstances Luss pier was closed in 1952, even before *Maid of the Loch* entered service. Ardlui pier followed in 1964, and with it went a popular out-by-train, return-by-steamer circular tour. Balmaha was closed in 1971, its owner making the point that *Maid of the Loch* was very much heavier than the steamers for which the pier had been built, with consequent long-term damage, and Tarbet was closed in 1975.

That left only Rowardennan and Inversnaid for the steamer to call at, and the *Glasgow Herald* pointed out in 1977 that Rowardennan's future was doubtful too, since its hotel-keeper owners were unable to afford repairs. The point was graphically made with a picture of the two young hoteliers crouched disconsolately beside a gaping hole in the deck of the pier that their deeds obliged them to maintain. This came in the two-part article, 'The Scandal of Loch Lomond' published on 1 and 2 April. It drew attention to vandalism and rubbish-dumping on the loch shores, but mostly it concentrated on the state of the piers. As it pointed out, the main street of Luss was the most attractive in the district but at the end of it, sticking out like a sore thumb, was the derelict pier.

Perhaps that article helped to prod the authorities into action, for it was announced in 1978 that £500,000 was to be spent by the local authorities and the Scottish Tourist Board in a five-year programme to rebuild the piers at Rowardenan, Luss, Tarbet and Inversnaid. The first beneficiary was Luss pier, which was rented by Strathclyde Region in 1979 for £5 a year, rebuilt, and re-opened in 1980. By then, Strathclyde Region was supporting operation of the steamer with a handsome subsidy, and traffic was on the increase.

Alloa Brewery and Countess Fiona

All of this, sadly, was not enough. In the 1981 season 114,000 passengers and a subsidy of £128,000 added up to a loss of £73,450. *Maid of the Loch*'s boiler was in poor condition and in January 1982 CalMac put her up for sale. She has lain at Balloch Pier ever since and has yet to re-enter service.

A future of that sort was not immediately forseeable. In 1982 the successful bidder for *Maid of the Loch* was Alloa Brewery Co. Ltd, a subsidiary of the brewing and catering group Allied Lyons plc. Also purchased was land at Balloch Pier. Firm plans for *Maid of the Loch* depended upon other possible developments at the foot of the loch. At that period this district was run-down, and had a tangle of ownerships and responsible authorities which meant that while there was much talk of improvement very little was achieved over the next few years.

What Alloa Brewery did do to maintain the shipping service to the piers up the loch in the meantime was to bring in another, smaller, ship. This was a motor vessel which had started life as *Countess of Breadalbane* on Loch Awe, as long before as 1936; after a varied career on that loch and elsewhere, she was brought to Loch Lomond overland, re-named *Countess Fiona*, and entered service for the 1982 summer season. She was named after – and by, on 8 June – the Countess of Arran, formerly Fiona Colquhoun. She operated between Balloch and Luss, Rowardennan and Inversnaid; Tarbet was added to her calls in 1984.

Some years later the author was advised by Alloa Brewery Co. Ltd that while *Maid of the Loch*, with her capacity for 1,000 passengers and her crew of 33, had required a large subsidy, *Countess Fiona* with a capacity of 180 passengers and a crew of 6 covered her costs without subsidy. She was also able to operate over a long season. *Maid of the Loch*'s season had been short, usually from the fourth week in May until the second week in September, but *Countess Fiona* usually ran from early April until the end of September. One can only regret that she had not been brought to the loch years before, to provide an off-peak service as consort to *Maid of the Loch*.

Initially, trains continued to connect with the ship at Balloch Pier as usual. Indeed Alloa Brewery must have expected sustantial traffic from this source, for they warned train passengers to obtain 'boat passes' at Glasgow Queen Street to guarantee that there would be room on board.

Balloch Pier Station Closed

At the end of the 1986 season, however, the train service over the final half-mile of line between Balloch Central and Balloch Pier was withdrawn. The proposal to do so had originated from a wish by Strathclyde Region to reduce the subsidy it paid to British Rail. This was paid through Strathclyde Passenger Transport Executive, which was controlled by the region.

Trains only traversed that half-mile when there was a connection to be made with *Countess Fiona*. Otherwise Balloch Central was the terminus. British Rail had produced the results of two censuses of traffic using Balloch Pier station in 1984. These showed traffic which was small but not non-existent – every train either brought passengers or took them away.

The Transport Users Consultative Committee for Scotland considered the closure proposal, as required by statute. Since all passengers were on pleasure bent, it found no evidence that closure would result in hardship – hardship being the principal criterion upon which such closures were judged – and reported so to the Secretary of State for Transport. British Rail was advised that it might close the line.

There were some curious features of the closure process. Strathclyde Region was with one hand paying for restoration of piers up the loch, but with the other removed funding for the rail link to the ship which served the piers. Strathclyde Passenger Transport Executive, with a duty to promote integrated transport, was here removing a central component from an integrated route.

Many of the savings which resulted from closure could have been made anyway. Balloch Central station was in those days located immediately north of a level crossing. Staff had to open and shut the gates every time a train arrived or departed, which meant several times an hour. Closure of the line to the pier was linked to a proposal to relocate Balloch Central station south of the road, and so eliminate the cost of the level crossing. All very well, but the station could have been relocated while retaining the line to the pier. In that event the number of trains using the level crossing daily would have been in single figures, and they would have been travelling slowly. In such circumstances a crossing with warning lights rather than gates would almost certainly have been permitted, and much of the anticipated saving made anyway. The TUCC did not appear to have considered this; it was under the impression that the unclassified road over the crossing was the A811.

Closure of Balloch Pier station also contrasted markedly with the reopening, in 1985, of the closed Loch Awe station and the establishment soon afterwards of steamboat cruises from the adjoining pier.

On 10 October 1985, the *Glasgow Herald* had reported the arrival at Balloch Pier of a train carrying more than 500 excursionists from the north of England. It is not clear whether any of them went on a cruise – this was after the end of *Countess Fiona*'s usual season – or whether the train was solely in the nature of a railtour traversing a line threatened with closure. Nevertheless it does accentuate the extent to which the train service to Balloch Pier remained wedded to Glasgow suburban services, while the line's potential for excursions from further afield seems latterly to have gone unexploited. Once the West Coast Main Line had been electrified from the south though to Glasgow in 1974, with the accelerations which resulted, Balloch Pier – and a cruise up Loch Lomond – were well within range of day excursions from the north of England – Blackpool, say, or Manchester. Or even from Euston, with the journey one way or the other made overnight. It would have been an attractive proposition.

The arrival of passengers by the trainload would have been just what *Maid of the Loch* needed. By 1986, however, it was becoming evident that any prospect of her early return to service was increasingly unlikely. Alloa Brewery Co. Ltd made no formal objection to the closure of Balloch Pier station. Nor did the Scottish Tourist Board, although it might reasonably have been concerned at the loss of the only station directly serving one of Scotland's most famous tourist attractions.

Alloa Brewery probably had ideas of moving *Countess Fiona*'s base to a point more obvious and accessible to road users. The company's ideas for *Maid of the Loch* seem to have been along the lines of a floating restaurant, static or, occasionally, mobile. Since her boiler had deteriorated markedly and needed replacement, there were thoughts of diesel power to drive the paddles.

What Alloa Brewery in fact did was sell out in 1988. The purchasers, jointly, were an Australian shipping line and a shipping company based in Barrow-in-Furness. They traded as Maid of the Loch Ltd, and promised much. *Countess Fiona* operated as usual for the 1989 season, and indeed according to the timetable started to call at Balmaha again. *Maid of the Loch* was to be restored to her former glory. A 350-passenger catamaran, *Lady of the Loch*, was being completed in Australia. But when I was allowed to see over *Maid of the Loch* that September it was evident all was not well. Nothing had been done: she remained a dilapidated sleeping beauty. Sailings by *Countess Fiona* were expected to resume at Easter 1990, but were instead suspended. On 8 August 1990 the *Glasgow Herald* reported that Maid of the Loch Ltd was in receivership consequent on, apparently, troubles with the Australian parent company. The two ships and the land were for sale again. This time the purchaser was Francis Leisure Group, based in Tyneside. Once again there were grandiose plans for restoration of *Maid of the Loch* – in conjunction with a large hotel development at Balloch Pier. And once again the owner went into receivership, early in 1992.

On this occasion Dumbarton District Council came to the rescue. Security staff had been withdrawn, and many fittings of value and importance had been stripped out of *Maid of the Loch*. She was in danger of sinking from accumulated rainwater. The council had her pumped out and provided 24-hour security. Subsequently it was able to buy both ships and the pier. It allowed members of the Paddle Steamer Preservation Society to start remedial work on *Maid of the Loch*.

We are now entering the realm of current events rather than history; the story of the revival of *Maid of the Loch* is still unfolding and its course so far is best summarised. Consultants were engaged to consider the ship's future and reported late in 1993. The essence of their extensive report was that *Maid of the Loch* should be restored to full operation, with steam power, as a 'flagship cruising experience', and her operational capacity reduced to about 500 passengers. On the other hand it was concluded that if this restoration programme proceeded, then *Countess Fiona* would not have a future cruising on the loch.

The outcome for *Countess Fiona* was sad. She was eventually put up for sale, and several bids were received. But no sale for re-use was concluded. Instead she was scrapped at Balloch in September 1999.

Maid of the Loch, however, was transferred in 1995 to a charitable company formed for the purpose, Loch Lomond Steamship Company, and the long, hard and laborious task of raising funds and doing the work got under way. Over £2 million was needed,and much of the restoration work has been done voluntarily. On appeal, many of the missing fittings re-appeared, no questions asked. Even so, it was 1997 before a new deck rendered the interior of the ship completely weatherproof for the first time in many years. This in turn made it possible to fit out the ship internally and so to use her as a restaurant and venue for events, and to open her to the public through the summer. A new boiler, to make her once again mobile, is at the time of writing still awaited.

Close by, the long-anticipated development of the south-west corner of the loch has materialised as Loch Lomond Shores, the leisure and retail complex which forms a gateway to the national park. Through the efforts of a public-private partnership comprising Scottish Enterprise (Dunbartonshire), the national park authority, Jenners, and Kilmartin Property Group, a once near-derelict area has become a popular attraction for visitors. So popular, indeed, that although the complex was opened only in July 2002, it welcomed its millionth visitor in August 2003.

The course of the railway to Balloch Pier has never been built over. We now live in an era when closed railways are regarded as ripe for reopening – to Alloa, and Galashiels, and from Airdrie to Bathgate, for instance. By comparison with these, reconstruction of this half-mile line would be a small task. Is it too much to envisage its restoration, to a terminal re-named 'Loch Lomond Shores', bringing visitors in quantity from far and wide to visit the national park gateway and embark on a restored *Maid of the Loch*?

8

ALONG LOCH LOMOND'S EASTERN SHORE

Paths or Not?

The lack of a modern road up the east shore of Loch Lomond is probably a consequence of – in equal parts – the difficulty of traversing its rugged slopes, and the ease of travelling up and down the loch. Yet there must always have been paths here, used by the inhabitants of the clachans along the shore. In September 1716 government troops intending to surprise Rob Roy attempted to use them by night. They left Buchanan House near Drymen at 8 p.m. to arrive at Inversnaid at dawn. Heavy rain in the evening brought the burns up in spate, flooded the fords and no doubt turned the paths into quagmires. It was broad daylight before they arrived, by which time Rob Roy had had ample warning.

Nonetheless, this route seems likely to have been one of those by which the Garrison was later supplied. The Ordnance Survey map, as recently as the 1924 revision, showed a path diverging from the shore path a couple of miles short of Inversnaid, and heading up easy gradients directly for the Garrison. It has disappeared from modern maps. North of Inversnaid, the 1924 revision showed no path beside the shore along its most rugged section to the head of the loch; land detail on the Admiralty chart, which was based on early Ordnance Survey work, clearly showed one. This duly reappeared on the Stanford's map of the 1970s; the publisher prudently inserted a note of warning to 'ramblers' that it was almost impassable in places and should only be used after seeking local information.

The path had remained in use from Inversnaid for a mile or so northwards as far as Rob Roy's Cave. This 'cave' is in truth a hollow among tumbled rocks above the shore; its association with the outlaw is traditional, and conjectural.

Robert Bruce

The cave has, equally, traditional association with Robert Bruce, who came to this part of the east shore of Loch Lomond late in 1306. This was during the time he spent in the western wilderness, between his contentious coronation at Scone – which was initially as unwelcome to his rivals in Scotland as it was to the king of England – and the start of his attempts to unify Scottish interests against the English. These would eventually culminate triumphantly at Bannockburn.

He came to the loch with a couple of hundred followers, hoping to cross to the west shore. But with no boats to be found and a winter's night coming on, Bruce and his companions took refuge in a cave. Hardly had the king and his party settled down in the dark, however, when they became alarmed at strange sounds of breathing and movement around them. They were, they feared, in the presence of a band of outlaws even more desperate than themselves.

A light was obtained and the supposed outlaws were found to be a flock of goats – goats which likewise had taken shelter in the cave. (Wild goats are to this day a feature of this part of Loch Lomondside.) For the rest of a cold night, the goats helped to keep Bruce and his men warm, and later in gratitude he ordained that on royal manors goats might graze rent-free.

By daylight the search for a boat was resumed more intensively than before, and one was eventually found – so small that it held only three people, and so full of leaks that while one man rowed the other two had to bale. With this the crossing began – and progressed so slowly that the impatient among Bruce's band swam across the loch, clothes on their backs and swords between their teeth. Even so the crossing took a day or more, but it was successful and enabled Bruce to meet up with his supporter the Earl of Lennox near Luss.

It was, however, the later association of the cave with Rob Roy that appealed most to nineteenth-century tourists. They came in droves, on foot, by rowing boat and by steamboat. Many on arrival found the little cave something of an anticlimax.

Ben Lomond

That could scarcely be said of the other great east-shore magnet for tourists, Ben Lomond itself. With its summit 3,192 feet above sea level it is both the most southerly and one of the most popular of the Munros. That popularity is due at least in part to its accessibility: a mere half-day's outing from Glasgow whence, as the Scottish Mountaineering Club's 1972 guide *The Southern Highlands* pointed out, it is possible to leave by car after lunch, ascend the hill and be back in time for supper.

Long before today's era of Munro-bagging, Ben Lomond was popular with tourists. They too found it accessible by the standards of their times, even though the rapidity of that round trip from Glasgow would amaze them. It was evidently the military road up the opposite side of Loch Lomond – from which Ben Lomond is in full view – which first made the mountain seem accessible. Sarah Murray, when she came to Tarbet inn in the 1790s, learned that there was a ferry across the loch to the foot of the mountain. Another visitor had been waiting a week for a favourable day for the ascent, and was that very day attempting it. A couple of decades later it was usual for parties of visitors from Dumbarton who wished to climb the mountain to leave between 2 a.m. and 3 a.m., and to have breakfast at Inverbeg before crossing by the ferry to ascend the ben, returning in the evening.

The introduction of steamboats to the loch made it easy to travel direct to Rowardennan. There, according to *Lumsden & Son's Steamboat Companion* of 1831, was a neat comfortable inn, where guides and every requisite for the journey could be obtained. The distance to the summit was about 6 miles. From his description, the writer of the guide had evidently made the ascent himself. 'The first part of the path will appear the most disagreeable, as it is principally over rock and heath' he wrote – a sentiment which hillwalkers everywhere must find familiar. He continued:

> Some green ridges are howevever met with, and frequently great portions of wet moss. Towards the summit, the track is more difficult and fatiguing, increasing in steepness, and passing over a very rugged or shelving surface; but when the ascent is gained, the toil is amply repaid by the sublime and wonderful prospect which is had in every direction . . . Below, the Lake appears wonderfully lessened in size, and the islands look like mere spots upon its surface.

He followed this with a page of eulogy about the extent of the view to be obtained on a fine day: Stirling Castle seems 'almost beneath

The eastern shore at Rowardennan on a sunny evening: a southbound steamer is perhaps picking up passengers who have been ascending Ben Lomond on the right (*Courtesy of St Andrews University Library*).

the mountain', the Isle of Man might be discovered in the distance 'if the atmosphere be clear', and to the north is seen 'the tremendous assemblage of ruggedness that constitutes the Grampian chain.'

Thirty-five years on, the proprietor of the Rowardennan Hotel was advertising a large extension for the greater comfort of his numerous customers. Rowardennan was the 'best and shortest road' to Ben Lomond, the only place where 'Ponies may be had by which parties can ride with ease and safety to the top'; the distance had mysteriously contracted to 4 miles.

Ward and Lock's *Complete Guide to Scotland* (1889) cautioned tourists never to undertake the ascent without a guide, for 'even on the clearest day, the mountain may suddenly become enveloped in clouds or mist', and in 1895 the Tarbet Hotel was advertising 'Guides to Ben Lomond'. Baedeker's *Great Britain* for 1910 told readers that the ascent from Rowardennan was easily accomplished in 2 to 3 hours and added 'guide not indispensible; pony with guide 8–10 shillings'.

A couple of years earlier, in 1908, Baddeley's 'Thorough Guide' *Scotland* (Part I) included a section on mountaineering with

Guides and ponies could be hired for the ascent of Ben Lomond (*Author's collection*)

directions for twenty-seven or so of the most popular hills. Ben Lomond was said to be second only to Ben Nevis in popularity. Three routes were described in detail: from Rowardennan – easiest and best; from Aberfoyle – more laborious but less hackneyed; and from Inversnaid – more shut in than the other two, and so recommended for the descent, after ascent by one of the others, so that the best of the scenery was kept in front.

In any case, the tourist who wished to economise on time was advised to choose a different route for the descent from the one by which he went up. That is a flexibility in which – particularly where Ben Lomond is concerned – the tourists of a century ago, with all the choices available to them for travel by train, steamer and coach, can only be envied by the hillwalkers of today, obliged as they so often are to return to parked cars as effectively as though attached to them by elastic.

Along the East Shore by Road or Rail?

There have been, from time to time, proposals for improved communications up the east shore of Loch Lomond. In 1841 the minister of Buchanan parish thought the then-existing road to Rowardennan should be extended up to Glen Falloch, and said so in the *New Statistical Account*. He was moved by the thought that population of his parish was likely to decline, since there was insufficient work for them all.

A similar consideration emerged almost a century later in the 1930s when, according to R.H. Aitken in *The West Highland Way*, Tom Johnston MP proposed construction of a road over this route as unemployment relief. Johnston was MP for West Stirlingshire between 1929 and 1931, and again between 1935 and 1945. His advocacy of such a road was to be less successful than his later advocacy of hydro-electricity.

In between these had come a proposal which, if carried out, would have seen the east shore traversed by a trunk route to Inverness: the Glasgow & North Western Railway. The Bill for this was presented in Parliament in 1882 and considered in great detail before Parliamentary committee in the spring of 1883. The only railway into the West Highlands at that date was the recently completed Callander & Oban, while the route from Glasgow to Inverness was a roundabout one via Perth and Forres. The Glasgow & North Western was to be much shorter. It was to diverge from an existing line at Maryhill, and run via Drymen, Balmaha and the east shore of Loch Lomond to Strathfillan, Glencoe, Fort William, the Great Glen and Inverness. For a line to traverse such a mountainous region, it was remarkable for the long near-level stretches beside Loch Lomond and Loch Ness.

In all that 167 miles the only place of importance not already served by a railway was Fort William, and after two months of argument in Parliament it became clear there was insufficient traffic to justify a further railway to Inverness. The Bill was rejected. The then-existing route to Inverness was later shortened, but no railway ever came up the east shore of Loch Lomond.

The West Highland Way

The route that was eventually established up the east shore was neither road nor railway, but – in reversion to the means of travel of our ancestors – long-distance footpath: the West Highland Way.

Proposals for such things seem to have grown out of, as much as anything, the outdoor movement of the 1930s. The Depression, particularly in and around Glasgow, at least gave those who were out of work the opportunity to head for the hills. Their budgets for doing so were minimal compared with those of earlier generations of tourists.

The prototype long-distance path was the Pennine Way in England. Parts of it have been in existence since 1951. In 1969 the Glasgow Group of the Holiday Fellowship, which numbered walkers and climbers among its members, joined with comparable organisations to produce a proposal for a walkers' way from Glasgow to Fort William; Tom Hunter, convenor of the relevant sub-committee of the fellowship, had as much to do with this as anyone. In December of that year the Scottish Development Department commissioned consultant F.J. Evans OBE to prepare a 'Study for a Footways System North of Glasgow'. Evans's later report on the Trossachs has already been mentioned. He produced his North-of-Glasgow report with commendable speed the following May; his 'footways' were for use by pedestrians, horse riders and cyclists.

On the map which accompanied his report, footway no. 1 was the 'Highland Footway', which endorsed the Holiday Fellowship proposal. The Highland Footway was to run from Clydebank to Glen Falloch, and to form part of a route which would extend further to the north. From Drymen northwards Evans considered a route via Stronachlachar and Glen Gyle, but concluded the east shore of Loch Lomond would be shorter and more popular. So after leaving Drymen the proposed route ran though forestry and then, passing to the north of the Conic Hill, gained the ridge of Beinn Bhreac and followed its continuation to the summit (and viewpoint) of Beinn Uird, 1,957 ft (596 m.) above sea level. Beinn Uird is a southern outlier of Ben Lomond itself.

Thence the way fell to the west, joining for some distance the path coming down from Ben Lomond to Rowardennan and then diverging northwards to join the forestry road which already extended up the east shore of Loch Lomond for several miles beyond the end of the public road at Rowardennan. About suggestions that this forest road should be made public and extended to Inversnaid – so making a circular route from Glasgow, out via Loch Lomond and back via Loch Ard – Evans was suitably scathing; this would ruin, he wrote, the high amenity for which this side of Loch Lomond was outstanding. His Highland Footway was to continue north of the end of the forestry road to Inversnaid and onward, although the 'fjord-like' terrain made the route difficult; at Rob Roy's Cave fallen boulders blocked the existing path, such as it was. But 'difficult' did not mean 'impossible', and after detailed survey the way could be made to reach Glen Falloch.

The Evans report was submitted to the Countryside Commission for Scotland. The Countryside Commission decided to make use of its powers under the Countryside (Scotland) Act 1967, to make a detailed study of the route from Milngavie (on the northern edge of the Glasgow conurbation), and to report its proposals to the Secretary of State for Scotland. The secretary of state could then designate the route for the local authorities (who had been consulted earlier) to implement.

As the Countryside Commission commenced its task, it became clear that the title 'Highland Way', as it had become, might conflict with further proposals for long-distance paths following some of the great traditional routes through the Highlands. Modified further, the name became the one which would become familiar, 'West Highland Way'. The over-riding principle in laying out its route was that it should capture the imagination: that it should be built on existing features, natural and man-made – rather than superimposed upon them. This meant that the way was to use, as far as possible, existing footpaths, rights-of-way, military roads, forest roads, farm tracks and so on. Much of the route was therefore already open to the public or in public ownership; but equally, much was not.

In negotiating the detailed route, the Countryside Commission was fortunate to have on its staff chartered surveyor Peter Bickmore Dundas who, after the first few months, took on this responsibility. Having trained on one of the great estates in Aberdeenshire he seems to have been well able both to sit down with his local authority colleagues, and to speak the same language as landowners and their agents, sharing their local knowledge and understanding their concerns. Sooner or later, initial hesitation on the part of landowners gave way to assistance. With their advice to avoid a boggy patch here, to work around a ridge to preserve the landscape there, to skirt a historic site somewhere else, some landowners all but laid out the route themselves. The process was doubtless aided by the general interest engendered by Bickmore Dundas and his local authority colleagues, and by the willingness of owners and others to contribute towards a project which caught the public imagination. It was helped too by the ability to restore dangerous old footbridges for continued use, with the occasional footpath bridge substantial enough to carry tractors and farm machinery at lambing time! One landowner, after initial and natural suspicion about the project, eventually offered use of a byre as a bothy for walkers.

Remarkably, some opposition to the proposal came from die-hard outdoor men. They considered that waymarked routes were not in the Scottish tradition; they feared that pampered and inexperienced people would wander off them and get into difficulty.

There were some diversions from the route as first proposed. Notably, the exposed high-level route along the ridge to Beinn Uird was replaced by a low-level route closer to the loch. This meant that north-bound walkers climbed up and over the Conic Hill to encounter that unique and astonishing view on p. 47 of the chain of islands which continues the line of the Highland Boundary fault straight across Loch Lomond. Reaching the shore at Balmaha, the way then turned northwards by adopting the route for a Loch Lomondside walk upon which the Forestry Commission was expecting to start work. North of Rowardennan, too, it followed an old path closer to the shore than the forest road.

Once access agreements had been achieved, the way had physically to be constructed. That meant waymarking and signs, gates and stiles, and, where there was no existing path, a path with drains and bridges. Funding came from central government. In building the way the principle adopted was to do, initially, no more than was needed to define the route, and to improve it subsequently to meet observed demand. So the standard of surface, it was decided, was to be 'suitable for a walker wearing stout boots', and where it crossed boggy ground it was not to permit feet to get wet – in normal conditions and with reasonable care.

One of the few sections – in the area covered by this book – which gave real trouble was to the west of Crianlarich, where the path crossed peat bog. For this, Bickmore Dundas and his local authority

The West Highland Way heads up Glen Falloch (*Author*)

colleagues approached an enterprising contractor experienced in the construction of hill roads. He developed a technique for building, in effect, a hill road 4 ft wide. The secret lay in the use of not a small digger but the largest available; its broad tracks spread its weight over a large surface, and its long reach meant that it could work over a large area while limiting its own movement – thanks to the skill of its driver Hughie. Along the line of the way, the peat was excavated down to the peat bog's gravel base; the gravel was then gathered up from sides to middle to form the path, ditches and landscape work.

Elsewhere valuable work was done by volunteers from the Scottish Conservation Projects Trust. Help also came from the Army. Members of the Royal Engineers Junior Leader Regiment, known as FREDs – Future Royal Engineer Disasters – built bridges and happily gave no evidence of justifying their nickname. Territorial Army and cadet units built bridges too, as training exercises. Bickmore Dundas recalls particularly one squad of part-time soldiers who, faced with the need to move a heavy bridge beam from one bank of the River Falloch to the other, hoisted it onto their shoulders and marched out into the deep and fast-flowing water.

Only the weight of the beam, it seemed, kept their feet on the river bed, and prevented them from being swept away until they had reached the far side.

By means such as this the West Highland Way was built, and opened officially in 1980. The numbers of people using it have since exceeded all expectations. This has meant that the path itself has needed to be upgraded steadily, and it is now a constructed track for most of the way. It has also benefitted the communities through which it passes. Bed & Breakfast signs which used to face the road appear to have been turned round to face the West Highland Way. Taxi firms found new business carrying heavy rucksacks from one overnight stop to the next. And in one remarkable instance, the proprietor of the Ardlui Hotel established the ferry across Loch Lomond between Ardlui and Ardleish, so that walkers – in the continuing absence of a bridge across the Falloch at its mouth – might have access to Ardlui.

9
TOURISTS, THE TROSSACHS
AND LOCH KATRINE

Early Visitors

The western waves of ebbing day
Roll'd o'er the glen their level way;
Each purple peak, each flinty spire,
Was bathed in floods of living fire.
But not a setting beam could glow
Within the dark ravine below,
Where twined the path in shadow hid,
Round many a rocky pyramid . . .
Here eglantine embalmed the air,
Hawthorn and hazel mingled there . . .
And now, to issue from the glen,
No pathway meets the wanderer's ken,
Unless he climb, with footing nice,
A far projecting precipice.
The broom's tough roots his ladder made,
The hazel saplings lent their aid;
And thus an airy point he won,
Where, gleaming with the setting sun,
One burnish'd sheet of living gold,
Loch Katrine lay beneath him roll'd . . .
High on the south, huge Benvenue
Down on the lake in masses threw
Crags, knolls, and mounds, confusedly hurl'd,
The fragments of an earlier world; . . .

Thus Sir Walter Scott, in the first canto of *The Lady of the Lake*,
represented the passage of his hero through the Trossachs and his
approach to Loch Katrine. The name 'The Trossachs' properly
applies, as is well known, to the short, rocky, bosky pass between
Loch Achray and Loch Katrine; it has been applied to a much

wider area by association. It is equally well known that the precise derivation of 'trossachs' is uncertain. Campbell Nairne, in *The Trossachs and the Rob Roy Country*, traced the familiar interpretation of 'rough or bristled territory' back to the Rev. Patrick Graham's *Sketches, descriptive of Picturesque Scenery on the southern Confines of Perthshire* . . . of 1806, where it is given but not explained. He mentioned a recent theory that 'Trossachs' is derived from the obsolete Gaelic *traisdachean*, a transverse glen joining two others, a description which he considered was not matched on the ground. W.H. Murray refers firmly to the pass of *Na Troiseachan*, the Cross-hills (anglicised to 'The Trossachs') – where a defile had been cut by the Achray Water. He does not elaborate.

Nairne was, perhaps, unduly dismissive: the last half-mile of the approach to Loch Katrine is indeed through a narrow pass linking two much wider-open spaces. But it is not, at least today, the route taken by the Achray Water as it leaves the loch through its defile – this, rather, forms a loop and the pass cuts across its head. Maybe that 'transverse glen joining two others' is not too inappropriate after all.

It is quite probable that the Achray Water did once leave Loch Katrine through the narrow pass. Nairne mentions a tradition that it changed its course during a tremendous storm in August 1621. The vicinity is certainly subject to severe thunderstorms, with associated avalanches, falling boulders and flooding, which appear to recur at long intervals. One such occurred in 1811, and there was another as recently as July 2002. Scott may well have been closer to the truth than he realised with:

> Crags, knolls, and mounds, confusedly hurl'd,
> The fragments of an earlier world; . . .

Lovers of the Picturesque

The way through the Trossachs today, a road terminating as it does in the expansive car and coach park at the steamer pier, gives little idea of what it must have been like formerly. Once it was what Scott describes, a path twisting and turning between the rocks though unspoilt heath and woodland, overshadowed by crags and mountains. As such it must have appealed greatly to lovers of the picturesque and followers of William Gilpin. Gilpin, in reaction perhaps to the planned artificiality of landscape which appealed to eighteenth-century men of taste, had since the 1780s taught people to appreciate the beauty and sublimity of mountains, rivers, lakes and woods in their natural state. He was doing so just as travel around the Highlands started to become reasonably practicable. Having published a work on the picturesque beauties of South Wales in 1782, he followed it with one on the Lake District and in turn with one on the 'High-Lands of Scotland'. This was published in 1789, although the travels upon which it was based had been made in 1776. I do not think Gilpin came to the Trossachs, although he had much to say about Loch Lomond.

In 1791, however, the minister of Callander, in whose parish the Trossachs lie, wrote in the old *Statistical Account*: 'The Trosacks (sic) are often visited by persons of taste, who are desirous of seeing nature in her rudest and most unpolished state.' They were accessible by a carriage road. He describes their 'wildness and rude grandeur' and, at 'the end of the lake', 'the several bays or creeks which . . . run boldly amidst the rocks and hills'. After three pages in this vein, he concludes with the information that 'The Hon. Mrs Drummond of Perth has erected booths of wicker work, in the most convenient places, for the accommodation of strangers, who visit this wild and picturesque landscape.' The 'booths' appear to have been small huts: Coleridge, having walked down the loch, took refuge in one of them, and called a greeting to the Wordsworths as they arrived by boat.

From the 1790s onward the Trossachs started to become well known, and were visited by travellers such as Sarah Murray. Her first glimpse of Loch Katrine in 1796 prompted her to write: 'I was astonished, I was delighted, a faint ray of sun was just then penetrating through the mist, still resting on the tops of the surrounding mountains and crags, tingeing the wood on their sides, and gleaming on the beautiful islands . . .' She had the good fortune to find, where the road met the water, a large boat in which timber had been brought down the loch; once it was unloaded, she was able to employ its boatmen to row her about the loch in it.

Sir Walter Scott and His Effect

Two people above all others have served, by their activities, to make the Trossachs and Loch Katrine famous. One of these was Rob

Roy MacGregor, the other Sir Walter Scott. Yet although the first of these remains famous and well-remembered the other, whose contribution was probably greater, is today largely overlooked.

The first leaflet produced to publicise the Loch Lomond & The Trossachs National Park, in 2002, reminds us that tourism in Scotland began here, points out that the landscape has for centuries fired the imagination of writers and poets, and mentions *The Lady of the Lake*. But the words 'Sir Walter Scott' appear only in connection with the steamship of that name! I mention this not to criticise the compilers of the leaflet, which is excellent in many ways, but rather to demonstrate how much the man himself is now forgotten.

Walter Scott, who lived from 1771 to 1832, was born and educated in Edinburgh; he was apprenticed to his father, who was a Writer to the Signet, and was called to the bar in 1792. His talents lay rather in literature, in composing and writing poetry and prose relating particularly to Scotland and her past. From the age of fifteen he went regularly to stay in the Highlands with an elderly client of his father, Stewart of Invernahyle, and from him absorbed the lore of the Jacobites and Rob Roy – Stewart had fought in the '45, and probably in the '15, and had also duelled with Rob Roy. Scott's first visit to Balquhidder has already been mentioned. It evidently left a lasting impression.

Scott became noted as a prolific author; he was eventually made a baronet in 1820. Four of his works relate to the Trossachs and their locality. *The Lady of the Lake*, an epic poem, appeared quite early in his career, in 1810; the novels which followed were *Waverley* in 1814, *Rob Roy* in 1817, and *A Legend of Montrose* in 1819.

All were set in earlier times than those in which they were written. Nevertheless, one of the features which distinguishes Scott's work is his use of named, identifiable locations, vividly described, as settings for his fictional events. Where he was particularly taken by a spot, he might use it more than once. The delightful Falls of Ledard – wilderness on a domestic scale – which lie to the north of Loch Ard appear as a setting in both *Waverley* and *Rob Roy*, although he seems to have moved the falls further up the burn than they are in reality.

Of the four works, *The Lady of the Lake* is in the present context the most important, with *Rob Roy* running it a close second. *The*

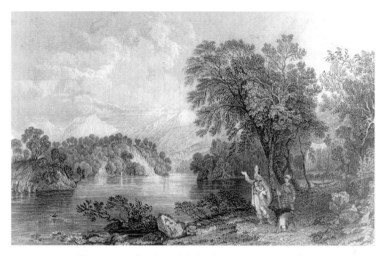

Beattie & Allom's *Scotland*, published in 1836, was illustrated with engravings of contemporary views – but this view of Loch Katrine and Ellen's Isle was peopled with characters from *The Lady of the Lake* (*Trustees of the National Library of Scotland: Beattie, W., Scotland, 1836*)

Lady of the Lake is a tale of adventure and romance, set in late medieval times. I do not propose to attempt any summary here, beyond mentioning that the lady herself is Ellen Douglas, resident upon her island in Loch Katrine, and that the plot hinges upon the habit of certain Scottish kings – James IV and James V – of wandering among their subjects unannounced and in disguise. While composing it Scott revisited the district on horseback to ensure that the travels he described were truly practicable.

In choosing his title, Scott must surely have been looking over his shoulder to that earlier 'Lady of the Lake' of Arthurian legend, while the use of 'lake' rather than 'loch' in a Scottish setting seems to have been commonplace in Scott's day and subsequently, even while retaining 'Loch' in proper names.

I must admit that generally I do not find poetry – especially long narrative poetry – particularly easy to read, nor historical fiction particularly enjoyable. So when, some time ago, I thought *The Lady of the Lake* worthy of study to find out what light it might throw on water transport on Loch Katrine, I deputed the task to my chief researcher – my wife. Having completed it she announced with delight that the tale was surely the stuff of the next Hollywood heather-and-tartan epic, fit to follow *Rob Roy* and *Braveheart*.

Popular though those films have been, however, their influence has been small compared with that of *The Lady of the Lake* when first published. The poem's effect was sensational. Crowds set off towards Loch Katrine, inns and houses were crammed with visitors, and revenue from the tax on horses available for hire in Scotland, for riding and for pulling carriages, showed a sharp rise. The first edition of 2,050 copies disappeared immediately, and was followed within a year by four more editions totalling more than 20,000 copies. Subsequent years saw further editions, so that by 1836 it was estimated that more than 50,000 copies had been sold in Britain alone, and the demand continued.

The reputations of the district and of Scott himself were alike enhanced still further by publication of *Rob Roy*. Set in the turbulent period immediately prior to the 1715 rising, it is a grand tale of derring-do and romance, with some hugely comic incidents too. Throughout most of the story Scott kept his characters firmly on the road, from London to the north of England, to Glasgow and eventually to Rob Roy Country, Aberfoyle and Inversnaid. Scott blends characters who are wholly fictional with characters drawn from history, to whom plausible actions are attributed.

Yet three of his principal characters seem to serve a greater purpose than simply to tell the tale: the young Englishman, Frank Osbaldistone, to whom everything north of the border is strange; the plain-living Lowlander, that worthy bailie of Glasgow, Nicol Jarvie; and his kinsman, whom he regards alternately with disgust and affection, the archetypal Highlander Rob Roy – seemingly out of place in a modern world yet retaining the virtues, as well as the vices, of an older one. Scott's readers, though they may have known little of the relationships between Englishmen, Lowlanders and Highlanders when they came to the book, must have absorbed unconsciously a great deal more by the end.

Towards the end of 1817, records Scott's biographer J.G. Lockhart, Scott sent a note to his publisher:

> With great joy
> I send you Roy.

'Twas a tough job,
But we're done with Rob.

He had not been at all well while writing the novel. Calling one day, his publisher had found Scott with a clean pen and a blank sheet of paper before him. ''Tis easy for you to bid me get on,' expostulated the great man, 'but how can I make Rob Roy's wife speak, with such a curmurring in my guts?'

When the book was published, an initial printing of 10,000 copies was insufficient, and a reprint of 3,000 was called for within a fortnight.

The flood of visitors brought to the Trossachs by Scott's writings proved to be no temporary phenomenon. Guidebooks to the district such as *Lumsden & Son's Steamboat Companion* of 1831 and Ward & Lock's *Scotland* of 1889 are larded with references to them, and indeed assume a familiarity with Scott on the part of the reader. Coachmen and boatmen pointed out the locations of fictional incidents in Scott equally with those of actual historic occasions. Theodor Fontane, in 1858, found copies of *The Lady of the Lake* laid out along with the newspapers at breakfast time in his Stirling hotel. Earlier, in 1846, Lord Cockburn had visited Loch Katrine and noted that 'the world is still paying homage to the genius of Scott at the Lake of his Lady'.

Where the genius of Scott had led, that of William McGonagall followed. From his 'Beautiful Aberfoyle':

Beautiful Loch Katrine in all thy majesty so grand,
Oh! How charming and fascinating is thy Silver Strand!
Thou certainly art most lovely, and worthy to be seen,
Especially thy beautiful bay and shrubberies green.

Of which the best that can be said is that it is no worse than a lot of his other poems, and a lot less morbid than some of them.

A good example of just how far the fame of the district had spread is to be found in Giuseppe Verdi's little-known opera *Aroldo*. The libretto was the work of F.M. Piave, who also provided the librettos for *Rigoletto* and *La Traviata*.

It needs a little explanation. *Aroldo*, which was first performed in 1857, was based on an earlier opera by Verdi and Piave, called *Stiffelio*. *Stiffelio* was set in Germany in the early nineteenth century and has a complex plot involving marital infidelity, misunderstandings, duelling and forgiveness. The hero is a pastor, a Protestant, but the concept of a man of God who is not merely married but forgiving of an unfaithful wife was apparently more than the Italian audiences of the day could cope with, let alone their censors. Hence the opera's eventual re-working as *Aroldo*.

In *Aroldo* the period has moved back to the thirteenth century and the hero, Aroldo himself, has become a Saxon knight, just returned from a crusade. While he has been away his wife Mina has been unfaithful, although she now regrets this. Until their final scenes the plots of the two operas are identical, with comparable characters and settings and some variation in the music. All of the early acts of *Aroldo* are set in and around the castle and home of Aroldo's father-in-law, in Kent. The final scene of *Stiffelio*, in which the hero forgives his unfaithful but penitent wife, is set in a church. This scene was abandoned in the re-working and a new last act provided.

In the last act of *Aroldo*, the setting has changed, abruptly and remarkably, to the banks of Loch Lomond. Here Aroldo and a friend, after the dramatic events of earlier acts, have gone to live in seclusion in a little hut (chorus of shepherds and hunters). A fierce storm breaks out and a boat is driven ashore. Who else should the villagers rescue from the wreck but Mina and her father? Even more remarkably, it seems they had set out across the North Sea, only to be shipwrecked on the shore of Loch Lomond! Inevitably, they knock at the door of Aroldo's hut to seek shelter. After a few more difficulties there is a happy ending. Verdi's music for the storm, writes C. Osborne in *The Complete Operas of Verdi*, is marvellous.

Scott's colossal influence on tourism to Loch Lomond and the Trossachs continued throughout the nineteenth century. Sir Archibald Geikie, in his *Scottish Reminiscences* (1904) cited a splendid instance of the manner in which Scott's fiction had become confused with fact. First however it is necessary to summarise – no easy task – the incident in *Rob Roy* to which he was referring.

Bailie Nicol Jarvie, Frank Osbaldistone and his servant, badly needing somewhere to stay the night, have entered the longhouse which serves as an inn at 'Clachan of Aberfoyle', against the advice of the landlady. There they encounter two Highlanders and a Lowlander. Whatever these three may be plotting, they do not wish to be disturbed. A scuffle breaks out; Osbaldistone draws his sword and acquits himself well. But Jarvie, when he attempts to draw his sword, finds that from lack of use it is rusted solid in its scabbard. Desperate for a weapon, he grabs from the fireplace the coulter of a plough, which has been used as a poker. (A coulter, in case readers have forgotten, is the iron spike on an old-fashioned wooden plough that stuck down into the earth and divided it ahead of the plough proper – just the thing to poke the fire with when its useful life is done.) Since the coulter has been in the fire, its end is red hot, and Jarvie brandishes it to such good effect that he penetrates his opponent Highlander's defences to the extent of burning a large hole in his plaid. The battle ceases as abruptly as it has started: honour is satisfied, no-one is injured. The Highlander, deeply offended by Jarvie's manner of fighting, demands and is promised a replacement plaid.

This blend of high adventure with comic absurdity appealed greatly to generations of readers. They came as tourists to Aberfoyle, wrote Geikie, in search of the inn, or at least its site, and were delighted to find, suspended from a tree on the village green for their benefit, the very coulter which Jarvie had extemporised as a weapon. Indeed they were so delighted that they carried it off surreptitiously more than once – and on each occasion the village blacksmith was obliged to manufacture another authentic coulter to replace it.

Such were the widespread effects of the work of Scott, 'The Wizard of the North'. He remained popular well into the twentieth century.

Providing for Tourists

Tourists brought to the Trossachs by Scott needed accomodation, and a farmhouse at the eastern end of the pass, Ardcheanacrochan, became an inn. Robert Southey, who stayed there in 1819, suggested the proprietor 'should put up the sign of Walter Scott's head'. In 1831 Lumsden & Son said the accommodation was excellent – perhaps a greater recommendation than was needed, for by 1838 Lord Cockburn was complaining of gross overcrowding. Nevertheless it was not replaced until the early 1850s, with the construction of the Scottish baronial Trossachs Hotel, and even then an early visitor, evidently accomodated in a tower room with slits for windows, considered it like a penitentiary. It was extended in 1877 and 1891; Campbell Nairne, in 1961, happily noted that it had been described as a Scott Monument. Today it is a holiday complex, Tigh Mor Trossachs.

From the Trossachs to Aberfoyle the route was for many years no more than a path, although one that was recommended to tourists for the views it offered. The carriage road was completed by the Duke of Montrose in 1882, doubtless to coincide with the opening of the railway to Aberfoyle. This road, over the 'Duke's Pass', remained for many years a private toll road upon which motors were not permitted; it was eventually improved, and freed from toll, in the early 1930s.

The route west from the Trossachs, by land or water, has been mentioned in connection with the Wordsworths. In earlier times, according to Nairne, the main track leading to the north shore of Loch Katrine avoided the pass of the Trossachs and ran more directly, high along the shoulder of Ben An. Hence descriptions, such as that quoted at the start of this chapter, of the path through the Trossachs to the end of the loch reaching a point beyond which it was possible to continue only by scrambling up a 'ladder' of roots and branches. By the 1790s, however, it is clear that this path had become a rough road for carts, and then or soon afterwards this was continued for some way along the north shore of the loch.

Nevertheless, just as the loch had formerly been navigated by clansmen in their birlinns, tourists later generally preferred to follow the example of the Wordsworths, or perhaps Ellen Douglas, and go by boat. Southey was among the many who did so, in 1819 – remarkably down-to-earth for a poet laureate, he railed against the Duke of Montrose for selling woods along the south shore for timber.

Many tourists merely rowed or sailed around the sights of the loch's eastern end, but some travelled further. Geikie recalled travelling by boat down the loch from Stronachlachar to the Trossachs in 1843. Sunset was approaching even as the boat started, so that the evening sunlight struck the mountain tops to be reflected in the calm waters of the loch, while shadows deepened about the lower slopes and, eventually, the full moon of autumn rose above Ben Venue. Four Highlanders rowed the boat, keeping time in the traditional way with Gaelic songs. The experience left a lasting impression on the young man. The boat was probably the galley *Waterwitch*, which carried people on Loch Katrine at this period.

As late as 1887, according to Alasdair Alpin MacGregor, the body of an expatriate member of Clan Gregor who had died in Cairo was rowed up the loch in a snowstorm to meet the deceased's last wishes that he should be buried with his ancestors at Glen Gyle.

The First Loch Katrine Steamers

By that date the more usual means of travel along Loch Katrine was the steamer. The first steamer, PS *Gipsy*, was brought overland from the Forth at Stirling in 1843, with immense difficulty and effort. It was in vain. The owners made the mistake of attempting to compete with the *Waterwitch*. On the first occasion, the crew of the galley rowed to such good effect that, having left the Trossachs at the same time as the steamer, they reached the west end of the loch first. A week or so later the *Gipsy* was missing, believed scuttled in deep water by the crew of the *Waterwitch*. She was never found, nor were the supposed culprits convicted – a case against them was 'not proven'.

A second steamer, the 70-ft long PS *Rob Roy*, was built only two years later, in 1845, at Dumbarton. She was brought by water to Inversnaid with the intention of taking her overland to Loch Katrine. This proved over-ambitious and she was dismantled, taken to Loch Katrine in pieces and re-assembled near Stronachlachar. She cannot have been very satisfactory, for ten years later, in 1855, yet another ship was built, as a screw steamer but with the same name. This time there was no attempt to take her overland, she was taken in sections to Stronachlachar and assembled there, an elegant vessel with a clipper bow which sailed the loch for many decades subsequently.

Drinking Water for Glasgow

It was at this period that the Corporation of Glasgow started to draw drinking water from Loch Katrine. In a growing city where water was sold from barrels on carts, where typhoid was common and cholera broke out in 1838 and 1848, a copious supply of good-quality water was very badly needed. The Glasgow Corporation Water Works Act of 1855 entitled the corporation to draw 50 million gallons of water per day from the loch. As an aid to this, it was also entitled to raise its level 4 ft above the previous summer level, and to draw it down 7 ft below. That such action was authorised in a location world-famous for its natural beauty is perhaps an indication of the urgency of the need.

The works required were designed by the talented civil engineer J.F.L.Bateman, and comprised a dam at the outlet of the loch, a covered aqueduct almost 26 miles long to carry the water as far as Milngavie, a storage reservoir there and trunk mains and distribution pipes beyond. The aqueduct was made 8 ft wide and 8 ft high, with a semicircular top, and a fall of 10 in. per mile. That meant that much of it was tunnelled through rock; and much of the rest was of masonry, wholly or partly in cutting; bridges carried it over rivers and siphons enabled it to cross wide valleys. Since so much water was being extracted from the loch which would otherwise have flowed down the River Teith, the corporation was obliged to provide compensation water down the river; Lochs Venachar and Drunkie were dammed to act as reservoirs for this.

The whole scheme was a fine example of Victorian engineering genius. It was inaugurated on 14 October 1859 by Queen Victoria who, accompanied by Prince Albert, travelled up the loch on the *Rob Roy* to the outlet works at Royal Cottage in order to do so. It was a day of thick mist and heavy rain – which, in view of the nature of the undertaking, might perhaps have been thought excusable.

Queen Victoria at Invertrossachs

The queen returned to the district to stay at Invertrossachs Lodge with some of her children in 1869. By then a reclusive widow, her appetite for expeditions had not diminished – indeed one is left with the impression that some of the entourage must have been gasping for breath.

On the first evening, after travelling from Balmoral, she drove out in her carriage as far as Kilmahog and Loch Lubnaig. The next day she set out by carriage – with two of the princesses, two members of her staff, and John Brown on the box – towards Callander, but turned off to go to the Lake of Menteith and Aberfoyle. A little further on they lunched on the grass, and then continued past Loch Ard to Stronachlachar. Here the party embarked on the *Rob Roy* and took a turn up Glen Gyle before heading down to the Trossachs, to join hired carriages for the return to Invertrossachs. By contrast with the 1859 visit the weather was fine – for the latter part of the expedition a golden evening produced scenes such as were described by Scott in the lines quoted above. This delighted the queen, who certainly knew her Scott, to judge from the frequency with which references to his works are scattered through her journal of the visit. The only drawback was that Invertrossachs Lodge came into view across Loch Venachar a full three-quarters of an hour before the party could reach it, after travelling the full length of the loch and then back again for most of it on the other side.

Subsequent days saw expeditions to Balquhidder, to Loch Lomond for the tour mentioned above, and to Lochearnhead. En route for Loch Lomond, to avoid the long drive round Loch Venachar the royal party embarked on small boats across the loch to join carriages sent on ahead. When they returned the same way in the evening, the wind had increased and the loch was rough; the queen's boat 'danced and rolled' and a smaller boat, able to carry only two members of the entourage and a single boatman, started to ship water.

The queen used the Loch Katrine steamer on three occasions during her stay. It was during one of these, according to Douglas Brown writing in the Clyde River Steamer Club's magazine, that it was discovered – when the royal party required tea – that the kettle had been left behind. John Brown was despatched to ascertain whether there was a kettle on board, but the only kettle to be found was the disreputable example that graced the crew's quarters. It was borrowed, and the tea was fine. But that is one incident the queen did not record in her journal!

SS Sir Walter Scott

SS *Rob Roy* provided the steamer service on Loch Katrine until 1900. In that year she was replaced by SS *Sir Walter Scott*. The replacement ship had been ordered the previous year, built by the famous builder

Passengers from *Sir Walter Scott* joined coaches for Callander and Aberfoyle at Trossachs Pier (*Author's collection*)

William Denny & Bros. Ltd of Dumbarton, delivered in parts to Inversnaid and brought over the hill to Stronachlachar for assembly. *Rob Roy* was kept in reserve until about 1908.

There seems to be a pattern that each successive steamship on Loch Katrine should last substantially longer than the previous one. The first ship lasted for about a week, the most recent for more than a century so far. That *Sir Walter Scott* should have lasted so long – when so much has changed beyond the hills which surround her loch – can be ascribed to several reasons. For a start, she was well designed and well built – though now a unique survivor, she was in her day a typical and up-to-date small passenger steamer: 110 ft long, two boilers, triple-expansion engine. She was well suited to the service she provided, and her run between Trossachs Pier and Stronachlachar has never been demanding. Her surroundings, since she is on fresh water, are less corrosive than those encountered by sea-going vessels. Two further reasons are unique to Loch Katrine. To prevent any possibility of contaminating Glasgow's water supply with oil, she has been kept not merely steam-driven, but fuelled by solid fuel. Since no public motor road follows the shore of the loch, she provides for visitors the only means – other than their own

A well-laden SS *Sir Walter Scott* heads down Loch Katrine below Ben Venue (*Author*)

efforts on foot or bicycle – by which they can experience to the full the beauties of Loch Katrine.

Two changes have happened during that long career. In 1953 she was acquired from her former owner by Glasgow Corporation, and so her ownership has subsequently descended to the successive authorities responsible for water supply to that city. Then in the late 1980s, after the Trossachs Tour had ceased, her afternoon return run between Trossachs Pier and Stronachlachar was replaced by two shorter out-and-back cruises from Trossachs Pier to suit operators of coach tours. She has continued to go up to Stronachlachar and back in the mornings.

Glasgow Waterworks and Their Effects

The Loch Katrine water supply scheme has been enlarged many times since 1859. It was found that the roughness of the rock sides of the tunnel sections of the aqueduct impeded the flow of water so that the full amount authorised could not be carried. Powers were obtained in 1885 to build a second aqueduct, to increase the amount of water extracted from the loch, and to raise its level further. Loch Arklet too was incorporated into the scheme. Its outflow was diverted from Loch Lomond to Loch Katrine and the dam built at its western end.

Even this was insufficient, and there were proposals to raise substantially the water levels of Loch Voil and Loch Doine, in Balquhidder glen, and transfer water from Loch Doine to Loch Katrine through a tunnel. A Bill to authorise this was rejected by Parliament in 1914. But an Act in 1919 empowered Glasgow Corporation to acquire extensive lands around Loch Katrine from which water was gathered, and to raise the level of the loch yet again. In the early 1960s Glen Finglas was dammed to make another large reservoir, from which water was fed to Loch Katrine.

The cumulative effect of raising the water level of Loch Katrine on those three occasions is that it is now some 14 ft higher than formerly. Clearly this must have had a substantial effect on the shoreline, the surroundings and the islands. The old cart track westwards along the north shore became submerged, and was replaced by a new private road at a higher level, extending through to Stronachlachar.

Alasdair Alpin MacGregor, writing *Wild Drumalbain* (1927), was understandably much concerned about the effect of all this on the home of his ancestors, Glen Gyle. A substantial acreage of good farmland on the floor of the glen had been submerged and more would be when the works then in progress were completed. He included photographs showing the Arcadian scene that was lost. It was, he considered, vandalism: Loch Katrine had become an eyesore.

Yet the passage of time has dealt lightly with the Loch Katrine waterworks. Many of the structures along the aqueduct have long since been listed as being of architectural or historic interest. In the 1920s MacGregor could drive from Glasgow to Stronachlachar early on an April Sunday morning and pass but one other vehicle in three hours. It is scarcely possible to contemplate how many other vehicles might be seen on such a journey now. Yet the effect of strict control over Loch Katrine and its surroundings for water supply has been to preserve them, almost entirely, from intrusion by motor vehicles. No main road sweeps past it with a constant roar of traffic; no by-road offers overcrowded, litter-strewn parking places along its shore.

Is there anywhere else, so well known, so beautiful, and so close to large cities, so innocent of the motor car and so unspoilt? Unless resident or on business we can enter only by our own efforts on foot or on a bike, or on a genuine coal-burning steamship: fragments of an earlier world indeed. Long may it continue.

10
LOCH EARN AND ITS SURROUNDINGS

Crannogs and Saints

Loch Earn has many of the features of Loch Lomond, but on a smaller scale, appropriate to its more limited extent; and much of its history has followed a comparable course. Natural islands are the most obviously absent feature – both of the islands in Loch Earn are crannogs, one at the west end, one at the east. The latter, called Neish Island, was inhabited until the seventeenth century and possibly more recently still. There are at least two more shallows in the loch which may or may not be the remains of crannogs.

On the shore close by the crannog at the west end of the loch – and apparently aligned on it so that one wonders if they are not related – are the remains of St Blane's chapel. Blane dates from the sixth century. His mother Ertha had crossed from Ireland to Bute with her brother, St Catan, only to give birth to her son by a father unknown or at least, apparently, not disclosed. According to legend, Catan sternly set mother and baby adrift on the sea in a boat without oars. However they floated back to the north of Ireland. There Blane spent his childhood, and eventually returned to Bute with the family evidently reconciled. From there he later travelled far and wide throughout Scotland, preaching the Gospel; he is associated particularly with Dunblane where he built a church, and at some time he also came to the head of Loch Earn to build his chapel there.

It was St Angus, however, who is credited with bringing Christianity to Balquhidder glen during the second half of the sixth century. He was, probably, an associate of St Columba, who came into Balquhidder from the east, and at his first sighting of Loch Voil and its surrounding hills, was so overcome by the scene

Loch Earn in winter. The view is that formerly seen from trains on the Callander & Oban Railway, which is mentioned in Chapter 12. (*Author*)

that he lifted up his hands and blessed them. The locality is still known as *Beannachadh Aonghais*, Angus's Blessing, and at that point it was formerly the custom for people going west to repeat (in Gaelic) 'Bless Angus in the Oratory' and remove their bonnets reverently. There are other traces of the saint around Kirkton of Balquhidder, most notably the Angus Stone, with a carved representation of an ecclesiastical figure holding a chalice, which may once have covered his grave and is today within the kirk, mounted upon the north wall.

The St Fillan after whom St Fillans is named is not the same as the well-known saint of that name whose works in Strath Fillan, in the neighbourhood of Tyndrum, are described in *Perthshire in History and Legend*. Saint Fillan of St Fillans was active some two centuries earlier, that is in the late fifth century, was related to the king of Munster and was known as *an lobar*, 'the leper', and also as 'the stammerer'. Yet there has evidently been much confusion between the two saints. Both are credited with having been able to transcribe the scriptures with the right hand, by night, by means of the light radiating from the uplifted left hand – the one while in Strath Fillan, the other while at Pittenweem before he came to

Strathearn. Both were associated with pools of sacred water which were supposed to cure diseases and particularly madness, preferably by immersion and accompanied by similar rituals – the one in Strath Fillan, the other in Strathearn.

The St Fillan who came to Strathearn based himself on Dundurn, the isolated mound that rises for some 600 ft from the floor of the strath a mile or so to the east of St Fillans. It was already being used as a fortress by the Picts, who were in those days the local inhabitants. Piles of boulders around the top of the hill seem too extensive to be of natural origin and may well be the material from which buildings and fortifications were formerly constructed. A natural seat formed in the rock at the summit was supposed to have been made miraculously for the saint, and two cavities in the rock before it were said to have been worn by his knees when at prayer. A well near the top of the hill, doubtless used by the Picts within their defences, also became associated with the saint. As St Fillan's well, it was credited with healing powers.

Travel and Trade on the Loch

Like Loch Lomond and so many other lochs, Loch Earn was used as a route for transport from prehistoric times. Probably the busiest period was during the late eighteenth and early nineteenth centuries. The main traffic was limestone from a quarry on the hillside above the north shore, about a mile from Lochearnhead. The stone was carried down the loch in large sailing boats to limekilns at St Fillans. There it was calcined to be used as fertiliser further down the strath. This was an enterprise of the Breadalbanes; quarry, boats and kilns were in full operation by the 1790s, at the date of the old *Statistical Account*, and continued into the 1840s at least. By the 1890s, it was described as something that happened 'in former times' because carriage, labour and fuel had become too expensive. That sounds as though the spread of railways through the Lowlands – but not, at that date, to upper Strathearn – had made it cheaper to get lime from places to the south which were rail-connected. Proposals of the 1790s and the ensuing decade for construction of a canal from Loch Earn down Stathearn, largely for distribution of lime as fertiliser, had come to nothing.

Even after roads had been made through the district, people continued to travel along the loch. In 1824 Edwin Landseer, then a young man of twenty-two, made a short tour into the Highlands with a friend; they visited Loch Lomond and Loch Katrine, and then came to Lochearnhead. Wishing to attend the Highland Games at St Fillans, they were rowed down the loch in a large boat in the company of many of the local inhabitants. The rowers kept them entertained by tales of the fairies and supernatural beings that allegedly lived on the shores of the loch. What the travellers in fact saw – and heard – on shore were parties of Highlanders in increasing numbers, dressed in tartan and headed by pipers as they too headed for the gathering. The voyage, with its accompaniment, left a lasting impression. The St Fillans Games had been established in 1819, among the earliest Highland Games of the sort still familiar. They included competitions in piping and dancing, tossing the caber and throwing the hammer; they also included shooting matches and a boat race on the loch.

In the 1830s Loch Earn was described as 'frequently visited by tourists', and in the 1870s it received its share of attention from the oarsmen of that period when touring by water first became popular. Not merely the loch, but the River Earn below it attracted their attention. Some oarsmen starting from its mouth near Bridge of Earn penetrated further and further west, others attempted to launch higher and higher up intending to navigate downstream.

Eventually in 1882 one particularly intrepid soul, having waited for a time of spate and high water levels, launched his double-sculling boat, 17 ft 6 in. long with a draught of 1 ft 4 in., at Lochearnhead. His first hour's journey took him to St Fillans without incident; the next section was quite the opposite, shooting rapids, crashing against rocks, being swept under bushes which overhung the banks. Nonetheless he made it, eventually, to Dundee. Fourteen years later *A New Oarsman's Guide* commented that that was the only time the river between St Fillans and Comrie had been navigated. Loch Earn, however, was 'one of the most picturesque lochs in Scotland . . . surrounded by bold and rugged hills.'

Most unusually, no passenger steamer plied Loch Earn in Victorian or Edwardian times. This may have been because, initially, no railway reached its shores; horsedrawn coaches carried

MV *Queen of Loch Earn* plied Loch Earn during the 1920s and 1930s
(*Collection J.Danielewski*)

tourists between the railhead stations at Balquhidder (at first called
Lochearnhead) and Crieff or Comrie, and followed the north shore
of the loch, until a railway was completed between these places in
1905 to serve Lochearnhead proper and St Fillans en route.

It was left therefore to the enterprise of a motor charabanc
operator, Peter Crerar of Crieff, to put not a steamer but a motor
vessel into service on the loch. This he did in 1922, with the intention
of operating it in connection with his motor tours. The vessel was
the twin-screw MV *Queen of Loch Earn*, which had a wooden
hull 70 ft long and was powered by two Rolls Royce 12-cylinder
petrol engines.

She was built in Fraserburgh and delivered, presumably by sea, to
Perth. There she was placed on a wheeled wooden cradle; this was
then hauled by a steam road locomotive from Perth to St Fillans,
taking just over twenty-four hours and arousing plenty of interest
from bystanders while passing through Crieff and Comrie. She was
launched early on 22 June.

Queen of Loch Earn's regular schedule was two trips up and
down the loch daily in summer, between piers at St Fillans and
Lochearnhead. Her pier at St Fillans was close to the war memorial,

on the opposite side of the river from the village (but with access by footbridge), where the shore of the eastern end of the loch forms a slight promontory. The pier at Lochearnhead was where the water sports centre is now. A poster advertising the service, noted recently by the author on display at Innerpeffray Library near Crieff, includes representations of two similar motor vessels, but this must surely have been no more than optimism on the part of the artist, or perhaps the operator.

Crerar's business was taken over in 1928, and again in 1930, this time by W. Alexander & Sons of Falkirk. *Queen of Loch Earn* changed hands with the rest of the business. Perhaps the latest owner had less enthusiasm than the originator for this small part of the undertaking; at any rate, when the Board of Trade demanded an extensive overhaul before the 1937 season, the vessel was sold off instead. She became a houseboat at St Fillans, latterly on shore, where she was for a long time a familiar sight.

Darnlinvarach

Loch Earn too has its connection with the writings of Sir Walter Scott. This is to be found in his *A Legend of Montrose*, published in 1819. It is a tale based, rather loosely, on the doings of James Stewart of Ardvorlich in Montrose's campaign during the Wars of the Covenant in the 1640s. Stewarts had settled at Ardvorlich, on the south shore of Loch Earn, in the 1580s and Stewarts remain there to the present day. Scott played tricks with the names of locations and of people – unlike his earlier stories set in specific locations – but his castle of 'Darnlinvarach' is evidently based upon Ardvorlich.

It was at Darnlinvarach that Scott set an incident in his tale, one that greatly appeals. Two travellers, one of them being Lord Menteith, with his servants, arrive there to learn from the old retainer Donald who greets them that McAuley the laird is out on the hill, with two English visitors who have arrived earlier. These visitors, says Donald, will be the ruin of the household. His master had earlier visited one of them, Sir Miles Musgrove, at home in Cumberland, and had found displayed for his benefit six great candlesticks made not of iron, nor brass, nor tin, but of solid silver. Nothing so grand as these would be found in his own poor country, McAuley had been taunted; and, stung to the quick, he had retorted that he possessed more and better candlesticks than any hall in Cumberland.

That was a mistake, for almost before he knew it he had found himself involved in a massive wager. The Englishman had arrived at Darlinvarach to see the point proved, or to collect his winnings. And that, says the old servant, is probably why the laird is so reluctant to bring them home from the hill, for not 'a candlestick, or ony thing like it, is in the house except the old airn branches that has been here since Laird Kenneth's time, and the tin sconces . . . made by auld Willie Winkie the tinkler . . .'; nor is there 'an unce of siller plate . . . about the house at a', forby the lady's auld posset dish, that wants the cover and ane o' the lugs.'

During the early part of the conversation, the laird's brother, tall and strong but imbecile, has been sitting quiet by the fire, taking it all in. By its end he has risen to his feet, furious; he bids those present to withdraw, for he must prepare the hall, in which they have been talking, 'for the reception of these southern guests'.

The travellers are taken to another room, where they are soon joined by McAuley and his English guests. It is a cheerful reunion, for almost all present are well known to each other. But so far as the laird is concerned, the coming loss of his wager casts a deep shadow; he confides in Menteith, a kinsman, and hopes that he will be able to help him out.

At this point the old retainer enters and announces that 'dinner is ready, and' – with emphasis – 'candles are lighted too.' A mystery. Laird and guests move towards the hall, the Englishmen entering first. Scott continues:

> . . . an unexpected display awaited them. The large oaken table was spread with substantial joints of meat, and seats were placed in order for the guests. Behind every seat stood a gigantic Highlander, completely dressed and armed after the fashion of his country, holding in his right hand his drawn sword, with the point turned downwards, and in the left a blazing torch made of the bog-pine. This wood, found in the morasses, is so full of turpentine, that, when split and dried, it is frequently used in the Highlands instead of candles. The unexpected and somewhat startling apparition was seen by the red glare of the torches, which displayed the wild features, unusual dress, and glittering arms of those who bore them,

while the smoke, eddying up to the roof of the hall, over-canopied them . . .

All this was the work of the supposed imbecile. Not only are the 'candlesticks' larger than anything possessed by the Englishmen but, as he points out, 'not one of these men knows any law but their Chief's command – Would you dare to compare to THEM in value the richest ore that ever was dug out of the mine?' The wager, of course, has been won by the laird.

Scott, apparently, based this tale upon an incident in the life of Alasdair MacDonald of Keppoch who in 1650 was entertaining Prince Charles, the future Charles II. The prince had earlier shown MacDonald two very fine candlesticks among his possessions, and MacDonald had rashly boasted that he possessed a pair both finer and larger. He made good his boast when they sat down to dine in the way described by Scott, with two tall Highlanders behind his chair holding torches. This account appears in the reminscenses of Keith Henderson, *Till 21*. He was a descendant of MacDonald.

The Bathymetrical Survey

During 1900 a rowing boat could be seen on Loch Earn carrying a boatman, two other men, one old, one young, and, clamped to the gunwale, a curious piece of apparatus. The boatman would row a little way and then hold the boat steady; one of the other men would then operate the apparatus, lowering a sounding weight quickly to the bed of the loch and hoisting it up again, while the third took notes of the results. Then the boatman would row a little further and the process would be repeated, over and over again. The older man was Sir John Murray, a distinguished oceanographer, and the younger his collaborator Fred. P. Pullar; they were engaged in the self-imposed task of surveying the inland lochs. This programme became known as the Bathymetrical Survey of the Fresh-water Lochs of Scotland.

The work of the survey combined scientific challenge with a very human story. The survey itself had been Murray's idea. Born in Canada of Scottish parents in 1841, he had come back to Scotland in his teens. He came to prominence taking part in the expedition by HMS *Challenger* which, between 1872 and 1876, had circled the globe investigating the physical, chemical, biological and geological conditions of the ocean basins, particularly at great depths. In the mid-1880s Murray turned his attention to the fjord-like sea lochs of Scotland's west coast, using the steam yacht *Medusa*, which was built for the purpose and financed by his friend Laurence Pullar of Bridge of Allan. Pullar's fortune presumably derived from the family dry-cleaning firm, Pullars of Perth. During the course of Murray's researches *Medusa* passed on several occasions through the fresh-water lochs which form part of the line of the Caledonian Canal, that is to say Loch Lochy, Loch Oich and Loch Ness. Murray was struck by the marked differences in the physical and biological conditions to be found in fresh-water lochs. Since fresh water is at its densest at a temperature of 39.2°F, for instance, water at this temperature sinks to the bottom while water at both higher and lower temperatures rises, which leads to different patterns of water circulation in fresh and salt water. In fresh water there is also far less profusion of life at great depths – 500–600 ft, but on the bottom organic matter decomposes less rapidly. All this suggested that a detailed survey of the fresh-water lochs would add usefully to the sum of human knowledge and be of particular interest to geologists, fishermen and engineers concerned with water power and water supply. The only information in this field then publicly available consisted of the Admiralty Charts of Loch Lomond and Loch Awe, together with soundings taken in limited quantity by the Admiralty in the lochs of the Caledonian Canal.

At Murray's instigation the Royal Societies of London and of Edinburgh had both represented strongly to the government, in 1883–4, that such a survey should be made – without result. The Admiralty, it seemed, would only undertake such work in the interests of navigation, while the Ordnance Survey operated only on land.

Some work was then done on an *ad hoc* basis. Soundings were taken in Lochs Morar, Lochy, Ness, and Katrine and elsewhere, by Murray and by J.Y. Buchanan. In 1888 J.S. Grant Wilson, a geologist, reported the results of a survey of Lochs Earn, Tay, Rannoch and Tummel. His main concern was to establish their relationship to the glaciation of the district, and his method was to take soundings 50 to 80 yards apart, along parallel lines across each loch at intervals of about a quarter of a mile. On Loch Earn he made use also of soundings taken by Mr Sandison of St Fillans. Grant Wilson reported that Loch Earn was a rock basin of the simplest form, produced by a great glacier moving in the direction east-south-east. Its bed sloped steadily from the west to the deepest point off Ardvorlich, and then rose steadily to the east.

Murray had many other calls upon his time. For instance, having found evidence of phosphate of lime in rock specimens from Christmas Island in the Indian Ocean, he prevailed upon the British Government to annex the island and then became one of the promoters of a company to exploit the phosphates. But first he sent a scientific expedition to the island to record conditions, flora and fauna. The Treasury, he said much later, had received sufficient in rents, royalties and taxes from the island to pay the cost of the *Challenger* expedition. He was knighted in 1898.

He did not forget the Scottish lochs, and about 1897 began a systematic survey. His collaborator Fred. P. Pullar was the talented son of his old friend Laurence Pullar. The earliest soundings in the lochs had been taken with hemp sounding-line, but this proved impracticable where lochs were deep. Not only was it slow, but while the line was being hauled up the boat was drifting, which made it difficult to record the position of the sounding accurately. The only commercially available sounding machine proved unsatisfactory and untrustworthy. Pullar designed his own. In those days before echo-sounders and electronics it was of necessity mechanical. Its framework comprised bicycle tubing and gunmetal brackets. Upon this was mounted a wire-spoked winding drum, operated by a handle through gearing to speed it up, and able to hold as much as 1,000 ft of three-strand galvanised steel wire. The wire was led round a measuring pulley, 1 ft in circumference, before passing through a grease box and over a guide pulley to descend vertically to the weight. This took the form of a tube able to recover a sample of material from the bed of the loch. The measuring pulley was connected to dials from which could be read the length of wire which had been run out. A smaller, simpler version was developed for use on shallow and remote lochs.

After trials of different sounding machines on various lochs,

Fred Pullar (top) and Sir John Murray (below) amused themselves by taking photographs of each other during what proved to be their last expedition together sounding the freshwater lochs (*Royal Scottish Geographical Society/Trustees of the National Library of Scotland: Scottish Geographical Magazine*)

and of different means to record the positions of soundings, the pair commenced work in earnest on the lochs of the Trossachs and Callander district. They took 775 soundings in Loch Katrine in 1899 and recorded a maximum depth of 495 ft. Other lochs surveyed the same year included Achray, Venachar, Drunkie, Lubnaig, Voil and Doine. The latter two they considered had been a single loch in the none too distant past, until divided by material brought down the Monachyle Glen by the river and deposited in the loch. Soundings showed the lochs to be deep close to the dividing promontory. The results of the summer's work were published in the *Scottish Geographical Magazine* and elsewhere. In 1900 Murray and Pullar turned their attention to the other lochs of the Forth basin, including Loch Chon and Loch Ard and the Lake of Menteith, and to those of the Tay basin. They expected to continue their task in 1901. In the winter of 1900–01 Murray had to make a visit to the Far East, including Christmas Island.

On the day of his return – 16 February 1901 – Murray was handed a telegram stating that Pullar had lost his life the day before. Pullar had drowned while attempting to rescue skaters who had fallen through the ice on Airthrey Loch near his home. That is the loch which now forms part of the campus of Stirling University. He had already rescued three people when he returned and attempted to rescue a fourth, only for his strength to fail while attempting to support her in the near-freezing water.

Murray's immediate reaction was to abandon the survey of the lochs altogether. But Laurence Pullar expressed a wish to see the work in which his son had been so interested brought to a conclusion – and to fund it as necessary. With the blessings of the Royal Societies, and the British Association, and various government departments – but without government money – the survey resumed. Staff were appointed, and 154 lochs were surveyed during 1902. More followed during the ensuing years until, by the end of 1906, a total of 562 lochs had been surveyed: all the important fresh-water lochs in Scotland, the only omissions being lochs which had no boats upon them or to which boats could not easily be transported. Details of the location and dimensions of each loch were recorded, with a map showing soundings and the contours of its bed. Water temperature and other features were measured too. The results of the survey filled six volumes, published in 1910. The deepest of the lochs was noted as Loch Morar at 1,017 ft; the longest, Loch Awe at 25.47 miles. The survey results also included a section on research into seiches – apparent tides resulting from oscillations in the level of the surface – carried out on Loch Earn by Professor Chrystal of Ardtrostan in 1905. It was all a worthy memorial to F.P. Pullar.

As part of the Bathymetrical Survey, Loch Lomond was surveyed in 1903 to establish what changes might have taken place since the Admiralty survey; the depths recorded agreed very closely. Its surface area was estimated to be 27½ sq. miles, the largest of all the fresh-water lochs.

Loch Earn was surveyed fully by two members of the survey staff on 14 to 19 May 1902, during which time they took 500 soundings. Murray and Pullar had taken 150 soundings in 1900; the contours on the eventual map of the loch, however, were drawn from the 1902 soundings. The shape of the bed of the loch, established by Grant Wilson's 180 soundings taken in the 1880s, was confirmed; the maximum depth recorded – 287 ft – also agreed well with his maximum of 288 . Nonetheless these figures may well have been seen as an affront by local inhabitants who, there as elsewhere, had thought their loch to be much deeper than in fact it was – Loch Earn had been supposed to be as much as 600 ft deep.

11

GLEN OGLE AND GLEN CROE: MILITARY ROADS, HIGHLAND ROADS AND TURNPIKES

Before the Military Roads

Much has already been written in earlier chapters about the manner in which people travelled, and trade was carried on, throughout the Highlands from time immemorial until the early eighteenth century: that is to say, either by water or by 'roads' which would seem to us no more than narrow, ill-marked paths, winding among the rocks and heather. Even the very substantial trade – legitimate or otherwise – in cattle droving – required no formal roads. So-called 'drove roads' could, at least in the Highlands, more appropriately be referred to as drove routes, the traditional routes which drovers followed, their charges spread out ahead of them across the moorland, snatching a bite to eat as they moved slowly onward. There was scarcely a glen or pass in the district covered by this book which was not used at one time or another by cattle drovers.

As early as 1617 an Act of the Scottish Parliament gave Justices of the Peace the power to order highway repairs, and a further Act in 1669 gave detailed instructions as to how they were to set about it. They were to list the highways, bridges and ferries within their shire and then, parish by parish, they were to convene tenants, servants and others to meet for several days each summer, bringing horses, carts and implements, to repair the roads; the cost of doing so was to be charged to the heritors, that is to the owners of property. The roads were to be made twenty feet wide, fit for horses and carts in summer and winter. In 1686 the Commissioners of Supply were joined with the Justices of the Peace in these responsibilities.

This was the 'Statute Labour' system. It remained the underlying basis of road maintenance in Scotland until the second half of the nineteenth century, although by then it had gradually become usual for liability for personal service to be 'commuted' by a money payment towards maintaining the roads.

An important point was that the justices, and the commissioners with them, were given powers rather than duties. Where roads were not included in any list, there remained no-one responsible for their upkeep. The legislation had some effect in the Lowlands, but it had little if any in the Highlands.

The condition of the road between Edinburgh and Fort William was surveyed by the military in about 1730, and the report gives an interesting glimpse of the state of roads in the area at that time. Parts of it are quoted by Ted Ruddock in 'Bridges and Roads in Scotland: 1400–1750'. From Edinburgh as far as Kilmahog, beyond Callander, there was already a cart road; the section between Doune and Kilmahog had probably been made shortly before 1700. Beyond Kilmahog, where the road entered the hills, was a horse road. But on this important route it was a wide one, for the surveyor was able to take a light two-wheeled chaise at least as far as Glen Ogle. Probably the road was similar to the road encountered by Hans Andersen between Stronachlachar and Inversnaid over a century later. To make it into a cart road, its surface needed to be made smoother, and hills made less steep. In Glen Dochart, there were many places where the road passed along ground which was too boggy and wet; there, the route needed to be altered. And so on, all the way to Fort William.

The condition of this road had been an essential element in a daring escape by Rob Roy in 1717. He had been captured in Balquhidder by a troop of cavalry, who were escorting him to Stirling. He was mounted, but unbound, and part of the troop was ahead of him, part behind. Towards the south end of Loch Lubnaig the road became narrow so that the troopers, who had been riding two abreast, had to change to single file. As the road rose away from the lochside, it also became rougher. The horse carrying the trooper behind Rob jibbed at a particularly craggy place; the troopers ahead, unaware, kept going. Rob was able to jump off, give his horse a smack to send it on and hinder the return of the troopers in front, and disappear uphill into the woods before his escort could do anything about it.

Wade and Caulfield

Such an incident must have done much to confirm to the military the need for better roads through the Highlands. They were needed for infantry on the march, for cavalry, for carriages and carts and, perhaps most importantly, for artillery. None of General Wade's initial network of roads passed though our district: the network comprised a road through the Great Glen and roads from the South via Drumochter to Fort Augustus and Inverness. In 1740 Wade, after being promoted, was moved away from Scotland and was succeeded by his Inspector of Roads, Major William Caulfield, who would eventually be responsible for the construction of far more roads than Wade himself.

So it was under Major Caulfield that work began in 1743 on the construction of a military road from Dumbarton to Inverary. It ran by Loch Lomondside to Tarbet, thence by Arrochar and Glen Croe, where it had to ascend from near sea level to a summit some 860 ft higher before descending again to the sea at Cairndow.

The manner in which the military roads were made has been so well covered elsewhere – in for instance William Taylor's *The Military Roads in Scotland* – that only the briefest resumé is needed here. They were usually built about 16 ft wide; upon a foundation of large stones was laid a surface of gravel – tarred roads only came in with the advent of pneumatic tyres, more than a century and a half later. Drains and ditches were provided. On the southern edge of the Highlands, into which cart roads already penetrated, it seems likely that the military contented themselves with upgrading such roads as lay along their route. The bridges built along military roads were almost as important as the roads themselves; the old horse roads and paths often crossed rivers and burns by fords, with all the problems that implied in a region where heavy rain brings burns up in sudden spate – as present-day hill walkers continue to be made aware. The builders of military roads tended to take a direct line where possible, to go up and over obstructions such as spurs from the hills, rather than round them; where the way forward was too steep for a direct line, they resorted to zig-zag traverses on the same general alignment. Such was the case at the head of Glen Croe, towards the summit soon to be known as 'Rest and be thankful'.

Butterbridge, on the descent from Rest and be thankful to Cairndow, is typical of bridges built on the military roads (*Author*)

The work was done by soldiers, with civilian assistance, and on the Dumbarton-Inverary road it came to an abrupt halt with the outbreak of the 'Forty-Five.

Work re-started in 1747, apparently at the behest of the Duke of Argyll, and the road was completed about 1749. At this date however there were no bridges over the River Leven and the road ran from Dumbarton up the east side of the vale as far as Bonhill, where a ferry crossed the river. Dumbarton bridge was built as part of the military road network in 1765, and from then onwards no doubt the road ran up the west side of the vale.

Meanwhile work had started in 1748 on the road from Stirling to Fort William. Its route was via Bridge of Allan, Callander, Loch Lubnaigside, Glen Ogle, Glen Dochart, Tyndrum, and thence north-westwards by Kinlochleven to Fort William. At the head of Glen Ogle, zig-zags were again needed to reach the pass, 945 ft high, then known as Lairig Eala or Larigalie – spellings varied. The road had reached Glen Dochart in 1751, but it was 1753 before it was complete throughout. A linking road between the two roads, at Tarbet and Crianlarich, was built between 1752 and 1760; Lt-Col. Wolfe and his men were working on it in 1753. Between Stirling and Dumbarton, soldiers did a lot of road work in the 1770s and early 1780s; this is late in the military road period, and the likelihood seems to be that they were rebuilding or re-aligning the then existing road via Kippen and Drymen in conjunction with the Commissioners of Supply.

Military Roads, Their Use and Their Maintenance

Built for military purposes, the new roads were welcomed by everyone, or almost everyone. 'Had you seen these roads before they were made,/You would lift up your hands and bless General Wade', runs the well known couplet, which has been attributed to Major Caulfield himself. Pennant, after riding along the Loch Lomondside road in 1769, commented, '. . . the whole [is] the work of soldiery: blessed exchange of instruments of destruction for those that give safety to the traveller.' Dr Johnson, having ridden over Rest and be thankful in 1773, wrote of Glen Croe that it was 'a black and dreary region, made easily passable by the military road'. Sarah Murray, travelling in her chaise in 1796, simply referred to the road over Rest and be thankful as 'the carriage road'. She knew its origin, however, for she stated that a friend of hers had been a lieutenant in the 24th Regiment which had built it and, when they had completed the zig-zags, set up a stone engraved with the words 'Rest, and be thankful' at the summit. The small loch immediately to the west is called Loch Restil, and it seems more than likely that this name contributed to the name given to the pass.

Only for cattle drovers were the military roads a mixed blessing. Roads which were narrow by droving standards and had hard surfaces were not the most suitable for cattle. But the roads helped to make possible the pacification of the Highlands, which in turn enabled the droving trade to flourish and increase. A good example is the origin of the Kingshouse – now the Kingshouse Hotel – beside the Stirling-Fort William road at the entrance to Balquhidder glen. The name 'King's House' had been applied originally to the inns which became established at the locations of construction camps along the military roads. But the building of this one, according to James Stewart in *Settlements of Western Perthshire*, was specifically petitioned by drovers in 1779. There seems to have been an earlier building at this location, and the new Kingshouse probably had a small garrison in its early days.

Certainly the roads, which had been built in a hurry, needed constant maintenance: repairs to surface and drainage, and re-alignment where found necessary from experience. Such work continued to be carried out by the military. In the 1790s the old *Statistical Account* for Balquhidder Parish noted that eight of the ten miles of the Stirling-Fort William road within the parish had lately been put into excellent repair, but two remained very bad. As civilian traffic increased, and military traffic declined, it became more and more evident that alignments selected for military purposes had shortcomings for civilian use. The Balquhidder *Statistical Account* continued: 'there is so much *up* and *down* hill in the present direction, that it cannot be made a tolerable road for carriages.' An alteration in the line had been proposed and, it was hoped, would soon be built. This sounds like avoiding the zig-zags at the head of Glen Ogle; a diversion, less steep and lacking sharp bends, was certainly built at some stage, and both lines can still be distinguished on the ground. Such concerns, and such actions, were echoed in many other places.

By that date too the continuing expense of maintaining military roads which were no longer of military significance was an increasing concern to the government – although, since they were generally the only roads for wheeled vehicles through the districts where they ran, they clearly had to be maintained. The government would have liked to hand them over to county authorities – by then, in effect, Commissioners of Supply – for maintenance by statute labour, but there were few places where the inhabitants were numerous enough or wealthy enough for this to be practicable. But such as there were tended to be on the southern edge of the Highlands. The road from Dumbarton to Stirling was handed over in the 1790s, and so was the road from Stirling via Bridge of Allan to Callander. The road between Callander and Lochearnhead, which had also been removed from the list of roads maintained by the military, had to be reinstated in 1810.

Highland Roads and Bridges

By then another government body had emerged which was relevant to the situation. This was the Commissioners for Highland Roads

Viewed from Rest and be thankful, the military road (as improved by the Commissioners for Highland Roads and Bridges) still descends into Glen Croe far more steeply than the modern road on the hillside to the left (*Author*)

and Bridges. They had been established by Parliament in 1803 in response to a comprehensive report by Thomas Telford, to build roads and bridges in those parts of the north and west Highlands to which the military roads did not penetrate. These roads and bridges were to be paid for half by the government, half by the landed proprietors, with the possibility in the latter case of reimbursement by means of an assessment on the inhabitants. The commissioners were also, after some initial hesitation by the government, given the responsibility for maintaining the roads and bridges they built.

The remaining military roads, in most of the counties through which they ran, were transferred to the commissioners in 1814. Argyll was numbered among the counties where the roads were transferred but, exceptionally, Dunbartonshire and Perthshire were not. Let us consider Argyll first.

The Inverary road passed into Argyll where it crossed the Loin Water at the head of Loch Long, so the section transferred included Glen Croe and Rest and be thankful. At the head of Glen Croe the new administration managed to ease the zig-zags to produce what Dorothy Wordsworth in 1822 described as 'a curious Jura, or Alpine, winding in the road'; Robert Southey, who toured the Highlands in 1819 with Thomas Telford, engineer to the commissioners, noted in his journal that the road descended 'with such volutions that a line drawn from the top would intersect it several times within a short distance. In mountainous countries,' he added, 'a fine road is a grand and beautiful work, and never so striking as when it winds thus steeply and skilfully.' Nevertheless, it cannot have been long after Southey's visit that an alternative route was surveyed. This, according to *Lumsden & Son's Steam Boat Companion* of 1828, was to run 'from the head of Loch-Long, in a direction north of the present one, to obviate the difficulty of passing through Glencroe'. It remained unbuilt, probably because of the expense, and looking at the map it is a little difficult to deduce exactly which route was proposed. In 1907, at which date the road as rebuilt by the commissioners was still in use, the gradients at Rest and be thankful were noted in the *Contour Road Book of Scotland* as successively, eastwards from the summit, 1 in 15 – 9 – 8 – 10 – 15; the book added the cautionary note: 'very dangerous turn'.

Turnpike Trusts

Continuing his 1819 journey from Rest and be thankful, Southey noted in his journal that about half a mile before Arrochar, 'the Military Road ends, and with it the power of the Commissioners. We entered Dunbartonshire, and the jolting was immediately such that with one accord we pronounced the Dunbartonshire roads to be worse than the Perthshire.' Earlier in his tour, after entering Perthshire near Tyndrum, he observed that the road formed a sad contrast to the fine smooth roads upon which they had been travelling further north, and earlier still, between Doune and Callander, one of the coach horses had stumbled and fallen, because of the bad state of the road. The cause, he wrote, 'lay in the obstinacy of the Perthshire people, Perthshire being the only highland county where they will not let the Commissioners interfere with the management of the roads.' He was wrong about Perthshire being the only such county, but right about the situation.

The problem was that transfer of military roads to the Commissioners for Highland Roads and Bridges meant a substantial charge on the inhabitants, county by county, for road improvement and maintenance. In Perthshire, most of the military roads lay in the north and west of the county and were used largely by travellers to and from places further north and west still; most of the inhabitants, however, lived in the south and east of the county, and not unnaturally resisted the proposal that they should have to pay for roads used mainly by others. No doubt similar considerations applied in Dunbartonshire. So while, it seems, maintenance of the remaining military roads in these counties was then left to the limited capabilities of the statute labour system, the condition of the roads themselves deteriorated to the extent that they became notorious.

The eventual solution lay in the formation of turnpike trusts to maintain these roads. Turnpike trusts had been a feature of main road travel in the Lowlands for many years. They were established by Acts of Parliament; each Act established a trust, whose trustees could borrow funds to improve a road, put up tollgates (originally, barriers called 'turnpikes'), and collect tolls, from which they would maintain the road and pay interest on borrowed funds. The first Scottish Turnpike Road Act had been passed, for Edinburgh roads and bridges, as early as 1713, but the system came into common use only after 1750. The length of road maintained by each trust was often, to modern eyes, quite short, and usually but not invariably within a single county. The lives of turnpike trusts were limited – often twenty-one years – and further Acts were needed to renew their powers from time to time. On Highland roads, it was considered, there would be insufficient traffic for the system to work.

Nonetheless, the military road from Dumbarton as far as Luss was made into a turnpike road as early as 1807; it had probably been handed over earlier to the county authorities for maintenance by statute labour. The relevant Act (and since there are others to be mentioned, brief details of all will be included at the end of the Bibliography) is entitled 'An Act for repairing and maintaining certain Roads in the County of *Dumbarton* (sic) and building Bridges thereon.' Such Acts, perhaps forbidding at first sight, with study reveal fascinating nuggets of information. This one begins:

WHEREAS the Roads from the West End of the Bridge of Dumbarton, leading into the County of Argyle, and the western Highlands and Islands of Scotland are very incommodious, and cannot be effectually repaired, amended, enlarged and made passable, and the Bridges thereon, or which maybe necessary over the River Leven, in the said County, to communicate therewith, cannot be built and kept in good Repair, according to the ordinary Course and Method appointed by the Laws and Statutes of this Realm: May it therefore please your Majesty, That it may be enacted . . . That every Person who is or shall be in his own Right or in the Right of his Wife, in the actual Possession and Enjoyment of the Life-rent or Fee of the Dominium Utile of Lands lying in the Parishes through which the said Roads shall pass, and valued in the Tax Rolls of the County, to the extent of One Hundred Pounds Scots, per Annum; and the Eldest Son of such Person, being the Heir Apparent to such Property, in the Absence of his Father, the Member of Parliament for the County for the Time being, and the Provost of the Town of Dumbarton for the Time being; and every Justice of the Peace for the said County, residing in the Parishes through which the said Roads shall pass, shall be, and they are hereby nominated and appointed Trustees, for the surveying, altering, making, maintaining, repairing, and keeping in Repair the said several Roads and Bridges leading from the west End of the Bridge of Dumbarton along the River Clyde, Gareloch, and Lochlong, to a Place called New Tarbet, and from the said west End of the said bridge of Dumbarton along the River Leven, and a Part of Lochlomond, to the School House at Luss, and the Roads communicating betwixt the said two Lines of Road, and for building and maintaining a Bridge or Bridges of Stone, Brick, or Wood across the River Leven, at or near Balloch and Bonhill, and making, repairing, and keeping in Repair the Passages to the same, and for putting in Execution all the other powers and Authorities hereby given and granted respecting the said Roads.

Here in the preamble to the Act we are told what is needed, who the trustees are to be, the roads and bridges with which they are entrusted, and what they are to do to them. A further fifty-five sections detail how they are to do it. The trustees themselves were for the most part drawn from people of the sort who already had responsibilities towards statute labour roads – indeed many individuals evidently served in the three roles of Justice of the Peace, Commissioner of Supply, and Turnpike Road trustee.

As well as the military road, the Act covers the road along the Gareloch and Loch Long as far as 'New Tarbet'. This place does not feature on modern maps, but appears to have been a name for the southern part of Arrochar. Assuming the military were still maintaining the military road northwards from Luss in 1807, it would have made sense to turnpike the roads from Dumbarton to Luss and Arrochar. Oddly, however, there was a length of road between New Tarbet and the military road which was made into a turnpike only by the 1828 Act, shortly to be mentioned.

The 1807 Act also authorised construction of bridges over the River Leven at Balloch and Bonhill. Neither bridge was built under the powers it provided, and it was not until the 1830s that they were built. Over their lines of road the trustees acted more conscientiously, although how quickly may be another matter – regrettably Southey does not mention any marked improvement in the road south of Luss. But after an interval of twenty-one years a further Act was needed in 1828 to renew the trustees' powers over their roads. This, at last, also extended their activities to the military roads from Luss to *Lochlonghead* on the Confines of *Argyllshire*', and from '*Tarbert* on *Lochlomond* Side . . . to the Confines of *Perthshire* at or near *Inverarnan*'. For 'Confines' read 'boundary'.

This Act was replaced in 1834 by the Dumbartonshire Road Act, which consolidated earlier legislation for turnpike roads in the county, and enabled them to be divided up into districts, each with its own trust. Probably these trusts had many trustees and officials in common, but their existence ensured that funds derived from tolls were applied to the lengths of road upon which they were collected. The road following the line of the military roads from Dumbarton to the head of Loch Long and from Tarbet to Inverarnan became the main component of the '5th District, or Luss Turnpike'. It had seven tollgates; in the 1850s it was stated that half its revenue came from the toll at Dumbarton, where the traffic was chiefly omnibuses, stone carts and printfield carts.

The Act also regularised the legal standing of Dumbarton Bridge. This had been in effect abandoned by the military authorities many years earlier, and had deteriorated badly. In 1834, however, when extensive repairs had become necessary, the government agreed to pay half the cost, most of the rest being raised from private subscriptions. Under the Act the bridge was administered by a trust of its own, with powers to levy tolls if further heavy repairs were needed.

'Ruinous and Utterly Impassable'

In 1820 was passed an Act with the title – in full – *An Act for maintaining and repairing The Military Roads in the County of Perth, and the several Branches or Roads of Communication therewith connected.* The preamble came quickly to the point:

> WHEREAS certain Roads passing through and pervading great Part of the County of Perth . . . and the Bridges upon each Line having been originally made for the Purpose of Military Communication, and ever since maintained, altered, amended, and repaired at the Public Expence until these few Years past, and known . . . by the general Denomination of 'The Military Roads': And whereas within these few Years last past the Annual Grant of Money, whereby the said Military Roads . . . were so maintained, altered, amended and repaired, as aforesaid, having been withdrawn, those Roads are now so dilapidated that in a short Time they will become ruinous and utterly impassable: . . .

The preamble goes on to enumerate the roads concerned, which, within the area of this book, were:

- The road from Larigalie where it joins the Callander road, by Tyndrum to the confines of Argyll, with a branch to Killin.
- The road from Crianlarich to Inverarnan in Glenfalloch.
- The road from Callander to Larigalie, or the confines of the parish of Balquhidder.

It also lists the road from Kenmore to Killin (which is remarkable, for this road is not usually described as a military road) and the many other military roads in north Perthshire.

The Act authorises formation of turnpike trusts for all these roads, district by district. But tolls were not to be taken until they had been put into as good a state of repair as adjoining military roads in Argyll and Inverness-shire – and they had to be kept to that standard, or payment of tolls would be suspended until they were returned to it. Southey must have been delighted.

The extent of detail in this Act is remarkable. Persons exempted from paying tolls, for instance, ranged from clergymen visiting the sick to horses ridden by yeomanry officers in uniform, and carts conveying vagrants and criminals. And actions specifically forbidden ranged from failing to keep a carriage to the left when meeting another, to playing 'at Foot-ball, or any other Game, on any Part of the said Roads, to the Annoyance of any Passenger or Passengers'. For such 'nuisances' the fine might be as much as forty shillings.

Yet such provisions were evidently not unusual, for in 1831 a general Act for turnpike roads in Scotland incorporated them among many other uniform provisions for administering the roads. They therefore disappeared from a further local Act for Perthshire in 1832, which consolidated the powers for all the turnpike roads in the county into a single Act. Among the 36 such roads listed is no. 11, 'The Road from the Turnpike Road . . . at *Lochearnhead*, along the North Side of *Lochearn*, by *Saint Fillan*'s Village, to *Comrie*, and . . . *Crieff*'. This had been turnpiked under an earlier Act of 1811 or thereabouts.

The Road Up Glen Ogle

The road maintained by the Callander Turnpike Trust (its name varied down the years) extended as far as Larigalie at the head of Glen Ogle. Some account books for its later years survive in the charge of Stirling Council Archives and offer an insight into the range of activities and events, large and small, involved in running a turnpike trust. In 1860 for instance 'the August Floods' damaged the road near Kingshouse, and the floods must have been severe, for repairs cost £57 7s 0d. The following year, Alex MacCrostie of Lochearnhead was paid £1 9s 6d for a snowplough. Presumably it was of the triangular wooden sort, to be pulled by horses. Earlier, in 1844, the trust's accounts show that it received 3s 4d from John McMartin, road surfaceman, for one shovel. That sum seems so high that I am inclined to suppose it in the nature of a fine for damage or loss.

Many deviations were made from the line of the military road to produce a road more suitable for horse-drawn carriages. That meant easy gradients, and curves rather than corners. Probably the largest deviation was the new road up Glen Ogle, which was built in the early 1840s and remains in use. Compared with the military road, it leaves the floor of the glen early and climbs by traversing along the eastern hillsides towards the pass, with no gradient steeper than 1 in 18.

By the early 1840s coach roads and long-distance coaches were being superseded, in England and in Lowland Scotland, by the rapidly expanding railway system. This had yet to reach the Highlands, where roads and coaching were still developing. Construction of the new Glen Ogle road was probably due to John Campbell, second Marquis of Breadalbane. He was already spending heavily on developing his vast estates, which extended from Kenmore to the West Coast, and reached down to the head of Loch Earn. He was also energetic in seeking to improve means of transport to and through his territory. We have encountered him already over the Loch Lomond steamers and the proposed canal from Loch Lomond to Loch Tay, and will do so again in connection with railway projects.

So on the same page of the accounts as John McMartin's 3s 4d, there is an entry for £500 received on 16 July 1844 as part of the Marquis of Breadalbane's 'advance for the Improvement of the road at Larigillie in Glenogle'. There is an advance of £250 from another source, and then on 22 October a further £650 'being in full his Lordship's advance'. The total expenditure exceeded these sums so clearly some funds from further sources were also used.

The progress of the work can be judged from the eight payments, totalling £1,500, made between 5 June 1844 and 17 January 1845 to Peter Dewar and James Campbell, 'in part of their contract for making new road from Lochearnhead to Larigillie'. There was a further payment to the contractor in June 1845, supposedly the 'final payment'. Yet, in the usual way of things, it was not, for there was a payment for extra 'surface work' the following December, and in May 1847 the trustees met a claim 'for extra work connected with the 3 upper bridges in Glen Ogle'. Even as late as the year ending 25 April 1849, by which date the trustees styled themselves the Callander & Larigillie Turnpike Trustees, there was an additional payment for the new road at Larigillie.

Three ways up Glen Ogle. In the centre is the military road, as improved for carriages – originally it climbed to the head of the glen by zig-zags. On the right is the easily graded turnpike road built in 1844–5 and still in use, and on the left the Callander & Oban Railway built in the late 1860s. (*Author's collection*)

During 1844–5 there were also substantial payments for improvements at Loch Lubnaig. These may refer to the curves alongside the river at the south end of the loch, and the long straight beyond, which are typical turnpike road improvement over the earlier, and still visible, up-and-over route of the military road past Anie.

Both of these large-scale improvements would be consistent with a wish to introduce a fast coach service over the road, and it is notable that the accounts for the summer of 1843 show 'Tolls of Kenmore Coach' for the first time. The following year the coach gets a name: the 'Queen of Beauty'. This four-horse coach was a summer-only phenomenon, but evidently became a lasting feature of the road. In 1848 it was advertised as running between Dunkeld and Callander, via Aberfeldy, Kenmore, Killin and Lochearnhead; at Dunkeld it connected with coaches between Perth and Blair Atholl. By 1866 the 'Queen of Beauty' was running between the railheads at Callander and Aberfeldy in connection with the trains.

The End of the Turnpike

It was a symptom of things to come. In 1870 the trustees of what had become called the Dunblane, Doune & Callander Turnpike recorded receiving £80 0s 0d from the Callander & Oban Railway Company for 'damage done to turnpike at Callander and Kingshouse'. This section of the railway was built during the late 1860s and the 'damage' was probably compensation for the bridges built at those places where the railway passed beneath the road.

As the railway system expanded, the importance of roads declined. In any case the annual government grant to the Commissioners for Highland Roads and Bridges had been terminated in 1862; in Argyll, since 1843, all roads had been maintained at the expense of owners and occupiers. Turnpike trusts, tolls and statute labour were abolished throughout Scotland by the Roads and Bridges Act, 1878. The Act came into operation over a period of time, but the accounts for the Trustees of the Dunblane, Doune & Callander Turnpike cease at Whitsun 1879. Road maintenance was subsequently funded from rates and administered at first by county road trustees; county councils took over the responsibility when established under an Act of 1889. Control of trunk roads was centralised on London in 1936, and transferred to Edinburgh twenty years later.

By then road traffic had long since revived, first cyclists, then motorists. The road built up Glen Croe by the military, and improved by the Commissioners for Highland Roads and Bridges, survived well into the era of motor traffic, but was eventually replaced by a new road, higher up the hillside, wider, and without any 'volutions'. In Glen Ogle, where the railway has come and gone, the road funded by the Marquis of Breadalbane continues in use carrying traffic far beyond the imagination or anticipation of its builders.

12
CRIANLARICH: THE CREWE OF THE WESTERN HIGHLANDS?

One Village, Two Stations

Crianlarich, of course, is not the Crewe of the western Highlands, and never has been. The point about a railway junction such as Crewe is that all the many railways which go there converge upon a single station, a convenient junction for passengers to change trains. Today Crianlarich appears not only far simpler, but quite straightforward. The railway comes up from Glasgow; at the north end of the station it heads straight on for Fort William and Mallaig, and a branch diverges to the left for Oban. Trains from Glasgow divide at Crianlarich, one section for each line. On the face of it, it could not be simpler.

There are some clues that there is more to it than that. The Fort William line, after crossing Strath Fillan by viaduct, swings left to run parallel to the Oban line for several miles. Before they finally part company the two lines provide Tyndrum with not one station but two. Tyndrum must be a strong contender for the smallest place to have two quite separate stations on the main railway network.

Leaving Crianlarich for Oban, the observant passenger notices that the train is descending quite steeply: a long and overgrown siding appears on the right at a lower level. The train descends some more, and the siding trails into the line upon which it is running. That siding is a vestige of the railway which formerly left the main Glasgow–Perth line at Dunblane and came to Crianlarich via Callander and Glen Ogle.

Crianlarich also used to have two stations, Crianlarich Upper and Crianlarich Lower, a quarter of a mile apart by road. The upper station, which remains in use, is located on the railway from Glasgow

A train for Oban leaves Crianlarich in April 2003. Grass-grown track on the left is a remnant of the former line from Dunblane and Callander. (*Author*)

to Fort William, and the lower was on the railway from Callander to Oban, two railways built and operated by separate companies. At Crianlarich, the former passed over the latter by viaduct. A line to connect the two routes, the 'Crianlarich spur', was provided: today it forms the initial half-mile or so of the Oban line, but for the first seven decades of its existence it saw contentiously little use. Train services on the two lines were almost entirely independent of one another. So deeply entrenched did this practice become that, even after nationalization in 1948 brought both lines into common ownership, it took another sixteen years before any fundamental rearrangement was attempted and by then – I shall return to the point – it was too late.

In *Scottish Railways* (1950) O.S.Nock wrote that there were no advertised connections at Crianlarich, and it was rare for trains on one line to be seen from the other. What this could mean for the ordinary user was well demonstrated by Margaret Leigh in *Spade among the Rushes*, her fascinating account of crofting, during and immediately after the Second World War, at Smirisary on the

Prior to 1965 the Crianlarich spur was little used by passenger trains so photographers had to take their chance with the weather. On a wet day in 1961 an excursion train is cautiously descending from the West Highland Line to the Callander & Oban. The locomotive is tender-first: probably it has been turned on the turntable at Crianlarich Upper, after coming from Glasgow and prior to 'running round' the train at the foot of the spur and heading for Callander (see p. 195). (*D. Stirling*)

west coast. Smirisary had no road for carts or other vehicles: it was reached by boat from Lochailort station on the Mallaig line. Needing a cow to provide milk, and butter, she journeyed to Oban market, not without difficulty for it was January, snowy, stormy, and she was sickening for flu. However she was successful in purchasing an in-calf cow, one of only two suitable beasts in the entire sale; the cow was despatched by goods train in a cattle truck consigned to Lochailort, and her new owner followed by passenger train. She alighted at Tyndrum and, feverish, found a warm bed for the night in the hotel.

To catch the only morning train for Fort William, Miss Leigh had to rise early, and head for the upper station through the half-light of dawn. Through deep snow, she trudged up the hill, weighed down by rucksack and suitcase. Half-way up, she saw in the far distance the lights of a train approaching from Crianlarich; after a moment's despair on her part, it turned away and she realised it was on the lower line. Seemingly now half-delirious with 'flu, she missed the bridge forming the entrance to the station, and floundered on through the deepest snow towards the goods yard, shouting for help. The stationmaster, gruff at first, realised she was in genuine distress, rescued her and sat her in front of a fire until the train came in.

She made it, eventually, to Lochailort. The cow, her truck having been shunted up the spur from one railway to the other at Crianlarich, arrived by goods train some time later.

The Scottish Grand Junction Railway

Clearly, the lack of a proper interchange station at Crianlarich over a long period was an extreme example of how competition sometimes fails the public, rather than benefitting it. To find out how the situation arose it is necessary to delve into the history of the railways concerned.

There might have been an interchange station in Strath Fillan, at or near Crianlarich, as early as the 1840s. By the middle of that decade, the success of early main line railways in the South led in 1845 to the 'Railway Mania', a speculative financial bubble on the grand scale. By comparison with the Railway Mania, the recent Dot. Com bubble fades into insignificance. Having filled up the map of England with railway proposals, speculators turned to Scotland and even in the Highlands there developed, on the map, a cat's cradle of projected railways. Stirred by proposals for railways in Argyll, Lord Cockburn commented that Britain had become an asylum of railway lunatics.

By comparison with some of its rivals, the Scottish Grand Junction Railway proposal of September 1845 was one of the least unsound. Behind it was the Marquis of Breadalbane. Since early the previous year he had been active in the promotion of the Scottish Central Railway; this was in due course built, running south-west from Perth by Dunblane and Stirling to join, near Falkirk, the Edinburgh & Glasgow Railway, and also the Caledonian Railway to the English border and Carlisle. Breadalbane was also closely concerned at this period with the railway from Bowling to Balloch, and with the Loch Lomond steamers.

These were peripheral to the Breadalbane estates; the Scottish Grand Junction would have been central to them. It was to run from Callander, where it would connect with a proposed branch from the Scottish Central, via Glen Ogle, Crianlarich and Tyndrum to Oban. There were to be branches to Killin, from Crianlarich down Glen Falloch to Inverarnan, where the steamer basin had recently been completed, and from Tyndrum by Loch Ericht to Dalwhinnie, where it would join a line proposed to run from Perth to Inverness.

All was not plain sailing. In Glen Falloch Breadalbane's men came to blows with surveyors for a rival promotion, backed by the Duke of Montrose. But, most unusually for mania proposals in the Highlands, the Scottish Grand Junction was authorised by Parliament in 1846 – although only between Oban, Crianlarich and Inverarnan. By then however the bubble had burst; funds proved imposssible to raise, and the railway remained unbuilt.

Building the Callander & Oban

By the 1860s the need for a railway to link Oban with the main railway system was increasingly clear. Such a line was promoted, but the initial problem for the promoters was to decide the route it should take. From Oban to Crianlarich was obvious; thence it could head either down Glen Falloch to join, eventually, one of the many existing railways near Glasgow, or it could continue via Glen Ogle to Callander, to which town the Dunblane, Doune & Callander Railway had been opened in 1858. But the Oban railway promoters needed more than a route. Since they were unlikely to be able to raise all the funds needed directly, they needed the support of an existing railway company in the Lowlands, which would both subscribe some of the capital and work the line when built – that is to say, provide locomotives and rolling stock, and employ personnel to run the railway, in return for a share in the takings. Such arrangements were common during the Scottish railway system's period of expansion. The Dunblane, Doune & Callander had been worked by the Scottish Central since it was built, and when the Oban railway promoters touted their scheme around the Lowland railway companies, it was the Scottish Central that took the bait and offered the best deal by far. It offered to put up one third of the capital, and work the railway for half the revenue. So the die was cast over the route, and the Callander & Oban Railway Company received its Act of Parliament in 1865. It had been agreed that five of its nine directors should be appointed by the Scottish Central, and also (and the point would soon become important) that the C & O should employ its own company secretary and staff to attend to legal, financial, and similar matters.

For a century or more, the history of railways in Scotland was one of amalgamation of small companies into ever-larger ones. In the 1860s, this process was at its most active. Only a few weeks after the Callander & Oban company was formed, the Scottish Central Railway and the Dunblane, Doune & Callander Railway were taken over by the Caledonian, which was well on the way to becoming one of the big five Scottish railways of Victorian and Edwardian times. The Callander & Oban company was not taken over, though the Caledonian inherited the Scottish Central's obligations towards it. But the Caledonian management saw greater profits to be made from new lines among the coalfields and ironworks of the Lowlands, rather than in venturing into the western Highlands, and the C & O was for many years an unwanted child. There were years of delay in construction and, when sections were eventually completed, inadequacies in operation.

The amalgamations of the 1860s did bring the C & O one great asset. John Anderson had been assistant to the general manager of the respected Edinburgh & Glasgow Railway when it was taken over by the North British Railway in 1865. Whether he then left voluntarily or not I do not know, but he was quickly appointed by the Callander & Oban to become its company secretary. The C & O could not have made a better choice. Assiduous in promoting the company's interests, he was to remain in post for forty-two years. Anderson set about drumming up subscriptions and encouraging contractors. With the two factions among its directors often at loggerheads, the progress of the railway fell very much on Anderson's shoulders.

So, gradually, the Callander & Oban was built – up the west side of Loch Lubnaig, through Strathyre, across the mouth of

It is difficult now to appreciate how much of the nation's goods traffic formerly went by train, particularly in places where there is now no railway at all. Here, a long goods train from the Oban direction trundles through Balquhidder station, probably in the late 1920s. (*Collection Niall Ferguson*)

Balquhidder glen, high along the hillside shelf behind Lochearnhead and up the west side of Glen Ogle. Where it came alongside the turnpike road at the head of the glen, a station was built and to it the Caledonian started to run trains in 1870. The station was called Killin, notwithstanding that the village proper lay 3½ miles further on and 550 ft below. No doubt financial editors were suitably impressed with progress, even though arriving passengers may have been less so.

At any rate, the line was continued to Tyndrum, opened in 1873, to Dalmally in 1877 and eventually to Oban, reached in 1880. From Killin Junction in Glen Dochart, a branch to Killin village and the Loch Tay steamer pier was added in 1886 – built, like the main line, by an independent company and worked by the Caledonian. After the branch was opened, the former Killin station became a passing loop called Glenoglehead, the names Larigalie or Lairig Eala seemingly forgotten. A further branch from Balquhidder to Lochearnhead, Comrie and Crieff was completed in 1905.

Meanwhile, once the line had been opened to Oban, John Anderson moved his office thither. His main task had become that of increasing his company's revenue, by encouraging traffic over its line – or indeed by exploiting any other opportunity. His activities ranged from tempting the Stornoway fish merchants to send their traffic via Oban, to letting a small piece of ground in Strathyre station yard to the owner of a Callander fruit and vegetable shop, so that she could establish a branch there. His efforts met with justified success, and the Callander & Oban Railway became a busy and prosperous undertaking – at least during the summer tourist season.

The West Highland Comes to Crianlarich

Completion of the Callander & Oban line had left gaps in the railway map: there was still no railway through Glen Falloch, nor was there a railway to Fort William. There were many attempts, unsuccessful, to fill these gaps – the most remarkable of them, the Glasgow & North Western Railway, has been mentioned in Chapter 8. Such proposals offered a substantially shorter route between Glasgow and Crianlarich than the then existing route via Dunblane. Everyone seems to have taken for granted that, when such a line was built, a connection with the C & O would be provided at or near Crianlarich, and that Glasgow-Oban trains would then use the shorter route.

The proposal that was eventually successful was the West Highland Railway. This was authorised by Parliament in 1889, to leave the existing railway at Craigendoran near Helensburgh, and to run by Garelochhead and Loch Long to Arrochar & Tarbet – the station situated midway between the villages of its name – thence beside Loch Lomond to its head, through Glen Falloch to Crianlarich and Tyndrum, and onward by Bridge of Orchy and Rannoch Moor to, eventually, Fort William. Its promoters, many of them from Lochaber, obtained the backing of the North British Railway, which agreed to work the line.

When the West Highland was proposed, the Callander & Oban had attempted to counter it by promoting its own branch from Crianlarich to Ardlui. From there, steamers would run to the foot of

Loch Lomond to connect with trains on the Caledonian-backed line to be built west out of Glasgow. No doubt this all had a bearing on the North British purchase of the Lochlomond Steamboat Company at this time, as mentioned in Chapter 7. The bill for the Crianlarich-Ardlui branch was rejected by Parliament during the same session that it passed the bill for the West Highland.

From the point of view of the potential user, it was self-evident that the West Highland should be connected to the Callander & Oban at Crianlarich. People in Oban looked forward to the short route to Glasgow – as much as 17 miles shorter than the route via Dunblane and Stirling. People in Lochaber wanted to send their livestock to the markets of Stirling, Perth and Falkirk by the quickest and most direct route. From the points of view of the Caledonian and North British Railway companies, the connection was more problematical: each wanted to retain as much traffic as possible for its own route.

However, the railways authorised by the West Highland Railway Act of 1889 included the spur line between the two railways at Crianlarich. It was to diverge from the West Highland and terminate 'at a junction with the Callander and Oban Railway at a point thereon eight hundred and ninety yards or thereabouts north-westward from Crianlarich Station booking-office.' The reference is to the C & O's Crianlarich station; it lay immediately to the north of the village, behind where the village hall is now. In other words, trains coming off the West Highland for the Oban line would not pass through the C & O Crianlarich station.

The Callander & Oban and Caledonian directorates seem to have accepted this with remarkable equanimity. At this period, however the independent directors of the Callander & Oban were in dispute with the Caledonian over the financial implications of working the C & O, a dispute which went eventually to arbitration, so it may be that eyes were taken off the ball.

However, when the West Highland bill had been before Parliament, the Caledonian had been successful in persuading the relevant Parliamentary committee that the North British should not be granted 'running powers' between Crianlarich and Oban. The North British had hoped for such powers, so that it could run its own trains into Oban. It had to be content with a formal agreement (made in 1891) with the Caledonian that through coaches would be exchanged at Crianlarich – to and from Oban, and also to and from Fort William. And a clause inserted into the West Highland Act obliged the West Highland, wherever it intended any works affecting the C & O, to submit plans and specifications beforehand: the works were to be made to the 'reasonable satisfaction' of the C & O's engineer. That meant that the C & O could veto any layout proposed for the junction between the two railways.

At this point, it seems, the Callander & Oban management woke up. The possibility of building a large station immediately to the west of the junction was considered. At this, passengers could change trains and through carriages could be exchanged. Successive plans were drawn up, and then rejected. The proposal would have meant stopping C & O trains twice within a few hundred yards.

At this belated stage all sorts of other possibilities were considered. One was to lay out the spur so that it diverged east from the West Highland and then swung round to join the C & O east of its Crianlarich station. Another was to build a station to the north of Crianlarich laid out for interchange of passengers, and trains, in all directions. A third was to build high and low level stations adjacent to one another with interchange by stairs or lifts. Yet another was to build a north-to-east spur to complement the authorised south-to-west one. All these were found wanting by one railway or the other.

The two companies went to arbitration over the problem late in 1893, and the consequence was that the spur was built very much as originally authorised. The West Highland had to pay for loops, sidings and signal boxes on the C & O at the junction. These enabled carriages and wagons to be exchanged between the two railways. Physically it was possible for trains coming from the south off the West Highland to run through in the direction of Oban, and vice versa, should the occasion arise. There were no passenger platforms, and no special provision was made for passengers to change from one line to the other: the new WHR station at Crianlarich was a quarter of a mile away from the C & O station, and uphill.

No further away than Perth and Stirling were examples of stations used by the trains of both the Caledonian and the North British Railways. One cannot help but feel that Parliament failed the public in not requiring a joint station to be built at Crianlarich, accessible by trains from all four directions, and with easy interchange between them – of both passengers and rolling stock, as appropriate. Yet that is written with the benefit of hindsight.

The West Highland Railway was opened in August 1894. Crianlarich, its mid-point, became important as a refreshment stop. A signboard which announced 'Refreshment Rooms: Lunches, Dinners, Teas' was more prominent than the station nameboards themselves. The refreshment rooms were privately operated and passengers could ask the guard of their train to telegraph ahead for refreshment baskets, to be ready when the train reached Crianlarich. Trains halted there long enough for them to be put aboard, or for passengers to visit the refreshment rooms themselves. Supply of refreshments became a lasting feature of Crianlarich, surviving the introduction of buffet cars on the trains and their eventual withdrawal in favour of refreshment trolleys. A framed selection of early telegrams, ordering refreshment baskets, is displayed in the station tea room, as it is now called.

The North British prepared a timetable for the West Highland which included a daily through-coach in each direction between Glasgow Queen Street, Crianlarich and Oban. In October 1894 it was reported that the Crianlarich spur, from the West Highland Crianlarich station down to the connection with the C & O at 'Crianlarich Junction', was complete and ready for opening. But it was not opened.

The cost of employing signalmen to work the junction, and providing a locomotive if necessary to work the spur, was to fall upon the newcomer, the North British. Deprived of the possibility of running its own trains to Oban, its management evidently now saw no advantage in going to this expense. Although the spur would enable passenger coaches to and from Oban to be exchanged, it would enable goods and livestock traffic between Fort William and places such as Stirling and Perth to be exchanged too, to be taken by the Caledonian via Callander. So long as the spur remained closed, such traffic had to be taken over the full length of the West Highland and via Glasgow – a much longer journey, but over NBR tracks almost throughout: it could be charged accordingly. Evidently the profit from this seemed likely to exceed that from the proposed through-coach to Oban.

So where the C & O had earlier obstructed making the junction, the North British now procrastinated over opening it. This did not go unnoticed by the public who would have used it. The Callander & Oban, in the person of John Anderson, started to receive complaints. Typical, probably, was John Macgregor, merchant of Dunblane, who sent hay and straw in the direction of Fort William. It was being routed via Glasgow and the full length of the West Highland, but unless he could offer quicker delivery via the Crianlarich spur his business would suffer. But whenever Anderson wrote to his West Highland counterpart to ask when the spur would be opened, he received only evasive replies.

On 7 March 1896 Caledonian Railway general manager James Thompson telegraphed Anderson at Oban:

> Crianlarich Junction with West Highland Railway write me today whether any traffic is presently being exchanged between the two companies at this Junction and if so how are passenger or goods vehicles exchanged or what is the modus operandi.

Anderson replied the same day:

> Dear Sir
>
> Your telegram.
>
> The works at the Junction have been finished for the last 15 months. They have not been inspected [by the Board of Trade Inspecting Officer] nor opened. Passengers have to walk between the two stations, a distance of nearly half a mile. We keep a pony and cart and have to convey the passengers luggage which we do without charge, as we have to take it up a hill while the N. B. Co are able to do the work with their porters. Goods have had to be carted and in some cases, sheep and horses have had to be untrucked and retrucked. No vehicles have been exchanged.
>
> Yours truly,

This telegram and its reply form part of the correspondence on the subject surviving among Callander & Oban records at the National Archives of Scotland.

At that period the North British had gone to Parliament for government financial aid towards the Mallaig line, and the Caledonian and others took the opportunity to oppose the bill, pointing out that if the NBR wanted public money towards the Mallaig extension, it should first act in the public interest by opening the Crianlarich spur. It was December 1897 before the Crianlarich spur was eventually opened for traffic, after more than three years of delay – and then only for exchange of goods vehicles. Even as late as 1912, tourists coming off the Loch Lomond steamer at Ardlui, and bound for Oban, were still being carried by four-in-hand coach between Ardlui and Crianlarich Lower.

The Maries *and the* Maid

From the beginning to the present day, and despite the previous sentence, summer tourists and the traffic they bring have been vital to the railways serving the western Highlands. Their managements have often gone out of their way to cater for them. John Anderson for example, once his railway was open as far as Tyndrum, arranged for the hotel keeper at Crianlarich to have a mountain guide available on Saturdays. As soon as the first train arrived from the south, he was ready to escort visitors to the summit of Ben More.

When the Caledonian Railway provided carriages specifically for the Callander & Oban in 1889, the first-class carriages had the end compartments arranged as coupés – that is to say, the seats faced windows let into the ends of the carriage. There were of course windows in the sides as well. So when one of these carriages was placed at the end of the train, it offered passengers in the coupé an unrivalled panorama of mountain and loch, slipping away past them.

The North British built special carriages for the opening of the West Highland; in days when railway carriages in Britain normally comprised a row of separate compartments, these were exceptional in that the central part of each carriage formed a large saloon, with large windows for passengers to enjoy the views. In 1913 the NBR too provided some carriages with coupé ends.

This trend towards carriages which enabled visitors to view the passing scene in ever-greater comfort reached its peak when the Pullman observation car *Maid of Morven* was placed in service between Glasgow and Oban. George M. Pullman had invented the Pullman car, as a luxurious sleeping car, in the USA in 1865; from the 1870s his cars were also running on certain railways in Britain. The Pullman parlour car was developed for daytime use – passengers paid a supplement to travel in luxury, and in due course meals were served too. Yet Pullman car operation had an equivocal element, for railway managements, once they had seen what could be done, often tended to decide they could do equally well in-house without troubling an outside contractor.

In 1907 the British Pullman Palace Car Company, which latterly had not prospered, was purchased from the trustees of G.M.Pullman by financier Davison Dalziel. Dalziel energetically set about promoting the use of Pullman cars. One of his biggest successes was to negotiate a twenty-year contract to provide, from 1914, all the restaurant cars on the Caledonian Railway, with the exception of those in trains going to and from England. For most routes Pullman dining cars were built (I shall return to them shortly), but for the Callander & Oban, the Caledonian's most scenic line, something better was evidently thought justified.

This was the first class Pullman observation car *Maid of Morven*. It was the custom of the Pullman Car company to name its cars, often with girls' names: 'Maid of Morvern' (as it is now usually spelt) is the title borne by the eldest daughter of MacLean of Duart, chief of Clan MacLean. Since Duart Castle, at the south-east corner of the Isle of Mull, is about the first landmark you see when crossing from Oban, and Morvern is the district on the opposite shore of the Sound of Mull, there could scarcely have been a more felicitous choice.

Influenced perhaps by experience of the earlier coupé-ended carriages, the bowed rear end of *Maid of Morven* was glazed from side to side and floor to ceiling: three panes only were needed. On either side, almost half its length was occupied by a door and four more deep, wide windows. Within the observation saloon thus formed were loose armchairs, tables, table lamps with silk shades, a heavy pile carpet, pearwood panelling and marquetry pilasters. Further along the car were chairs with dining tables between, and the pantry from which refreshments were served. If *Maid of Morven* was not the most luxurious railway carriage running in public trains in Britain at the time, it must have come very close to it. Probably its nearest rivals were carrying the rich and famous between Brighton and Victoria. That is an indication of the high regard in which the Pullman Car company and the Caledonian Railway then held the Callander & Oban Line.

The *Maid of Morven* made its first run on 3 August 1914. This could hardly have been a worse moment; the long, settled period of wealth and prosperity, which alone had made such a vehicle possible, came crashing to an end the very next day when Britain entered the First World War. The observation car ran until the following February, and was then withdrawn for the duration. It did not re-enter service until March 1919, after which it became a popular feature of the line despite changed times.

On the Callander & Oban the observation car was then joined by some of the Pullman dining cars. These seem, wherever they ran, to have been available to any passenger in the train who wanted a meal, while those who wished to spend the entire journey in the car paid a supplement, although arrangements probably varied. At any rate the dining cars were furnished with the full Pullman splendour, inlaid panelling, table lamps and all. The chairs, however, were dining chairs rather than Pullman armchairs. Some of the cars were described from time to time as buffet cars, but for simplicity here I will use the term dining cars throughout. Initially the Pullman dining cars were used on main routes such as Glasgow to Edinburgh and Glasgow to Aberdeen, but there were some less likely routes as well. For a time one car started out in the morning from St Fillans, in a train running via Comrie, Crieff and Gleneagles to Glasgow: its patrons no doubt enjoyed a good breakfast on the way.

The Pullman dining cars running on the Caledonian were named for the most part after heroines of Scottish history, Scottish folklore, or the works of Sir Walter Scott (or, in some instances, after individuals who were all three simultaneously). One such was *Helen MacGregor*, named after Rob Roy's wife; it would have been nice to be able to say that this car passed regularly through Balquhidder, but this does not seem to have been the case. Rather, the Pullman dining cars which did normally run over over the Callander & Oban were *Mary Beaton, Mary Seaton* and *Mary Carmichael*. There was a fourth car in the same series called *Mary Hamilton*. Encountering these undistinguished-sounding names in a list of railway rolling stock, I pondered aloud who the four Maries might be. They were, my

Pullman dining car *Mary Beaton* was one of the cars which ran regularly
in Callander & Oban line trains (*National Railway Museum*)

chief researcher responded instantly, the ladies-in-waiting to Mary
Queen of Scots.

She was right, yet there was more to it than that. The four Maries
of Mary Queen of Scots, the daughters of nobility who accompanied
her to France for their upbringing and returned to Scotland to
become part of her court, were Mary Beaton, Mary Seton, Mary
Fleming and Mary Livingston. For Mary Hamilton and Mary
Carmichael we must look elsewhere. They are found in the ballad
Mary Hamilton. This tells the sad, tragic, macabre story of Mary
Hamilton, a young lady at court who, it is learned, 'gangs wi' bairn
to the hichest Stewart of a'.' She does away with the baby – and pays
the price on the scaffold. The last verse runs:

> Last nicht there was four Maries,
> The nicht there'l be but three;
> There was Marie Seton, and Marie Beton,
> And Marie Carmichael, and me.

The ballad appears to relate to the Four Maries of Mary Queen
of Scots – who seem in reality to have been no great models

of rectitude – but the names do not tally and there are other inconsistencies. F.J.Child in *English and Scottish Popular Ballads* showed convincingly that, at the court of Peter the Great of Russia, a Mary Hamilton, of Scottish origin and a maid-of-honour to the empress, suffered just such a fate, except that the father of the child was an aide-de-camp to the tsar, rather than the tsar himself. She was executed in 1719, in the presence of the tsar. The writer of the ballad, first recorded in the 1790s, probably took this story and set it at the court of Mary Queen of Scots.

I seem to have strayed rather far from the true subject of this chapter. Yet one of the attractions of an interest in railway trains is the illumination sometimes cast upon incidentals. One does wonder just how much whoever it was who chose the names for the Pullman cars knew of the Four Maries. To sit down to afternoon tea in a Pullman car, and then to find it named after a convicted child murderess, would quite put one off the buttered toast – however tragic the tale.

No such qualms affected a regular user of *Mary Beaton*. Much later he corresponded with John Thomas, and Thomas quotes in *The Callander & Oban Railway* his correspondent's mouthwatering description of the breakfasts he had enjoyed in the Pullman, travelling home for school holidays on the 8.00 a.m. from Glasgow Buchanan Street to Oban.

In 1923 the London Midland & Scottish Railway absorbed the Caledonian Railway (and the Callander & Oban Railway Company, and for that matter the Killin Railway Company too) and it inherited the Pullman Car contract. Initially the LMS expanded the use of Pullman dining cars to other railways in Scotland which it had absorbed. But in 1933 it chose not to renew the contract. Instead it bought the Pullman cars and employed the staff, and operated dining cars and observation car itself.

The *Maid of Morven* ran until some date in the late 1930s – sources differ as to the year that it was withdrawn. It can scarcely have been worn out; its wealthy clientele, however, were of the class likely to defect early to the motor car. Observation cars re-appeared on the Callander & Oban line – and appeared on the West Highland – in the late 1950s and 1960s, using cars handed down from distinguished express trains elsewhere. At least one of the conductors of the Oban line observation car had, long before, performed the same function on the *Maid of Morven*.

The Pullman dining cars survived much longer than the observation car. Some lasted long enough to pass into the ownership of British Railways on nationalisation in 1948. With their names long since removed and bearing mundane numbers instead, they were still serving meals to passengers on the Callander & Oban line in the early 1950s.

Passenger Trains Use the Crianlarich Spur

Though patronage of the *Maid of Morven* by the wealthy may have dropped away in the 1930s, the railway companies of the time found a new leisure traffic in the form of Sunday excursions for the masses in the Lowland towns and cities. These ran from Glasgow to Fort William over the West Highland, now part of the London & North Eastern Railway, and over the LMS from Glasgow, Edinburgh and Dundee to Oban. The Dundee trains came via Crieff and joined the Callander & Oban line at Balquhidder.

It was excursion traffic that eventually brought the Crianlarich spur into use for passenger trains. The LMS and the LNER were two of the big four companies which ran most of the railways throughout Britain at this period. Nominally competitive, they were well aware that road competition was best fought with a united front, and came to cooperate with one another far more than the former railway companies had done. The LMS and the LNER for instance published a fine series of pictorial posters, to encourage holidays in the Highlands, in their joint names. Such a spirit of cooperation did not extend to any great co-ordination of the regular train services on the two lines through Crianlarich, but it did at last allow through-excursions between one line and the other.

So the first passenger train to traverse the Crianlarich spur ran on 10 June 1931, more than thirty-three years after it had been opened to goods traffic (and even longer since it had been built). It was an excursion to Oban, run in connection with a cruise to Staffa and Iona on MacBrayne's brand new ship the *Lochfyne*, and it ran over the LNER from Glasgow Queen Street to Crianlarich, and thence over the LMS to Oban. According to John Thomas in

The Callander & Oban Railway it took 83 minutes less time for the journey than the best regular train via Dunblane, but presumably it did not have to make all the usual stops, of either line, en route.

Subsequently the Crianlarich spur was used by circular tour excursions, operated by the two companies in cooperation: they ran from Glasgow, out by the West Highland and back by Dunblane, or vice versa. Since they reversed at Crianlarich Junction, they must have been awkward to operate. Steam locomotives normally run facing forwards, so the locomotives of these trains had to be detached from them to be turned on the turntable at Crianlarich Upper. Assuming the same locomotive was used for the whole journey, it would also have to run round the train, that is to say be moved from one end to the other, at Crianlarich Junction.

LMS and LNER were absorbed into the nationalised British Railways in 1948, and for the summer of 1949 the Scottish Region of BR proudly announced a new train to run over the short route from Glasgow Queen Street to Oban, via the West Highland line as far as Crianlarich. This was the first regular passenger train service to use the Crianlarich spur. The train ran from Glasgow to Oban in the morning, and back again in the evening. That was all very well, but it was very little use to people living at the Oban end of the line; nor, indeed, did many people seem to want to use it for a day out in Oban. In 1950 and 1951 it ran only during July and August; by 1954 it had disappeared from the timetable, although it reappeared in some subsequent summers, 1962 for example.

Far more successful were the 'Six Lochs Diesel Land Cruise' trains. By the late 1950s BR's Scottish Region was being provided with diesel multiple-unit trains. With large windows, and a view obtainable front and back through the glass partitions which separated passengers from driver, they were well suited to excursions through fine scenery. Furthermore, reversing them meant only that the driver had to walk from the driver's cab at one end to the cab at the other. Enterprisingly, BR exploited these features to reinstate the circular tours from Glasgow, out via the West Highland to Crianlarich and back via Killin and Callander, or vice versa. This involved reversing not only at Crianlarich, but also at Killin Junction. The title associated the excursion with favourite Clyde steamer cruises, and the whole operation became very popular in the early

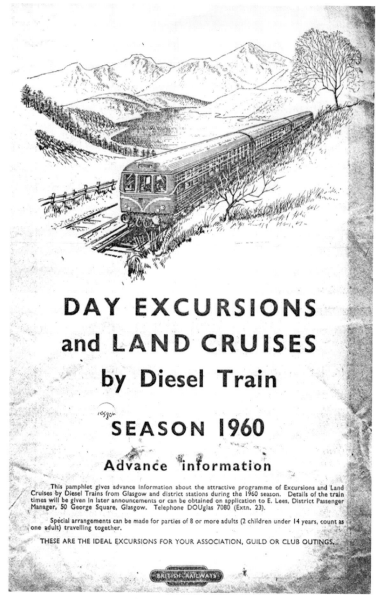

British Railways publicises 'land cruises' in 1960 by newly-introduced diesel trains. Some of these cruises were circular tours, outward from Glasgow to Crianlarich over the West Highland line, and back via Callander and Dunblane. (*Collection R.N.Forsythe, courtesy British Railways Board*)

1960s. At the same period, diesel locomotives started to replace steam locomotives on the regular trains.

More than successful excursions, however, would have been needed to keep the Callander & Oban line open east of Crianlarich. Throughout Britain in the early 1960s car ownership was booming and the road network rapidly expanding; correspondingly, railway finances were disappearing down a black hole. The Beeching Plan of 1963 proposed that railways should be used for the things they did well – carrying passengers in quantity and freight in bulk – and that they should cease to be used for the things they did badly, which meant closing country stations and rural railways. The latter in truth was no more than to accelerate an existing trend – the railway between Comrie and Balquhidder, for instance, had been closed as early as 1951, and the Killin–Loch Tay section before that, although it remained in place for locomotives to reach the shed and water supply at Loch Tay.

In those circumstances it is surprising that any railways in the West Highlands survived. Between the Lowlands and Crianlarich, it must have been clear that there was not sufficient traffic for two railways, and that one should be closed. Given that trains could run direct between Oban and Glasgow over the West Highland in less time than they took via Dunblane, while trains could only run between Fort William and Dunblane by reversing twice at Crianlarich, it was clearly going to be the eastern section of the Callander & Oban which was closed.

In preparation for this, goods trains for Oban were diverted to run over the West Highland line as far as Crianlarich in 1964, and the stations between Callander and Crianlarich were closed to goods traffic. Closure to passengers of the line from Dunblane to Crianlarich, with the Killin branch, was announced in 1965, to take place from 1 November; from that date, Oban trains would run over the West Highland as far as Crianlarich and the Crianlarich spur would become, in effect, the start of the Oban branch of the West Highland.

On the night of 26–27 September, a landslide in Glen Ogle blocked the track. In normal circumstances, a bus link would have been provided past such a blockage until it had been cleared and the line re-opened. Circumstances were abnormal, and the

**WITHDRAWAL OF PASSENGER
TRAIN SERVICES BETWEEN
DUNBLANE AND CRIANLARICH
AND BETWEEN
KILLIN JUNCTION AND KILLIN
ON AND FROM
MONDAY 1st NOVEMBER, 1965**

Alterations to Passenger Train Services
and
Alternative Road Services

The Scottish Region of British Railways have announced that on
and from MONDAY 1st NOVEMBER, 1965 ALL passenger train services
will be withdrawn from the DUNBLANE–CALLANDER–CRIANLARICH
and KILLIN JUNCTION–KILLIN lines and that Glasgow to Oban trains
will be re-routed to run from and to Glasgow Queen Street Station via
Dumbarton and Crianlarich Upper. From the same date the following
stations will be closed to passenger traffic:–

BRIDGE OF ALLAN	KINGSHOUSE	LUIB
DOUNE	BALQUHIDDER	CRIANLARICH LOWER
CALLANDER	KILLIN JN.	LOCH AWE
STRATHYRE	KILLIN	FALLS OF CRUACHAN
		ACH–NA–CLOICH

This pamphlet contains details of:–

(i)   The revised train services which will operate between GLASGOW QUEEN
      STREET, CRIANLARICH UPPER and OBAN and between OBAN, CONNEL
      FERRY and BALLACHULISH to replace the services shown in the timetable.

(ii) The alternative road services which will be available including certain
      additions and alterations required by the Minister of Transport.

British Rail announces closure of the line between Dunblane and
Crianlarich in 1965 (*R.N. Forsythe, courtesy British Railways Board*)

Killin Junction in September 1965, with a train leaving for Killin
(*D. Stirling*)

line was not re-opened. For the benefit of local passengers, the
service was maintained by a bus link between Callander, Killin
and Crianlarich until the official closure date; the Glasgow-Oban
train service was diverted to the West Highland route immediately.
The long-established through sleeping car service between Oban
and London was withdrawn. So were through coaches between
Oban and Edinburgh. A regular bus service started to run between
Stirling, Callander and Crianlarich, connecting with trains to and
from Oban, but as so often happened it did not last.

There were some odd consequences. The locomotive which had
been used on the Killin branch – steam to the end – had to leave for
the last time via Crianlarich. The royal train was affected when it
carried the queen from Ballater to Dalmally to open the Cruachan
pumped-storage hydro-electric scheme on 15 October. It would,
presumably, have used the Callander route: it had, of course, to
use the West Highland. But when, hauled by diesel locomotives, it
reached Crianlarich Junction in the small hours, there was (if plans

were carried out as intended) a steam locomotive waiting, to draw it back towards Crianlarich Lower, and there quietly to provide steam heating while the royal party slept. In the morning the royal train continued behind diesels. That must have been one of the last occasions, if not the last, when a steam locomotive was used on the West Highland lines prior to the introduction of steam excursions with preserved locomotives.

Crianlarich Lower station took on a new lease of life as a loading point for timber, carried by the trainload to the pulp and paper mill at Corpach near Fort William. Operation of these trains at Crianlarich was eased by allowing the locomotives to push, rather than pull, their trains up and down the spur. The traffic lasted for about fifteen years and was, probably, the saviour of the West Highland line at that period.

No attempt was made, in 1965, to integrate the train services to and from Oban with those to and from Fort William; rather, the Oban-Glasgow train service was superimposed on the existing West Highland train service, with trains running at about the same frequency, and times of day, as before. Only in 1989, when new diesel trains were introduced, was the opportunity taken to recast the timetable, with trains for Oban and Fort William dividing at Crianlarich. Even then, no connecting train was provided to enable Oban passengers to join or leave the London-Fort William sleeper at Crianlarich. This remains the position at the present day, a timetabling – and marketing – remnant of days gone by when each line was operated independently of the other. In the meantime, operation of all regular passenger trains to Oban and Fort William passed to ScotRail Railways Ltd on privatisation.

Eye-witness Memories

The eastern part of the Callander & Oban, from Dunblane to Crianlarich, is now represented for the most part by farm roads, cycletrack and grass-grown roadbed. My own recollections of travel over it when it was a railway are limited to journeys to and from a family holiday on Mull in 1951: going to bed in a sleeping berth somewhere around Crewe, and waking up near Luib to look out at an early morning Glen Dochart. And to seeing more of this part of the line in the evening on the way back, and admiring the neatness of the station gardens at Balquhidder and Strathyre.

So I am greatly indebted to David Stirling, who for many years edited the Scottish Railway Preservation Society's magazine *Blastpipe*, for two eye-witness accounts. As a young man he knew the line well in its last years. He writes:

We travelled to Oban in the summer of 1960 on the way to a family holiday in Barra. This involved taking the Sunday train to Oban – in the summer the mail ran on Sunday instead of early on Monday morning. We left Glasgow early, about 7 am, and changed from the Glasgow-Aberdeen train into the Oban one at Stirling, settling in a comfortable old carriage with double doors to the compartment. The train left the main line at Dunblane and turned west, stopping at each station to change the tablet for the single line sections. As an economy measure the train crews saw to this themselves on the mail train, saving the cost of the signalmen. It certainly slowed the journey but nobody seemed to mind. Callander was an important stop for there was a tea trolley on the platform, the only available refreshment before Oban . . .

We crossed the Leny followed by some fields and then, with suitably energetic sounds from the two steam engines, climbed through the Pass of Leny. The trees, rocks, heather and bracken combined to make this a spectacular section, enlivened by crossing and re-crossing the Leny near the falls. Soon enough the land opened out and we were on level ground, running alongside Loch Lubnaig, on the side opposite the road. This was isolated territory and there was a private wooden halt for railway staff at Craig na Cailleach, near the rocky promontory of the same name. Here the railway squeezed itself between a scree slope and the water at a point where rocks were occasionally sent hurtling down the slope. The line was protected by a high fence whose wires were connected to some automatic signals protecting trains from any rock that might have fallen.

On [past Strathyre] to Balquhidder, where no-one got on or off at a large, empty and, to a teenager interested in railways, fascinating station. Most steam trains took water at Balquhidder – even the fast summer Saturday relief trains stopped – because of its absolutely reliable water supply . . . subsequent experience showed that few days at Balquhidder were entirely free of rain . . .

After Balquhidder the line climbed steeply, giving a magnificent

view of Loch Earn before it turned into . . . Glen Ogle. The glen
narrowed progressively, with a spectacular viaduct part way along,
until we reached a small loch at the summit, where Glenoglehead
crossing loop lay. Here the signalman came out to offer the tablet
to the train, saving a stop and doing the train crew a favour . . .
The view opened out almost immediately afterwards as we rolled
downhill with views over to Killin and Loch Tay – the countryside
was not then covered in forest. After a few minutes the branch line
came up from Killin to join us at another spot of railway interest,
Killin Junction . . . The timetable labelled Killin Junction 'exchange
platform only' but I later found out that it had a booking office
and functioned as a normal station, although originating traffic
was slight. By this time too much leaning out of the window had
ensured a good crop of cinders in my hair, and my mother declared
an embargo . . .

That was a typical journey of the period. The next is quite
untypical:

Partly in the knowledge that this was the last chance as the
Dunblane–Crianlarich line was due to close at the end of October
and partly because it was a splendid trip, my mother and I booked
on the Six Lochs Tour from Glasgow for the Glasgow holiday
Monday of 27th September 1965 . . . outwards to Crianlarich by the
West Highland and back via Callander. The day dawned fine and
our spirits were high, to be slightly dampened by a hand written
notice in Queen Street [station] advising that the service between
Killin and Callander had been interrupted . . . [We joined the train
nonetheless and were soon] enjoying the view over . . . Loch Long.
At this point the railway representative on the tour . . . announced
that we would have to travel from Killin to Callander by bus, as the
line was obstructed by an avalanche in Glen Ogle . . .

The train ran uneventfully to Crianlarich through the grand
but rather austere scenery of the West Highland – I always found
that the route through Callander was much gentler, more colourful
and less forbidding. At Crianlarich the train turned left and crept
down the spur to the Callander & Oban line – trains always seemed
to take the spur cautiously in those days. Here the driver changed
ends and we were now looking out of the front windows. We headed
off eastwards, collecting the [single line] tablet at Crianlarich East
Junction [signal box] and onwards under the looming bulk of Ben
More. There was no cause to delay at Luib and we ran straight

into the branch platform at Killin Junction, where we stopped. After a pause the station master wearing the red armband which declared him to be the pilotman, came over to the train and gave the driver a ticket for [use of] the single line to Killin. (For special occasions like this there was so much traffic to Killin that the usual 'one engine in steam' arrangements would not cope.) The signal remained at danger, however, and after a while the Killin branch engine . . . appeared from the Glenoglehead direction. There was much conferring and the station master collected his ticket from the tour train and dispatched the light engine towards Killin instead. We had more time to admire the pine trees around Killin Junction.

After a while we set off for Killin ourselves, arriving there to find no trace of the steam engine and the line between Killin and Loch Tay filled with several other diesel multiple unit trains – other Six Lochs tours from other places. Presumably the steam engine had been shunted past these trains and escaped to the engine shed and water supply at Loch Tay.

For our tour Killin meant lunch, so . . . lunch we had . . . By the time we returned to the station there was a large fleet of buses to take the train load of people onwards to Callander . . . We passed similar fleets of buses coming the other way, with those who were doing the Six Lochs tour in the opposite direction; on public holidays there could be several trains going round the circuit in each direction. As we started to descend through Glen Ogle everyone looked over to the railway on the other side of the glen for a view of the avalanche which had closed the line, but nothing was evident. This was rather disappointing, for if this mishap had cheated us of our last run over the line and the best views of Loch Earn and the Falls of Leny, the least it could have done was to be spectacular.

Callander was inevitably busy, with a flotilla of diesel multiple unit trains waiting for their various participants on Six Lochs tours.

Sadly, we must now return to the twenty-first century. Since I have so rashly written earlier of railways being ripe for re-opening, a comment is needed as to whether I think that this line could or should be re-opened. The answer, I regret to say, is 'no'. I cannot see sufficient traffic being generated by anything short of, say, a major oil strike in Loch Linnhe, or a draconian ban on through traffic over the roads of the national park. Regrettably, although Crianlarich is also a nodal point in the road network, it remains as innocent of effective bus/rail interchange as it was formerly of interchange between the two railways. It is a pity too that the railway could not have been retained from Dunblane as far as Callander, as an economical single-track branch without points or signals, to give access to the Trossachs. In just this manner the Windermere branch was retained to give access to the Lake District.

Should the eastern part of the Callander & Oban ever have been closed? When its trains were diverted over the West Highland route south of Crianlarich, Oban gained the most direct route to Glasgow, but lost the most direct route to Stirling, Edinburgh, the South, and indeed the North. Fort William had never even had the benefit of the latter, at least for through trains: the layout of the junction at Crianlarich saw to that. As to which line between Crianlarich and the Lowlands should have been closed, the die had been cast long before, in the 1890s. If Parliament then had done its job properly and insisted on a joint station at Crianlarich accessible from all directions, then perhaps . . .

13

LOCH SLOY HYDRO-ELECTRIC: GENERATING THE REGENERATION OF SCOTLAND

The Viewpoint Among the Trees

'The Rt Hon. Thomas Johnston CH (1881–1965) created the North of Scotland Hydro-Electric Board in 1943'. The inscription surrounds the circular dial of a viewpoint indicator on top of a low pillar. It is evidently a memorial, and it is situated on the promontory that juts out into Loch Lomond at Inveruglas. The dial shows the direction and distance of hills, islands, Rob Roy's Cave and suchlike.

It is an inscription that reveals itself to readers as they work their way around the pillar. It must surely baffle most of them. Firstly, they probably do not know who Thomas Johnston was. Secondly, they probably do not appreciate the significance of forming some obscure board quite a long time ago. Thirdly, there is no apparent reason why the memorial should have been located where it is. That is certainly so for visitors who have approached down the road from Crianlarich, and largely so for those who have approached from the south.

The knoll upon which the memorial stands forms part of a picnic site between the main road and the loch; the memorial itself is approached, from the car park, up a path through a thick grove of trees. From the indicator, gaps in the trees allow views to the loch and the hills beyond; but in the direction from which the visitor has approached, the trees have closed in to allow no view at all.

Only by continuing down the path towards the point, and then following it round the south side of the promontory, does the visitor suddenly find himself facing inland at a point clear of trees. Now the view previously hidden is revealed: from high on the hillside, four huge pipelines sweep downwards to the hydro-electric power station

Pipelines sweep down the hillside to Loch Sloy Hydro-electric power station, Inveruglas, in April 2003. The ferryboat to Inversnaid waits at the pier in the foreground. (*Author*)

at their foot. They may not be things of beauty – and indeed trees planted alongside the pipes now partially screen them from the public gaze from other directions – but they are mightily impressive.

Pipes and power station together symbolise the great venture – I almost wrote adventure – of harnessing the great resource of the Highlands, the rain that falls upon them, to provide light, heat and power for the inhabitants: a wholly green source of energy, established long before peoples' minds were much exercised by such things. That was what the hydro-electric board achieved. Its Loch Sloy scheme – so-called after its principal reservoir – was the first to be completed and was an early jewel in its crown. So by creating the board, that was Thomas Johnston's achievement too. The inscription is eloquent in its simplicity. It picks out the single most important element in a long and distinguished career. It might well have added, but does not, that in 1943 Johnston, a committed socialist, was serving as Secretary of State for Scotland under a great Conservative, Winston Churchill, which gives some indication of Johnston's calibre. To Johnston and to members of the board he created, completion of Sloy in 1950 was far more than just a great technical achievement. In an era when pre-war economic depression had been succeeded by wartime austerity, it was a huge step towards improved standards of living, more employment and increased production: the replacement of depopulation and despair with hope for better things to come.

The promontory upon which Johnston's memorial stands has not always been covered with trees. It seems evident that the memorial was sited so that those who come to it should first observe the great natural beauty of the scene ahead, and then swing round to see it complemented by the great human achievement behind. More's the pity they cannot.

The Beginnings

Using the force of gravity to generate electricity though the medium of falling water seems an obvious thing to do. It is something of a surprise to learn just how extensive, and how intense, has been the controversy attending proposals actually to do so. Controversy arose on two main counts. Firstly, although the 'fuel' for hydro-electricity is free, the capital costs of schemes to use it are high. They need dams, tunnels, aqueducts and pipelines as well as power stations and extended transmission lines – extended, because hydro-electricity has often to be generated far from where it is to be used. So there was plenty of scope for contention over how much, or even whether, the electricity produced would be cheaper than that produced by other means. Secondly, the dams, reservoirs, pipelines, power stations, and transmission lines seemed likely to become blots on the landscape in places famous for their natural beauty; the reservoirs further meant inundating land used for something else. The consequence was controversy compared with which the present-day controversy over electricity generation by wind farms is a pale shadow.

There have been hydro-electric schemes operating in Scotland since the 1880s – the first in the Highlands was installed by the monks of Fort Augustus to light both monastery and village. Such schemes were small, and early private schemes were even smaller. The Inversnaid Hotel was generating its own electricity by water power as early as 1900. The earliest large-scale hydro-electric schemes in Scotland were linked to the production of aluminium, which required large amounts of electricity. Such were the schemes based on Foyers, Kinlochleven and Fort William, put into operation between the 1890s and 1930s.

For public supply, the first large-scale hydro-electric scheme in the Highlands was built by the Grampian Electricity Supply Co. between 1928 and 1940. It used the waters of Loch Ericht and Loch Rannoch, their tributaries and even watercourses further afield, which were diverted to feed power stations at Loch Rannoch and at Tummel Bridge. As well as supplying electricity throughout much of the north of Scotland it was linked to the newly established national grid at Abernethy. Such schemes required Parliamentary powers to authorise their activities over a necessarily large area. In the Lowlands, the Falls of Clyde scheme was built during the 1920s and the much more extensive Galloway scheme, authorised by Parliament in 1929, completed in the 1930s.

During the 1930s and early 1940s no further hydro schemes in Scotland were authorised by Parliament. One by one, six bills for hydro-electric schemes were promoted, and six bills were lost. The opposition came from the coal mining lobby, immensely powerful in those days before North Sea oil and gas, and from a 'hands-off the Highlands brigade'. The latter comprised three main factions – those dependent on tourism, those concerned with the preservation of natural beauty, and owners of sporting estates. These were joined, increasingly, by those who saw the likely benefits, such as attracting industry and stemming depopulation, that hydro-electricity might bring, but felt that the powers it demanded were too all-pervading to be handed to private industry. It was, rather, something to be undertaken by the state. Among the latter was Tom Johnston.

Johnston, Churchill and Hydro-Electricity

In 1941 Tom Johnston, a native of Kirkintilloch and a product of Glasgow University, was about sixty years of age and had had a varied and distinguished career. He had been a journalist and historian, and he was well known as a Labour Member of Parliament. At that point Churchill, as prime minister, invited him to join his wartime

National Government. Johnston was initially far from eager to accept. But, as he put it in *Memories* (1952), a rabbit cornered by a boa constrictor would have had about as much chance of escape. Before, however, he was 'hypnotised' into accepting the post of Secretary of State for Scotland, he managed to establish the condition that he should be supported by a council of state composed of all living former secretaries of state, of whatever political persuasion, and that when they were agreed upon an issue, the prime minister would give them his backing. In the event, all the former secretaries of state agreed to serve.

The council of state acted promptly and one of its first actions was to set up a committee to enquire into hydro-electric development. This, the Cooper Committee, was chaired by Lord Cooper, a senior Scottish judge; its membership comprised four other suitably distinguished and qualified persons, ranging from the chairman of the Scottish Co-operative Wholesale Society to the civil engineer who had designed the dams for the Galloway hydro-electric scheme. In its report, late in 1942, the committee castigated those sectional interests who had allowed the whole subject to descend into an atmosphere of grievance, suspicion, prejudice and controversy. Then, with safeguards for amenity and fisheries, it came down unanimously in favour of a new public service corporation to be called the North Scotland Hydro-Electric Board, which would undertake, in its area, the development of all further generation and transmission of electricity.

Based largely on the committee's recommendations, the Hydro-Electric Development (Scotland) Bill was brought to Parliament by Johnston early in 1943. There were impassioned speeches from MPs and peers who thought the bill went too far, and equally impassioned speeches from those who thought it did not go far enough. But overall it was received with goodwill and, amazingly, passed through both Houses without a division. Johnston later wrote that it was the first time since the Reform Bill of 1832 that such a thing had happened to a major Scots measure.

So the Bill had become an Act, and the North of Scotland Hydro-Electric Board (as it had become) was formed. There were two particularly remarkable features of the Act. One was the extent of safeguards and checks placed upon the board. Not only did every 'constructional scheme' proposed by the board have to be approved, in detail, by the secretary of state, it had also to be laid before Parliament, where it could be annulled. The other was the 'social clause' which gave the board wider responsibilities than the simple generation of electricity. Section 2, sub-section 3 stated 'The Board shall . . . collaborate in the carrying out of any measures for the economic development of the North of Scotland District or any part thereof.'

Johnston probably had much to do with the appointments to the board. The first chairman was Lord Airlie, a Scottish banker and landowner, who had been – uncharacteristically for his class and background – enthusiastic in support of the bill in the Lords. The deputy chairman and chief executive was an innovative electrical engineer, A.E. MacColl. MacColl's early career had been with Glasgow's corporation tramways; he had later had much to do with the construction of the Falls of Clyde hydro scheme, and had subsequently been largely responsible for the establishment of the grid system in Scotland. As a promoter of hydro-electricity, he became second in importance only to Johnston himself. Airlie and MacColl, particularly MacColl, started to build up a team of engineers, administrators and negotiators, all highly competent and enthusiasts for hydro-electricity.

Loch Sloy

High among the hills which line the northern part of the west shore of Loch Lomond lay a small glen, once used as a hiding place for stolen cattle, containing a little loch. This was Loch Sloy. The possibility of incorporating it into a hydro-electric scheme had been considered as early as 1906, and again in 1925. In 1936 MacColl himself had examined the district and considered enlargement of Loch Sloy into a reservoir for a hydro-electric sheme – not just a hydro-electric scheme, but a pumped storage scheme. Surplus power from the grid would be used to pump water from Loch Lomond to Loch Sloy when demand for electricity was low, and water from the top reservoir would be released to generate electricity when demand was high. This scheme, conceived on a large scale, was ahead of its time and, despite modifications, lay fallow.

A hydro-electric scheme based on Loch Sloy, however, became part of the North of Scotland Hydro-Electric Board's first construction scheme, which was promoted in 1944. It was the largest part by far; the remainder comprised two small schemes in the north-west. The advantages of Loch Sloy were several. Much was already known about the locality. The catchment area of Loch Sloy combined high rainfall with a lack of houses, cultivation, and fisheries. Though small, it could be enlarged; there was a suitable location for a dam to enlarge the loch, and its altitude meant that a high head of water could be obtained for a power station beside Loch Lomond. Not too far away lay the industries of Glasgow and the central belt; they desperately needed power, while the board equally needed the income from this to help finance less economic schemes further north.

Despite so much in its favour, the scheme went to public enquiry, and all the old objections to hydro-electricity seem to have been trotted out, with some new ones as well. The board, new to the game, did not help itself by issuing documents ten days before the enquiry which showed that the proposed site of the power station was being moved by half-a-mile – detailed examination of the earlier site having shown it to be unsuitable. The principal objector was Dunbarton County Council, which wished to retain control over Loch Sloy for possible use for water supply. The objections, in due course, were over-ruled, The construction scheme was confirmed by Tom Johnston as Secretary of State and, since no objections were raised in Parliament, became operative on 28 March 1945. Soon afterwards Mrs Tom Johnston ceremonially 'dug the first sod' – using an 18-ton bulldozer for the purpose.

The principal works in the scheme were these:

The dam, which was built of concrete, of mass buttress type, in which water pressure is resisted by the buttresses. It was the first of its type in Scotland. With a height of 160 ft and a length of 1,160 ft, it raised the water level of Loch Sloy by 115 ft and doubled its length.

An extensive system of aqueducts and tunnels which increased the catchment area of Loch Sloy from 6½ sq. miles to 27½ sq. miles – and, later, to about 32 sq. miles.

The main tunnel, which is 2 miles long, to carry water on the first part of its journey from dam to power station. It passes beneath Ben Vorlich to emerge on the hillside at the valve house above the power station; most of it was made of horse-shoe section, 15 ft 4 in. diameter. Connected with this, and excavated within the mountain, is the surge chamber into which the moving mass of water surges when valves controlling admission to the turbines are closed.

The four steel pipelines down the hillside, each of which is 6 – 7 ft diameter, and mounted on concrete anchor blocks weighing between 1,700 and 3,600 tons.

The power station itself, with four Francis type turbo-alternators, in which each turbine is mounted on a vertical shaft in common with its alternator. Able to produce 130 megawatts, when installed these were the most powerful hydro-electric generating sets in Britain. A Pelton wheel auxiliary set was installed to produce 450 kW for local needs.

Twin 132,000-volt transmission lines which, from a switching station behind the power station, took a 36-mile route evidently intended to make them no more obtrusive than was inevitable – between the hills to a point above Arrochar, high above Loch Long, through Glen Fruin, across the Vale of Leven, and through the Kilpatrick Hills to a switching station north-west of Glasgow.

The earliest tasks of construction were none of these, but to build access roads – some 15 miles of them – and hutted encampments for the work force. After Mrs Johnston's promising start, progress was slow. It was ironic that the first manifestation of a programme, which was intended to arrest depopulation and provide work, was occuring at a time when labour was extremely scarce. The war in Europe was just over, but in the Far East it continued. The immediate solution was to employ, in addition to a core of local workers, German prisoners-of-war who had still to return home. To take them and locals to and from work a temporary railway station was built on the West Highland line at Inveruglas, close to the power station site. Trains then brought workmen from Garelochhead (and possibly further afield), from Faslane where a temporary halt was built to serve the prisoner-of-war camp, and from Arrochar & Tarbet, to Inveruglas and another temporary halt in Glen Falloch. The latter I assume to have been used by men making the aqueducts

Loch Sloy power station under construction in 1948. The partly completed pipelines pass beneath a new bridge carrying the West Highland Railway. Beyond the skeletal power station building, there can be seen moored some of the lighters used to carry sand up Loch Lomond. In the distance extreme right is Ben Lomond; the reservoir for the abortive Craigroyston pumped storage scheme would have been in the corrie between the summit and the near ridge. (*Scottish & Southern Energy plc, Hydro Generation*)

and tunnels which diverted water from some of the burns flowing into Glen Falloch and took it to Loch Sloy.

The Inveruglas station was additionally much used for supply of materials; plant and machinery also arrived in quantity by road. The board purchased so far as possible in Scotland; the heavy industries of the Clyde found an opportunity to turn from armaments to hydro-electric generating equipment.

A diesel generating station was built early on, to provide light and power to camps, roads and working sites. True to its mission, the Hydro Board provided a public supply of electricity from it to Tarbet and Arrochar. As peacetime conditions slowly returned, the prisoners went home and the workforce came to include men – and women – from all over Scotland, and from further away: miners from Cornwall to drive the tunnels, refugees from many countries in Europe. Men who had worked on earlier hydro schemes between the wars re-appeared to offer the benefit of their experience. Yet with full employment there was much turnover of staff. The weather in the hills, blizzards, rain and gales caused problems – which might perhaps have been foreseen in view of the nature of the undertaking! Yet the average rainfall for Loch Sloy, estimated at 115 to 120 inches a year, was handsomely exceeded in 1948 when it reached 168 inches. All this took place against a background of national austerity: food and clothes were still rationed, raw materials were in very short supply, and there were acute shortages of fuel. So the work went on, but far less quickly than at first envisaged.

Threats to the Board

While slow progress was being made at Sloy, there were problems elsewhere. The Hydro-Electric Board's next constructional scheme, Tummel-Garry near Pitlochry, resulted in a public enquiry at which the board suffered a very rough ride indeed. Opposition degenerated into personal attacks on Lord Airlie, and then on his family. Understandably, he felt unable to carry on, and resigned as chairman in 1946. By then, Tom Johnston was no longer in Parliament. He was induced, by MacColl and others, (without, one suspects, too much difficulty) to take Lord Airlie's place.

Johnston's political skills were almost immediately called back into play. Even while secretary of state he had had to resist proposals that, post-war, a national electricity generating board, with local distribution boards, should be established to cover the whole of Britain including the North of Scotland: in this the Hydro Board, and its social purpose, would have been lost. There was no immediate outcome, but from 1945 the Labour Government was committed to a programme of nationalisation. Full nationalisation of the electricity industry – it was already, in part, publicly owned – was high on the list, and in 1946 the threat to the Hydro Board became real. That it survived seems to have been due, as much as anything, to Johnston's personal contacts in the cabinet. Both Herbert Morrison, who was in charge of the nationalisation programme, and Emmanuel

Top: Cabinet ministers inspect the Loch Sloy scheme in 1946. Emmanuel Shinwell MP, Minister of Fuel & Power, is holding the plan; Tom Johnston is second from the left, and holding his lapels extreme right appears to be A.E.MacColl. Bottom: Herbert Morrison MP (wearing glasses), who was in charge of the Labour Government's nationalization programme, jokes with construction workers.

Behind the scenes, Tom Johnston was battling to prevent the hydro-electric board from being swallowed up by an all-Britain electricity generating authority. (*Scottish & Southern Energy plc, Hydro Generation*)

Shinwell, Minister of Fuel and Power, were invited by him to come
north to see for themselves what the board was doing. Both came,
separately, to inspect the Sloy scheme, in the late summer of 1946,
and Shinwell also visited Pitlochry. If they had had reservations about
the Hydro Board previously, they were reassured. When electricity
was nationalised in 1947, the North of Scotland Hydro-Electric
Board survived, although (a bone of contention) new schemes for
generating had to be vetted by the British Electricity Authority. But
in its own district the board's responsibilities were enlarged: into
it were merged all other existing generators and distributors of the
public electricity supply.

The Royal Opening Ceremony

On the Loch Sloy scheme, the main tunnel beneath Ben Vorlich
was driven through in April 1949, and in February 1950 for the first
time one of the turbo-alternators was set in motion by Sir Edward
MacColl – he had been knighted a few months before.

On 18 October 1950 the scheme was formally opened by Queen
Elizabeth – still then queen consort and yet to become the Queen
Mother. She herself arrived by car; for the board and its guests, a
special train, with dining car, left Edinburgh Waverley at 10.50 a.m.
and, after calling at Dumbarton and Helensburgh Upper, ran direct
to the temporary station at Inveruglas. On a wet and windy day,
guests found two large canvas-covered stands erected on either side
of the tail race in front of the power station. They faced a smaller
covered dais erected beside the power station itself. A crowd of
onlookers gathered on the hillside immediately to the north of the
power station. Assuming the programme went as planned, the queen
was met at the north gate of the power station. She was presented
with a very fine bouquet. She and Thomas Johnston then mounted
the dais and, after an introduction by Johnston, the queen formally
pulled a lever to start up two of the hydro-electric generators. She
was then taken on a tour of inspection of the power station.

One point remains uncertain. At 3.45 p.m., according to the
programme, it 'may be possible to visit Loch Sloy dam by bus'.
Evidently the board, with all too much experience of late-October
weather in that vicinity, was hedging its bets. I do not know whether,

in fact, any of the guests made it to the dam. At any rate, the special train was to stand in the station for them from 4 p.m. onwards, with tea served on board, before setting off on the return journey at 5.22.

It was a day when dreams came true.

Success Story

Thomas Johnston remained chairman of the North of Scotland Hydro-Electric Board until 1959. By 1964 the board had built 53 dams and commissioned 51 large power stations, of which Sloy remained the most powerful by far. The men who built these hydro schemes, and the hardships and hazards they overcame, have their own worthy record in James Miller's *The Dam Builders*.

Among the many constructional schemes was no. 25, Breadalbane Project, authorised in 1953. One section of this incorporated Loch Earn, and had its principal power station at St Fillans. Water used there includes some which would naturally have flowed into Loch Tay, but has been collected and brought by aqueduct, reservoir and tunnel to St Fillans power station; it is discharged into Loch Earn. The level of the loch is maintained by a weir at St Fillans, whence most of the flow of water is diverted though a tunnel to the power station at Dalchonzie. These two stations came into operation in 1957 and 1958 respectively.

How successful was the board's programme in meeting the hopes and aspirations of its promoters? In one respect it failed. There had been great hopes of attracting to the Highlands heavy industries with processes which demanded large amounts of electric power, but it proved impossible to produce electricity cheaply enough, compared with other countries such as Norway. At least this was so initially: an aluminium smelter did operate at Invergordon for a decade from 1971.

Little or no consideration seems to have been given to harnessing hydro-electric power for the electrification of railways in the Highlands. This is surprising, for electrification of the railways of Switzerland and Norway in the first half of the twentieth century was closely linked to the availability of hydro-electricity, while electricity generation in Britain was in its early years closely linked to power supply for electric tramways. That, indeed, was A.E. MacColl's background. Maybe the coal lobby was the problem.

The hydro board was more successful in encouraging light industries than heavy, and its programmes to connect electricity to existing homes, farms and other premises were very successful indeed. In 1940 it had been estimated that even in the area supplied by the Grampian Electricity Supply Co. only one in five premises was connected; elsewhere in the Highlands and Islands, outside the few main towns, people were still mostly dependent on the paraffin lamp and the peat, or coal, fire. In 1948 there were some 41,100 farms and crofts in the board's area, of which 1,950 had mains electricity, that is 4.7 per cent. By 1966 there were 38,201 farms and crofts, and 34,191 of them, that is 89.5 per cent, had mains electricity. By the late 1980s, almost every potential consumer of electricity had been connected.

All this had been achieved without the total desecration of the Highlands. Salmon still returned every year, and so did tourists. Yet there remained a certain disenchantment with the effect of hydro-electric schemes upon the landscape. Inevitably, where the water level of a reservoir is subject to frequent fluctuation, there is a rim of bare boulders, innocent of vegetation, which jars the eye. At least, it does so for the author, who has to work hard to remind himself, in such circumstances, that this is the price to be paid for the fridge and the freezer and the washing machine and the video recorder and the dishwasher, all humming away at home.

Then there are power stations, and pipelines. The chairman of the Loch Sloy enquiry looked across Loch Lomond to the Inversnaid Hotel, standing out on the unspoilt eastern shore, and concluded in effect that since its appearance, though plain, was acceptable there was no reason why a power station in itself should not be. So it is a pity, perhaps, that most of the board's power stations were built during a period when what may be called the 'functional oblong box' school of architecture was in the ascendant – whether for power stations, office buildings or blocks of flats. This is not to discount the great efforts to which the board did go to make the appearance of its later power stations inoffensive. Its demand for building stone, with which to clad its buildings, effectively revived a moribund quarrying industry.

Few if any of the Hydro Board's subsequent power stations were fed with water by pipelines so conspicuous as those at Sloy, and many of them were fed by tunnels. Indeed some power stations themselves were hidden underground. This is the case at St Fillans, where most visitors are probably unaware of the existence of a power station. Yet even that seems to smack of hiding the light under a bushel. How are people to appreciate the achievements of hydro-electricity in the absence of visual evidence?

Craigroyston

Latent concerns welled to the surface in the mid-1970s when the board proposed a pumped storage scheme at Craigroyston on the flanks of Ben Lomond. By then, although construction of conventional hydro stations had ceased, the board had recently completed pumped storage schemes at Cruachan beside Loch Awe and at Foyers beside Loch Ness. The attraction of pumped storage is its ability in effect to use surplus electricity at slack periods to produce electricity when demand is high. The attraction of Ben Lomond was its proximity to the cities and towns where the demand arose. The conversion of Sloy to pumped storage had been considered, and found to cost more in order to produce less. Output from Craigroyston was planned to be as high as 1600 MW, with potential for later increase to 3200 MW.

Looking at the details, it is evident the board went to immense trouble to make its scheme acceptable on amenity grounds. There were to be no pipes down the hillside, no oblong-box generating station: all of this was to be underground. The high-altitude reservoir, in a corrie to the north-west of the summit, was to have its dams made not of concrete but from rock quarried on site; the main dam, facing north-east, would have been largely hidden from view; a small subsidiary dam, facing west, was to be covered with natural vegetation. Transmission lines would be led away to the east. The fluctuations in the water level of Loch Lomond were to be no more than those already caused by wind and rain. The public road to Rowardennan would be improved, the access roads beyond remain private (the board had decided against water transport). Learned and extensive studies were made into the environmental impact of the scheme.

Yet the scheme caused a furore. In its concern for details, it seems to me, the board had overlooked a more fundamental question: whether any development on Ben Lomond would be acceptable at all. After the loch itself, the Ben is by far the most prominent feature of the district – as can be judged from the frequency with which it appears in the background to the illustrations in this book. And this was in the 1970s, when residents around the loch were faced with – increasingly – crumbling piers, littered banks, crowded beaches, speeding boats and, up the west shore, a trunk road which was narrow, winding and congested. About all or any of this, authority seemed unable or unwilling to do very much. By contrast with the west shore, the east remained relatively unscathed – and now, I suspect it seemed, authority was likely to give official sanction to desecration not only of the unspoilt and remote east shore, but of the very Ben itself.

Fragmented opposition came together with the formation in 1978 of the Friends of Loch Lomond – the concept was based on a similar organisation in the Lake District. This voluntary society was to tackle not just the one big problem but also the many lesser ones. Founder members of its council included Hannah Stirling – who had set the ball rolling with a letter to the editor of the *Glasgow Herald* – Josephine Colquhoun, Gavin Arneil, W.H.Murray and Tom Weir, together with representatives of many of the local community councils. Support gathered rapidly – not just local support, but world-wide. As an influential voluntary conservation group the society became a great and continuing success, not only in successful opposition to inappropriate developments and encouragement of appropriate ones, but in taking practical action in, for instance, building footpaths and arranging for the archaeological survey of the islands.

The Craigroyston proposal seems meanwhile to have withered away. Its most exceptionable feature in my opinion – apart from disturbance during the construction period of at least eight years – would have been the opening up of the east shore. By 1982 the scheme was described as 'postponed', and it has never been submitted formally for approval. The North of Scotland Hydro-Electric Board itself was privatised during 1989–90. It is ironic, and I am aware that I have already used the word once in this chapter, that from Tom

Johnston's memorial at Inveruglas the successful Sloy scheme is at present invisible – but the site proposed for the unsuccessful one at Craigroyston is in full view. Yet there is another irony which would not I think have been unappreciated by the man; that the actions of the board he founded should have been responsible for crystalising concern for the conservation of Loch Lomond itself.

14
TO INVERARY VIA LOCH ECK

David Napier in Argyll

The abilities of Glasgow engineers of the early nineteenth century are famous. It is no surprise to find that the first self-propelled vehicle to ply for hire, and one of the first steamships to be built with an iron hull, were associated with that city. What is a surprise is to find that they were put to work not around the city but in a Highland glen which is, at least today, little known (if I may say so without offence to its inhabitants) and seemingly remote.

The man responsible was David Napier (1790–1869) whom we have already encountered as the man who put the first paddle steamer onto Loch Lomond. Napier was one of those people who had the good fortune to be in the right place at the right time. He was, too, a rare example of a talented engineer who was also a skilled entrepreneur. His father had an ironfounding and engineering business in Dumbarton, of which town he was a native, but moved it to Glasgow in 1802. At the time that the *Comet*'s boiler was built, David Napier was managing the foundry for him. After the father died in 1813, the son took over the business and did well. Steamships were rapidly increasing in popularity and numbers, and he built their machinery and boilers. He made successive improvements to these. He branched out into shipowning, operating the ships fitted with steam plant he had built. He was responsible for the first steamers to ply successfully across the Irish Sea.

By 1826 he had prospered sufficiently to buy for himself a 2,000-acre country estate at Glenshellish in Argyll. Glenshellish is inland from Strachur on Loch Fyne, three miles or so in the direction of the head of Loch Eck. There he built himself a mansion house as a summer residence. He also, from 1828, bought land on the north shore of Holy Loch, including the ancient clachan of Kilmun, and subsequently extended his holdings beyond Strone Point along the shore of Loch Long. These purchases seem to have been in the nature of speculations; steamboats on the Clyde, including his own, were making this formerly remote area easy of access. At Kilmun he built a pier, villas and a hotel; and he built a residence for himself, to use when he did not wish to travel as far as Glenshellish.

He evidently spent time there in winter as well as in summer, for an anecdote which survives gives a pleasant picture of the man. One of the other residents, walking to the kirk on a winter Sunday, overtook him. Napier was drawing with his walking stick in the snow at the side of the road. Upon enquiry, it appeared that the idea for an improvement to the steam engine had occured to him, and he needed to sketch it out to see if it would work. He had satisfied himself on the point. It would work: which was fortunate, for only then could he dismiss it from his mind and pay proper attention to whatever the minister might say in his sermon.

What, you may be wondering, has all this got to do with iron ships and self-propelled vehicles? The answer lay far to the west, at Inverary. Ever a centre of importance, it was never easy to approach from Glasgow and central Scotland. The military road had improved matters, but it still wandered to the north of a direct route and involved the climb over Rest and be thankful. By sea the route was more indirect still – ships had to head south down the Firth of Clyde and pass either north or south of Bute before heading north up Loch Fyne.

Evident advantages were offered by direct routes leading from the western shores of the Clyde across the Cowal peninsula by road and then over Loch Fyne by ferry. One possibility was via Lochgoilhead and St Catherine's. Another was via Ardentinny, on Loch Long, and Strachur. Early in the nineteenth century the Commissioners for Highland Roads and Bridges had built roads over both of these routes, primarily to make the Loch Fyne herring fishery more accessible than hitherto. The Ardentinny–Strachur road headed up Glen Finart and over the hill to reach Loch Eck at Whistlefield – as a by-road it still exists, apparently little altered – and then followed the east shore of the loch and passed within half a mile of Glenshellish.

To Napier it must have been clear that there was another option. In those days water was seen not as an obstruction to travel but, if it could be navigated, as an aid to it. On the direct route between Kilmun and Strachur lies Loch Eck, which is about 6½ miles long (although scarcely more than ⅓ mile wide at the most). The distance from Kilmun to the foot of Loch Eck is about 3½ miles, and from the head of the loch to Strachur about 4½ miles; if he ran a steamer on Loch Eck, there would be only those short distances to be covered by land in the entire journey between Glasgow and Inverary. It would be a route as direct as any, and one over which Napier himself could provide the means of transport with little fear of direct competition.

Aglaia

The ship which he built in 1827 for Loch Eck was the *Aglaia*, named, like *Euphrosyne*, after one of the three graces. For delivery to the loch, the engine and boiler were removed and taken by land. The lightened hull was then taken up the River Echaig. The Echaig forms the outlet from Loch Eck to Holy Loch; I doubt whether it was normally considered navigable for it appears neither wide, nor deep, nor slow-flowing, but perhaps to a veteran of the Leven it seemed less forbidding. At any rate, with the assistance of the residents – many of them presumably Napier's tenants – the hull was dragged up to the loch and the little ship there re-assembled.

Maybe it was the need to resist damage during the ascent of the Echaig that caused Napier to build the hull of iron. Or maybe it was to resist damage from the winter's ice – this was likely to be a problem on fresh water, and although it does not seem to have caused difficulties on Loch Lomond, Loch Eck is much much more sheltered and could have been seen as more likely to freeze. The first iron boat built in Scotland had been *Vulcan* of 1819, a horse-drawn passenger boat for the Forth & Clyde Canal, and it was certainly to resist ice-damage that her hull was made of iron rather than wood. The first iron-hulled steamers had also been associated with fresh water. The first of all, *Aaron Manby*, had been built (in sections) at Tipton, Staffordshire in 1822 for service on the River Seine; the second, *Marquis of Wellesley* of 1825, for service on the

River Shannon. *Aglaia* is said to have come next in precedence after these. The first iron-hulled steamer to ply the Clyde proper was *Fairy Queen* of 1831.

Captain James Williamson in *Clyde Passenger Steamers* (originally published in 1904) related an odd little story about *Aglaia*. The engineer had been renewing the jointing material beneath the cylinder cover and, when he had re-assembled it, found that the engine would not turn over. He could not work out why. A boy employed on board pointed out the reason: the 'pot lid' – i.e. the cylinder cover – was on the wrong way. The boy, whose name was Homish McLean, later became a well-known character on Clyde steamers.

The inference is that the top of the cylinder cover was similar but not identical to its lower side, so that when replaced upside down it fouled the piston approaching top dead centre. To have replaced it thus, the engineer must have been unskilled and inexperienced even by the standards of the period. Maybe, since the joint had evidently been blowing steam, he had deliberately turned over the cover in an attempt to make a better seal. If so, perhaps a little too much was attributed to the perspicacity of the wee boy. If nothing else, the story tells us something about engine-room conditions in those early days.

For a contemporary mention of *Aglaia*, we can turn again to Felix Mendelssohn and his travelling companion Carl Klingemann. They used this route to travel back from the Hebrides to Glasgow in 1829. Klingemann recorded that they had been told the steamboat was made of iron, but the 'walls' at which they knocked were of wood. One visualises the young composer and his friend prodding at the sides of the ship! I would have been inclined to suppose they were knocking at an internal wooden lining, were it not that E.C.Smith in his authoritative *A Short History of Naval and Marine Engineering* (1937) described *Aglaia* as having had an iron bottom but wooden sides above the water-line. He did not, unfortunately, give any reference to his source. Such construction would be compatible with either of the two possible reasons which I suggested above, but there seems to be no hint of it in Napier's autobiography.

Napier seems to have had at least four steamboats working on the Clyde over the next few years, bringing passengers to his pier at

Arcadian scene beside Loch Eck – with the *Aglaia* in the background steaming up the loch. The author sought the location of this engraving unsuccessfully at the head of the loch, and decided to stop for a picnic on Dornoch Point further down – from which place the outline of the hills started to look familiar . . . (*Trustees of the National Library of Scotland: Leighton, J. M.,* The Lakes of Scotland, *1834*)

Kilmun. He also had at least one on Loch Fyne, variously identified as *Thalia* – the third of the three graces – and *Cupid*. Duckworth and Langmuir, in *Clyde River & Other Steamers*, mention that in 1827 *Thalia* was advertised to sail from Inverary at 7.30 a.m. for Cairndow (whence passengers could make their way to Tarbet and Napier's Loch Lomond steamer) and at 10.00 a.m. for Strachur and the Loch Eck route.

Napier's Steam Carriage

Between Strachur and the head of Loch Eck Napier doubtless provided a coach using the road built for the herring fishermen a decade or so before. Between Kilmun and the foot of the loch whatever road there may have been was so inadequate that Napier himself had to have a proper road built.

It was here that he ran, or attempted to run, the steam carriage. Successful propulsion of vehicles by steam power had been a dream in mens's minds for a very long time. The first steam vehicles which actually worked had been built in Paris by Joseph Cugnot in the late 1760s. James Watt's assistant William Murdoch built an excellent working model in the 1780s; Watt himself would have nothing to do with it. Richard Trevithick built the first successful full-size steam vehicles in Britain during the first decade of the nineteenth century. By the 1820s many engineers and experimenters were at work. James Nasmyth – whose ancestor may or may not have built Inversnaid Barracks – built a steam carriage in 1827 and successfully carried his friends up and down Queensferry Road near Edinburgh. Since the steam carriage was not seen to have a commercial future, he then dismantled it again.

To an accomplished engineer such as Napier, the potential for using a steam carriage to provide the link between his ships on the Clyde and Loch Eck must have been self-evident. Unfortunately we know very little in detail about the vehicle. What he himself wrote about it later in his autobiography was:

> This steam carriage was, I believe, the first that carried passengers for hire on common roads, being long before there were any public railways in either England or Scotland conveying passengers by steam; but from the softness and hilliness of the roads, and more particularly from want of knowledge of how to make a boiler, we could not obtain the speed I expected.

Since it was intended to carry a steamer-load of passengers, Napier's steam carriage must have been big. That no doubt contributed to the problems with the road, even a new road. As for the boiler, steam boats at that period had large, heavy boilers to produce a lot of steam at low pressure. Steam carriages were going to need lightweight, compact boilers to produce high pressure steam – satisfactory designs were only then being developed and may well have been outside Napier's experience.

A contemporary, if slightly derogatory, brief description of the steam carriage in 1829 is provided by Mendelssohn and Klingemann. They had expected to travel on it but did not. Horsedrawn transport was provided instead. The steam carriage stood idly by the roadside, noted Klingemann. It had been used but 'not found quite practicable yet'; to him it looked ridiculous with a high funnel and a rudder. Presumably there was a tiller steering-arrangement of some sort.

The practicability of steam carriages was well demonstrated in the 1830s by the public services run by Goldsworthy Gurney between Cheltenham and Gloucester, by John Scott Russell between Glasgow and Paisley, and by Walter Hancock in London. Then the whole topic was swept aside by the rapid development of the railway system. Some years later, however, Napier wrote with remarkable prescience:

> I feel . . . confident that steam carriages can be made to do all the work that is done by horses on common roads, as well as a good deal of what is done by steamboats, at one half the expense . . .

He was wrong only about the means of propulsion.

Just how long *Aglaia* continued to ply on Loch Eck is not clear; she may have been superseded by another steamer for a few years. I suspect that the rather complex arrangements needed for this through route may have demanded the personal interest of Napier, whose main residence was in London after 1837. When Lord Cockburn travelled that way on circuit in September 1843, he used his own carriage from Strachur direct to Dunoon. Loch Eck he found gloomy, and commented 'it is never enlivened by sound, and its dead surface is rarely broken by an oar or a sail'. In view of that, it seems unlikely that a steamer was then operating.

Tour No. 45

The Loch Eck route was revived in 1878 by the Glasgow and Inverary Steamboat Company. This had the steamer *Fairy Queen* assembled at the lochside, and then operated her with coach connections to and from Dunoon and Strachur. The high summer of Victorian and Edwardian tourism was approaching, and the route became part of the vast network of interconnecting rail, steamer and coach services that was provided for visitors to the Highlands.

In 1887 for instance the North British Railway's 'Circular Tour No. 45' ran from Edinburgh and Glasgow by rail to Craigendoran, steamer to Dunoon, coach to the foot of Loch Eck, steamer up

The foot of Loch Eck, with SS *Fairy Queen* at her pier (*Collection J. Danielewski*)

Loch Eck, coach to Strachur, steamer to Inverary and thence back via the Kyles of Bute to Rothesay, another steamer to Craigendoran and home by train. That took two days, but timings were such that a real hustler could do it in one day by going round the opposite way – which meant leaving Edinburgh Waverley at 7.20 a.m. and returning at 9.15 p.m.

The Loch Eck steamer seems to have lasted only until shortly before the First World War, although between the wars the same company was operating buses between Dunoon and Strachur. Comparable round tours were on offer for as long as Clyde steamers went to Inverary, that is until the early 1970s. Latterly they incorporated a motor coach between Inverary and Dunoon, which passed alongside Loch Eck on the way.

Change as well as movement has been a constant feature of Loch Lomond and the Trossachs and the surrounding region: change, that is the constant rise and decline in human affairs, set against the unchanging – on a human time-scale – background of lochs and hills. Just how much change has been for the better, and how much for the worse, has often been in doubt. That is a continuing problem, one which it is to be hoped the national park authority will be able to tackle with success. Certainly there is much to be learnt from those who have gone before.

BIBLIOGRAPHY

Agnew, J., *The Story of the Vale of Leven*, Famedram Publishers Ltd, Gartocharn, 1975

Aitken, R., *The West Highland Way Official Guide*, HMSO, 1980

Anderson, A. O., *Early Sources of Scottish History*, Stamford, 1990

Arneil, G.C., *The Friends of Loch Lomond: Memories of 21 Years*, Friends of Loch Lomond, 1999

Baddeley, M.J.B., *Scotland (Part I)* (Thorough Guide Series), Thomas Nelson & Sons, 1908

Barnett, T. R., *The Road to Rannoch and the Summer Isles*, John Grant Booksellers Ltd, Edinburgh, 1946

Barrington, J., 'Trossachs Clearances' in *Scots*, no. 15, 2002

Beauchamp, E., *The Braes o'Balquhidder*, Heatherbank Press, Milngavie, 1981

Behrend, G., *Pullman in Europe*, Ian Allan Ltd, 1962

Bredsdorf, E., 'Hans Andersen and Scotland' in *Blackwood's Magazine*, April 1955

Brown, A., *Loch Lomond Passenger Steamers 1818–1989*, Allan T. Condie Publications, Nuneaton, 2000

Brown, D., 'Tales from Loch Katrine' in *Clyde River Steamer Club Magazine*, no. 15, 1979

Bruce, J.G., 'The Railways and Loch Lomond' in *Back Track*, vol. 10. no. 7, July 1996

Bruce, M.B. & Brown, A., *Drymen and Buchanan in Old Photographs*, Stirling District Libraries, Stirling, 1988

Calder, C. & Lindsay, L., *The Islands of Loch Lomond*, Famedram Publishers Ltd, Formartine, 2002

Campbell, J., 'A Tram Ride to Loch Lomond' in *Scottish Transport*, Magazine of the Scottish Tramway Museum Society, no. 23, January 1973

Child, F.J., *English and Scottish Popular Ballads*, 1882

Chirrey, J., *The Loch Lomondside Military Road*, Dumbarton District Libraries, n.d.

Cleary, R., *Maid of the Loch*, Caledonian MacBrayne, Gourock, 1979

Coats, R.H., *Travellers' Tales of Scotland*, Alexander Gardner, Paisley, 1913

Cockburn, Lord H., *Circuit Journeys*, Byway Books, Kelso, 1983 (originally published 1888)

Craigroyston, North of Scotland Hydro-Electric Board, Edinburgh, c.1977

Danielewski, J., *Loch Lomond in Old Picture Postcards*, European Library, Zaltbommel, Netherlands, 1987

de Selincourt, E. (ed.), *Journals of Dorothy Wordsworth*, 1941

Duckworth, C.L.D. & Langmuir, G.E., *Clyde River and Other Steamers*, Brown Son & Ferguson, Glasgow, 1972

Ellis, H., *Railway Carriages of the British Isles . . .*, George Allen & Unwin, 1965

Evans, F.J., *The Trossachs Report*, Countryside Commission for Scotland, Perth, 1972

Fatal Accident Inquiry . . . Determination by Robert Colquhoun Hay Esq. CBE WS, Sheriff Principal of North Strathclyde following an Inquiry held at Dumbarton on 26, 27 and 28 January and 1, 2 and 3 March 1994 into the death of Ann McAuley, Dumbarton Sheriff Court, Dumbarton, 1994

Fenton, A. & Walker, B., *The Rural Architecture of Scotland*, John Donald Publishers Ltd, Edinburgh, 1981

Ferguson, J., *The Law of Roads, Streets and Rights of Way, Bridges and Ferries in Scotland*, Edinburgh, 1904

Ferguson, J., *The Law of Water and Water Rights in Scotland*, 1907

Fontane, T., *Across the Tweed: Notes on Travel in Scotland, 1858*, J.M. Dent & Sons Ltd, 1965

Ford, R., *Vagabond Songs and Ballads of Scotland*, Alexander Gardner Ltd, 1899

Forsyth, R.N., *To Western Scottish Waters*, Tempus Publishing Ltd, Stroud, 2000

Fryer, C.E.J., *The Callander and Oban Railway*, The Oakwood Press, Oxford, 1989

Geikie, Sir A., *Scottish Reminiscences*, James Maclehose & Sons, Glasgow, 1904

Gilpin, W., *Observations, relative chiefly to Picturesque Beauty, made in the Year 1776, on . . . the High-Lands of Scotland*, R. Blamire, 1789

Glover, J.R., *The Story of Scotland*, Faber & Faber Ltd, 1977

Gracie, J., 'The Men who Plumbed the Depths' in *The Scots Magazine*, June 1994

Graham, D., *Sunset on the Clyde*, Neil Wilson Publishing Ltd, Glasgow, 1993

Haldane, A.R.B., *New Ways through the Glens*, Thomas Nelson & Sons Ltd, 1962

Haldane, A.R.B., *The Drove Roads of Scotland*, Thomas Nelson & Sons Ltd, 1952 (reissued Birlinn Ltd, Edinburgh, 1997)

Hamilton, H., *The Industrial Revolution in Scotland*, Oxford University Press, 1932

Henderson, K., *Till 21*, Regency Press, 1970

Hunter, T., *A Guide to the West Highland Way*, Constable 1979

Inglis, H.R.G., *The 'Contour' Road Book of Scotland*, Gall & Inglis, Edinburgh, 1907

Irving, J., *The History of Dumbartonshire . . .*, Dumbarton 1857

Jenkins, D., & Visocchi, M., *Mendelssohn in Scotland*, Chappell & Co., 1978

Johnston, T., *Memories*, Collins, 1952

Knight, G.A.F., *Archaeological Light on the Early Christianizing of Scotland*, James Clarke & Co. Ltd., 1933

Lamond, H., *Loch Lomond: A Study in Angling Conditions*, Jackson, Wylie & Co., Glasgow, 1931

Langmuir, G.E., 'Loch Lomond Passenger Steamers' in *Clyde Steamers*, Magazine of the Clyde River Steamer Club, no. 26, spring 1991

Lawrie, P., 'Clanship and Feudalism' in *The Clan Gregor Society Newsletter*, winter 2002

Leigh, M., *Spade among the Rushes*, Phoenix House, 1949 (reissued Birlinn Ltd, Edinburgh 1995)

Lindsay, J., *The Canals of Scotland*, David & Charles, Newton Abbot, 1968

Loch Sloy Hydro-Electric Scheme . . ., North of Scotland Hydro-Electric Board, Edinburgh, 1950

Lockhart, J.G., *The Life of Sir Walter Scott*, Constable, Edinburgh, 1902 (containing text of 1839 edn)

Lumsden & Son's Steam-boat Companion or Stranger's Guide to the Western Isles and Highlands of Scotland . . ., James Lumsden & Son, Glasgow, 1828; 1831

McAllister, R., *The Lure of Loch Lomond*, Forth Naturalist and Historian, Stirling, 1997

MacDonald, J.G. et al, *A Natural History of Loch Lomond*, Glasgow University Press, Glasgow, 1974

MacGregor, A.A., *Wild Drumalbain*, W. & R. Chambers Ltd, 1927

McGregor, John, *100 Years of The West Highland Railway*, ScotRail, Glasgow, 1994

MacGregor, Jimmie, O*n the West Highland Way*, BBC Publications, 1985

McLeod, D., *Loch Lomond Steamboat Companies*, Bennett & Thompson, Dumbarton, 1889

McNaughton, D.B., *Upper Strathearn From the Earliest Times to Today*, Jamieson & Munro, Perth, n.d.

MacPhail, I.M.M., *Rowing on Loch Lomond*, Bennett & Thompson, Dumbarton, 1963

McQueen, A., *Echoes of Old Clyde Paddle Wheels*, The Strong Oak Press, Stevenage, 2001 (first published 1924)

McTaggart, T., *Pioneers of Heavy Haulage*, Alloway Publishing, Ayr, 1985

Miller, J., *The Dam Builders*, Birlinn Ltd, Edinburgh, 2002

Mitchell, J., 'Loch Lomondside Depicted and Described: 1, Myths, Marvels and Monsters' in *Glasgow Naturalist*, vol. 23, part 3, 1998

Mitchell, J., *The Shielings and Drove Ways of Loch Lomondside*, Jamieson & Munro, Stirling, 2000

Morrison, I., *Landscape with Lake Dwellings: The Crannogs of Scotland*, Edinburgh University Press, Edinburgh, 1985

Murray, Sir J. & Pullar, L., *Bathymetrical Survey of the Fresh-Water Lochs of Scotland*, 1910

Murray, S., *A Companion and Useful Guide to The Beauties of Scotland*, Byway Books, Hawick, 1982 (originally published 1803)

Murray, W.H., *Rob Roy MacGregor: his life and times*, Richard Drew Publishing, Glasgow, 1982

Nairne, C., *The Trossachs and the Rob Roy Country*, Oliver & Boyd Ltd, Edinburgh, 1961

Napier, D., *David Napier: Engineer*, James Maclehose & Sons, Glasgow, 1912

Nasmyth, J., *James Nasmyth: Engineer*, John Murray, 1883

Neill, J., *Records and Reminiscences of Bonhill Parish*, 1912

New Statistical Account, 1830s

Nock, O.S., *Scottish Railways*, Thomas Nelson & Sons Ltd, 1950

Old Statistical Account, 1790s

Osborne, B.D., *The Ingenious Mr Bell*, Argyll Publishing, Glendaruel, 1995

Osborne, C., *The Complete Operas of Verdi*, Knopf, New York, 1977

Paget-Tomlinson, E.W., *The Complete Book of Canal & River Navigations*, Waine Research Publications, Albrighton, 1978

Payne, P.L., *The Hydro*, Aberdeen University Press, Aberdeen, 1988

Pearson, J., *Loch Lomond: The Maid and the Loch*, Famedram Publishers, Gartocharn, n.d.

Pennant, T., *A Tour in Scotland 1769*, Birlinn Ltd, Edinburgh, 2000

Pennant, T., *A Tour in Scotland and Voyage to the Hebrides 1772*, Birlinn Ltd, Edinburgh, 1998

Porteous, A., *Annals of St Fillans*, David Phillips, Crieff, 1912

Power from the Glens, Scottish Hydro-Electric plc, Edinburgh, c.1993

Prothero, F.E. & Clark, W.A. (eds), *A New Oarsman's Guide to the Rivers and Canals of Great Britain and Ireland*, George Philip & Son, 1896

Purser, J., *Scotland's Music*, Mainstream Publishing, Edinburgh, 1992

Report of the Commissioners for enquiring into matters relating to Public Roads in Scotland, 1860

Rixson, D., *The West Highland Galley*, Birlinn Ltd, Edinburgh, 1998

Robertson, C.J.A., 'Railway Mania in the Highlands: The Marquis of Breadalbane and the Scottish Grand Junction Railway' in Mason, R. & MacDougall, D. (eds), *People and Power in Scotland . . .*, John Donald, Edinburgh, 1992

Rocks and Rapids: a narrative of the first voyage from Lochearnhead to Dundee . . ., G. Girdwood, Dundee, 1883

Ruddock, Ted, 'Bridges and Roads in Scotland: 1400–1750' in Fenton, A. & Stell, G. (eds), *Loads and Roads in Scotland and Beyond*, John Donald Publishers Ltd, Edinburgh, 1984

Salmond, J.B., *Wade in Scotland*, The Moray Press, Edinburgh, 1934

Scott, Sir W., *A Legend of Montrose*, 1819

Scott, Sir W., *Rob Roy*, 1817

Scott, Sir W., *The Lady of the Lake*, 1810

Scott, Sir W., *Waverley*, 1814

Shearer, J., *Antiquities of Strathearn*, 1836

Smith, W.A.C., 'The Oban Line' in *The Railway Magazine*, January 1952

Smollett, T., *The Expedition of Humphry Clinker*, 1771

Southey, R., *Journal of a Tour in Scotland in 1819*, James Thin, Edinburgh, 1972

SS Sir Walter Scott on Loch Katrine, Strathclyde Water/Jarrold Publishing, Norwich, 1994

Stewart, J., *Settlements of Western Perthshire*, Pentland Press Ltd, Haddington, 1990

Stirling, I.E. & Walden, N., *Loch Lomond: An annotated bibliography . . .*, University of Strathclyde, Glasgow, 2002

Stott, L., *Enchantment of the Trossachs*, Creag Darach Publications, Aberfoyle, 1992

Stott, L., *The Ring of Words: Literary Loch Lomond*, Creag Darach Publications, Aberfoyle, 1995

Taylor, W., *The Military Roads in Scotland*, David & Charles, Newton Abbot, 1976

The Islands of Loch Lomond, Friends of Loch Lomond, Helensburgh, 2001

The Historic Landscape of Loch Lomond and the Trossachs, Royal Commission on the Ancient and Historical Monuments of Scotland/Historic Scotland, Edinburgh, 2000

The Loch Lomond Water Board Order 1966, Statutory Instrument no. 281, 1967

The Loch-Lomond Expedition . . ., Glasgow 1715

The West Highland Way: A Report on a Proposed Long Distance Route from Milngavie to Fort William presented to the Secretary of State for Scotland Countryside Commission for Scotland, Perth, 1973.

Thomas, J. & Turnock, D., *A Regional History of the Railways of Great Britain vol. XV The North of Scotland*, David & Charles, Newton Abbot, 1989

Thomas, J., rev. Paterson, A.J.S., *A Regional History of the Railways of Great Britain* vol. VI *Scotland: The Lowlands and the Borders*, David & Charles, Newton Abbot, 1984

Thomas, J., *The Callander & Oban Railway*, David & Charles, Newton Abbot, 1966

Thomas, J., rev. Paterson, A.J.S. & Ransom, P.J.G., *The West Highland Railway*, House of Lochar, Isle of Colonsay, 1998

Trubridge, M., *The Inversnaid Hotel and its Surroundings*, M.F. Wells (Hotels) Ltd, Inversnaid, 1992

Trubridge, M., *The Loch Achray Hotel and its Surroundings*, M.F. Wells (Hotels) Ltd, The Trossachs, 1993

Victoria, Queen, *More Leaves from the Journal of a Life in the Highlands*, 1882

Vine, P.A.L., *Pleasure Boating in the Victorian Era*, Phillimore & Co. Ltd, Chichester, 1983

Weir, T., *The Scottish Lochs*, vol. 1, Constable, 1970

Whetstone, A.E., *Scottish County Government in the Eighteenth and Nineteenth Centuries*, John Donald, Edinburgh, 1981

Williamson, J., *Clyde Passenger Steamers 1812–1901*, SPA Books Ltd, Stevenage, 1987 (first published 1904)

Wordsworth, D., *Recollections of a Tour made in Scotland A.D. 1803*, David Douglas, Edinburgh, 1894

Youngson, A.J., *Beyond the Highland Line: Three Journals of Travel in Eighteenth Century Scotland*, Collins, 1974

Periodicals

Dumbarton and Vale of Leven Reporter
Glasgow Herald
Lennox Herald
Newsletter of the Friends of Loch Lomond
Newsletter of the Friends of the West Highland Lines
Newsletter of the Loch Lomond Association
Paddle Wheels (Paddle Steamer Preservation Society)
The Railway Magazine
Scotland on Sunday
The Scots Magazine
The Scotsman
Scottish Geographical Magazine
Scottish Industrial Heritage Society Review
Stirling Observer
Waterways World

Principal Turnpike Acts affecting former military roads in the area covered by this book:

Act	Date	Roads
47 G. III s.2, c. II	1807	Dumbarton–Luss
1 G. IV c. xlvii	1820	Larigalie–confines of Argyll Crianlarich–Inverarnan Callander–Larigalie
9 G. IV c. lxxxii	1828	Dumbarton–confines of Argyll Tarbet–Inverarnan
1 & 2 W. IV c. xliii	1831	General turnpike Act for Scotland
2 W. IV c. lxxxii	1832	General turnpike Act for Perthshire
4 W. IV c. lxi	1834	General turnpike Act for Dunbartonshire including Dumbarton Bridge

INDEX

Note. It is clearly impracticable to include an entry for 'Loch Lomond', and for 'The Trossachs' as applied to the large district to the east of the region. Please consult the appropriate entry for the subject concerned. Other lochs do have entries, and so does 'The Trossachs' in its strict sense as the small area at the east end of Loch Katrine.

Index of People